LITERARY MONOGRAPHS · *Volume 7*

Thackeray, Hawthorne and Melville, and Dreiser

LITERARY MONOGRAPHS

Volume 7

Thackeray, Hawthorne and Melville,
and Dreiser

EDITED BY

Eric Rothstein

AND

Joseph Anthony Wittreich, Jr.

Published for the Department of English by

THE UNIVERSITY OF WISCONSIN PRESS

Published 1975
The University of Wisconsin Press
Box 1379, Madison, Wisconsin 53701
The University of Wisconsin Press, Ltd.
70 Great Russell Street, London

First printing

Printed in the United States of America

ISBN 0-299-06620-7; LC 66-25869

Publication of this volume has been made possible in part
by a gift to the University of Wisconsin Foundation from
the estate of Beatrice T. Conrad, Davenport, Iowa.

PREFACE

The Department of English of the University of Wisconsin continues with this volume a series of monographs in English and American literature. The series was inaugurated in 1967 to serve scholars whose work might take a form too lengthy for journals but too brief for a separate book.

For future volumes of *Literary Monographs* we invite works of high quality, scholarly or critical, that contribute materially to English or American literary studies. We welcome not only conventional literary essays but also those involving experimental critical theories and methods whenever they are eloquent and persuasive. And we will be flexible enough to welcome monographs involving comparative literature or comparative aesthetics, so long as they significantly illuminate literature in English.

The editorial board of *Literary Monographs* would like to express its appreciation to the University of Wisconsin Foundation for making possible the publication of this volume through a gift from the estate of Beatrice T. Conrad, Davenport, Iowa.

Eric Rothstein
Joseph A. Wittreich, Jr.

Madison, Wisconsin
April 1974

NOTES ON SUBMISSIONS

Manuscripts should be from 15,000 to 35,000 words in length. They should be submitted, with return postage and self-addressed envelope enclosed, to

The Editor
Literary Monographs
Department of English
Helen C. White Hall
600 N. Park Street
University of Wisconsin
Madison, Wisconsin 53706

Manuscripts should follow the *MLA Style Sheet*, with a few exceptions or amplifications included in the specific instructions given below.

1. Paper should be 16-pound or 20-pound weight bond in normal quarto size; do not use highly glazed paper (sold under such trade names as "Corrasable"). To make satisfactory photocopying possible, the paper should be white and the typewriter ribbon black. Handwritten corrections may be made in pencil or washable ink; avoid ballpoint pen. Leave margins of 1 to 1 1/2 inches on all sides.

2. Manuscripts should be double spaced throughout, including notes and all excerpts, prose or verse. Do not indent prose excerpts, but mark them with a pencil line along the left margin to the full length of the quotation and allow an extra line of space above and below.

3. Brief references should be inserted in the text (see *MLA Style Sheet*, Sec. 13f). In notes, first references should be cited in full. Succeeding references to books should use short titles rather than *"op. cit."*; e.g., Taylor, *Problems,* p. 12. Short references to journal articles should use author's name, journal name, volume, and page; e.g., McKerrow, RES, xvi, 117.

As can be seen from this volume, *Literary Monographs* reserves the use of footnotes for information that is needed in order to follow the argument of the text or to understand a system of in-text citation. Endnotes supply documentation, or they may extend or parallel the text discussion. Contributors are requested to organize their manuscripts so that endnotes and footnotes are on separate pages, with separate numbering sequences.

CONTENTS

HENRY ESMOND:
THE ROOKERY AT CASTLEWOOD

Elaine Scarry

Yes, this is Vanity Fair; not a moral place certainly; nor a merry one, though very noisy. . . . But the general impression is one more melancholy than mirthful. When you come home, you sit down, in a sober, contemplative, not uncharitable frame of mind, and apply yourself to your books or your business.

"Before the Curtain," *Vanity Fair*

*H*enry Esmond might have been called *Coming Home After the Fair*: its world differs from that of the fair not in the degree to which its values are fatuous but in the degree to which its fatuousness is funny. The tonal distance separating the two novels reflects the difference in narrative perspective: the man describing the world of Vanity Fair is characteristically an anonymous spectator; the man describing the world of Henry Esmond is Henry Esmond. The vanity that often intoxicates and amuses the first instills in the second sobriety and sadness. Only one can afford the bravado of satiric insight; the other, as he himself confesses, is not given to huzzas.

Like *Vanity Fair, Henry Esmond* is a sustained argument against the reality of moral absolutes. Esmond himself does much of the arguing, for he is proficient at identifying illusory values and beliefs. His sophisticated scepticism, however, is itself founded on a dedication to one surviving absolute: truth. The very act of writing an autobiography assumes that the truth about oneself is able to be known and transmitted to others. For this particular autobiographer, the assumption is a studied conviction: throughout his memoirs, he continually alerts us to the pains he is taking to describe his world with an accuracy unaltered by beneficence. Esmond's belief in the reality of truth, however, is not shared by Thackeray. Early in the novel occurs an incident in which several sermons are burned; the single

3

passage surviving the fire warns of the disjunction between the tree of knowledge and the tree of life.[1] When the novel, like the fire, is spent, it is again this message which survives; for while the narrator "has taken truth for his motto" (81), the author has taken the absence of truth for his theme.

Thackeray, it would seem, has endowed his trusting hero with a particular belief for the purpose of proving that belief untenable. His techniques will be examined in detail after first setting forth the specific definition of truth to which Esmond subscribes. A loyal heir of Cartesian enlightenment, Esmond rejects all authorities external to himself, trusting only his own perceptions. His random comments on truth consistently reveal his distrust of formal abstractions: social ceremony, political principle, religious doctrine, and aesthetic design are all dismissed as falsifications of the single knowable reality, the intimate thoughts and feelings of the individual. To this personal sphere he attributes an integrity as absolute as that which is traditionally, and erroneously, ascribed to canons and creeds: "Our great thoughts, our great affections, the truths of our life, never leave us. Surely they cannot separate from our consciousness, shall follow it withersoever that shall go, and are of their nature divine and immortal" (383). In effect, Esmond denies the existence of an objective sphere of truth but affirms the existence of a subjective sphere of truth.

Esmond's concept of personal truth has as corollary the concept of personal history advocated in and exemplified by his memoirs. While *The History of Henry Esmond* is like all histories in its attempt to bestow on the future a knowledge of the past, here past and future belong to intimately related individuals: as Esmond emphasizes in periodic asides to his reader, his history records not the past life of the nation but his own private past; his history is to be read not by the public of an anonymous future but by his own private future, his grandsons (203, 267, 273, 350). Here, then, the unit of historical continuity is the family and the proper historical perspective, personal intimacy. If Esmond includes in his private memoirs public events and figures, it is because his life included a personal acquaintance with those events and figures, and he maintains the perspective of personal acquaintance when describing them. We see the part Steele played in Esmond's daily affairs, not Steele's contribution to mankind. We see the War of Spanish Succession only as a fragmented series of military incidents in which Esmond himself participated: he makes no attempt to formulate an objective overview summarizing or clarifying the pattern of issues and events. His portrait of Marlborough, he tells us, is shaped by his subjective response to the man rather than by an impartial, objective estimate of the man's career. In these and many other details, Esmond practices the belief announced in his preface, that a work of history is more valid when ceremony and formality are replaced with familiarity.

Esmond's narrative, then, offers subjective truth as an alternative to objective truth, subjective history as an alternative to objective history. But Esmond's narrative is not Thackeray's novel. As will be shown, Thackeray manipulates the narrative to demonstrate that personal truths are as elusive and illusory as the objective truths Esmond rejects. This essay will examine the three basic verbal patterns through which this subversion is accomplished before showing similar patterns visible in the novel's larger structural elements.

I

The first verbal pattern is one which weakens, but does not necessarily destroy, the reader's confidence in subjective truth. Esmond has a peculiar habit of expression with which he inadvertently discredits the very world he wishes to praise. He consistently describes his private experiences in language borrowed from the formal doctrines he has ridiculed. For example, despite his professed hostility to certain religious mythologies (142, 200, 275, 335, 402), he invariably relies upon images from those mythologies when describing his beloved "saint," "goddess," and "angel," Rachel Castlewood. Significantly, those passages in which he scoffs at deities and those in which he deifies Rachel often occur in close succession:

When [Esmond's] early credulity was disturbed and his saints and virgins taken out of his worship to a rank little higher than the divinities of Olympus, his belief became acquiescence rather than ardour. (104)

It was [Rachel's] disposition to think kindnesses, and devise silent bounties, and to scheme benevolence for those about her. We take such goodness, for the most part, as if it was our due; the Marys who bring ointment for our feet get but little thanks. (105)

. . . .

"Dearest saint [Rachel]" says [Esmond], "purest soul, that has had so much to suffer, that has blest the poor lonely orphan with such a treasure of love. 'Tis for me to kneel, not for you." (332)

[Frank] reminded Colonel Esmond that he too was, by birth, of that church and that his mother and sister should have his lordship's prayers to the saints (an inestimable benefit, truly!) for their conversion. (335)

While a saint need not be a metaphysical reality to be an effective metaphor, Esmond unintentionally deprives sainthood of its metaphorical as well as metaphysical powers.[2] The Ptolemaic system, though itself untrue, can be used metaphorically to express the truth of a personal vision; but the Ptolemaic system will not be an effective metaphor if prefaced with disdainful comments on the idiocy of Ptolemy.

Esmond first divests a particular idiom of its original meaning and authority; he then calls upon the now weakened idiom to bestow meaning and authority on his private world. Brief examples from two additional vocabularies, the political and the aesthetic, will suggest Esmond's fondness for these weakened idioms. While Rachel is described in the language of deceased spiritual deities, Beatrix is described in the language of discarded political principles. In Esmond's estimation, the divine right doctrine—"that monstrous pedigree which the Tories chose to consider divine" (323)—is an arbitrary and empty claim, neither entitling a mortal to rule nor exempting a ruler from his mortality. Yet all that Beatrix is and is not, she is and is not by divine right. The idiom is used in a physical capacity: she is an "imperious beauty," a "lovely queenly creature" (383) who carries "her head with a toss of supreme authority" (362). The idiom is used in a psychological capacity: it explains "the conquering spirit which impels her" (389) as well as the eagerness of others to be conquered by that spirit. Most importantly, and most disturbingly, the idiom is used in a moral capacity: it bestows privileges and immunities on one who, born to rule, "can neither help her beauty, nor her courage, nor her cruelty" (389). The vocabulary of divine right enables Esmond to translate her faults into signs of superior humanity:

She never at that time could be brought to think but of the world and her beauty, and seemed to have no more sense of devotion than some people have of music, that cannot distinguish one air from another. Esmond saw this fault in her, as he saw many others—a bad wife would Beatrix Esmond make, he thought, for any man under the degree of a prince. She was born to shine in great assemblies, and to adorn palaces, and to command every-where—to conduct an intrigue of politics or to glitter in a queen's train. (338)

While the idiom is compelling, it is also discomforting: Esmond's repeated insistence that a king is merely a man (17, 420) necessarily disrupts his attempt to convert a mere woman into a queen.

Again, Esmond convincingly demonstrates that whatever virtues reside in formal art, truth is not among them: his own elegy for Nancy Sieveright, he confesses, was inspired by the desire to write a Latin elegy rather than by a sense of loss at the young girl's death (94); the view of the war presented in Addison's "Campaign" is dictated more by the poem's genre than by the nature of the actual events (258, 260). In the opening passage of his memoirs, Esmond protests the inflated formality of dramatic and historical works, and promises that his own life story will be told in a style "familiar rather than heroic" (18). Despite these arguments, protests, and promises, Esmond calls upon a large number of biblical, mythological, and literary heroes, presumably to clarify "the truth" of his personal experiences. Each of the major participants in his life story is, in the course of the narrative, endowed with a repertoire of aesthetic antecedents. Aeneas, Ulysses, Hamlet, Macbeth, Othello, Oedipus, Orpheus, Diogenes, Esau, and Lazarus are a few of the figures to whom Esmond, sometimes facetiously but often soberly, compares Esmond. The discrepancy between his sceptical attitude toward formal art and his reliance on its allusive powers becomes even more emphatic when any one particular allusion is examined. On three separate occasions, for example, he satirizes the painting by Sir Peter Lely portraying Isabella Castlewood as the huntress Diana: if the aging dowager ever resembled the ageless nymph of mythology, time has falsified the relation, once more demonstrating the incompatibility of art and truth (20, 110, 186). Yet the same Esmond who prides himself on this satiric insight eagerly and innocently offers the reader a lengthy description of Beatrix in which he sincerely compares her to "the famous antique statue of the huntress Diana" (136, 137). The aesthetic vocabulary, like the political and religious, is called upon to express after having been deprived of its expressive potential.

Through these discredited metaphors, Thackeray is inviting us to witness the failure of Esmond's language to support his assertions: Esmond offers personal truth as an alternative to and asylum from the precarious instability of formal truths, but his reliance on the vocabulary of those formal truths arouses in us the suspicion that his subjective perceptions are equally precarious. This suspicion is amplified by the second, far more damaging way in which Thackeray manipulates Esmond's narrative.

II

Through Thackeray's second technique, Esmond's narrative violates the primary criterion of subjective truth. If Esmond claimed to be the exponent of objective truth, if he claimed his memoirs were an objective record of public history, we might consult other historical records, check his chronology of battle dates, quarrel with his judgment of Marlborough (as did Winston Churchill[3]), and condemn as fantasy his portrait of the Stuart Pretender. External certification is, however, a wholly irrelevant measure of Esmond's truth: in subjective truth the source of consistency or stability resides not in the external object perceived but in the perceiver himself; consequently, the primary criterion of subjective truth is not external certification but internal consistency.

The claim of internal consistency is implicit in the two basic qualities Esmond attributes to his narrative perspective in the memoirs, stability and precision of perception. He has, at the time he is writing, a single stable overview of his life: he is narrating the events not as they occur but "in his old age, and at a distance" (273). This perspective carries with it the assurance of simplicity and serenity:

Now, at the close of his life, as he sits and recalls in tranquillity . . . (78)

[Young Esmond was] of a hotter and more impetuous nature than now, when care, and reflection, and grey hairs have calmed him. (158)

We get to understand truth better, and grow simpler as we grow older. (94)

This narrative distance stabilizes his vision without diminishing its accuracy. Convinced that great significance often resides in apparent "trivialities" (92, 136), he demands that his history be precise and detailed in its descriptions: it is with a sense of self-obligation that he specifies the location of a smallpox scar on Rachel's forehead, the existence of a wart on the nose of an anonymous nun, or the occurrence of a dinner party "three days after the fifteenth of November, 1712" (379). According to Esmond, both the stability and the precision of his narrative perspective are made possible by the power of memory. His confidence in the permanence of memory is made explicit in continual, casual reassurances to the reader—

How those trivial incidents and words . . . remain fixed on the memory. (24)

He will remember to his life's end . . . (35)

I have good reason to remember it. (83)

He sees them now (will he ever forget them?). (102)

Esmond minds him well of the date. (379)

—and is made emphatic in studied declarations:

Our great thoughts, our great affections, the truths of our life, never leave us. Surely they cannot separate from our consciousness, shall follow it whithersoever that shall go, and are of their nature divine and immortal. (383)

We forget nothing. The memory sleeps but wakens again; I often think how it shall be when, after the last sleep of death, the *reveillée* shall arouse us forever, and the past in one flash of self-consciousness rush back, like the soul, revivified. (394)

The history of the changes and growth experienced by a young Esmond is, then, being told through the stable perspective of the aged Esmond who has, according to his own self portrait, a matured, fixed identity, an immutable core of remembered facts, feelings, and thoughts. This insistence on the accuracy and the stability of his narrative perspective contains the promise of an internally consistent work of history.

Esmond's history, however, fails to fulfill the promise of internal consistency. Thackeray subverts the narrator's assumptions about subjective truth by allowing him to contradict himself incessantly: the trivial factual details to which Esmond assigns such significance, as well as the "great thoughts and affections" he believes "divine and immortal," tend to collapse in the course of the narrative. The novel is a tissue of small, almost imperceptible contradictions, each in isolation insignificant; collectively, devastating. This pattern of mutation will be demonstrated below with a handful of representative examples. "Truth," the word which tolls throughout Esmond's history, means "open to proof"; "truth" calls for a test.

Question 1: Esmond periodically describes the intricacies of his ancestral lineage. His paternal grandfather, Thomas Esmond, had two brothers. What were their names?[4]

> Answer 1: Thomas Esmond had an elder brother, George, and a younger brother, "Francis, in holy orders, who was slain whilst defending the house of Castlewood against the Parliament, anno 1647." (26)

> Answer 2: Thomas Esmond had an elder brother, George, and a younger brother, "Edward, who had embraced the ecclesiastical profession, was slain on Castlewood tower, being engaged there both as preacher and artilleryman." (18)

Question 2: As a young child, Henry Esmond lived at Castlewood with Isabella Esmond, Thomas Esmond, and Father Holt. During one period of political upheaval, the child was left at home alone. Was he made happy or sad by his separation from Father Holt?

> Answer 1: The chapter devoted to this period (I, 4) opens with a description of young Henry's love for Father Holt, and continues: "After being at home for a few months in tranquillity (if theirs might be called tranquillity which was, in truth, a constant bickering) my lord and lady left the country for London, taking their director with them; and his little pupil scarce ever shed more bitter tears in his life than he did for nights after the first parting with his dear friend, as he lay in the lonely chamber next to that which the Father used to occupy." (43)

> Answer 2: The same chapter (I, 4) concludes: "He liked the solitude

of the great house very well; he had all the play-books to read, and no Father Holt to whip him, and a hundred childish pursuits and pastimes, without doors and within, which made this time very pleasant." (49)

Question 3: The first chapter of Esmond's memoirs describes the day on which Francis and Rachel Esmond take possession of the Castlewood estate, previously possessed by Thomas and Isabella. In what year does this event occur?[5]

Answer 1: 1691.

"When Francis, fourth Viscount Castlewood, came to his title, and presently after to take possession of his house of Castlewood, county Hants, in the year 1691, almost the only tenant of the place besides the domestics was a lad of twelve." (20)

Answer 2: 1690.

On the first day of his arrival at Castlewood, Francis mentions the present year when he describes his age in an arithmetic riddle: " 'I was but two years old [when the Roundheads attacked the clock-tower],' says he, 'but take forty-six from ninety, and how old shall I be, kinsman Harry?' " (23)

Question 4: What is the age difference between Esmond and Rachel's son, Frank?

Answer 1: On the day Harry Esmond first meets Rachel's family, Harry is "a lad of twelve years of age" and Frank is "a child of two years old." (21, 23)

Answer 2: "Harry Esmond, who was [Frank's] tutor and eight years his little lordship's senior, had hard work sometimes to keep his own temper and hold his authority over his rebellious little chief and kinsman." (99)

Question 5: Esmond frequently interrupts the flow of the narrative to share with us his vivid memory of physical details, often the details of a beloved person's beauty. At the time the boy Esmond was tutoring the child Beatrix, what color was Beatrix's hair?

Answer 1: "He sees them now (will he ever forget them?) as they used to sit together of the summer evenings—the two golden heads over the page—the child's little hand and the mother's beating the time, with their voices rising and falling in unison." (102)

Answer 2: "And Harry remembered all his life after how he saw his mistress at the window looking out on him, in a white robe, the little Beatrix's chestnut curls resting at her mother's side." (109)

Question 6: Esmond lived his adolescence at Castlewood with Francis and Rachel Esmond. According to Rachel, was it she or her husband who insisted that the child share their home?

Answer 1: "You were but an orphan child when I first saw you—
when *he* [Francis] first saw you, who was so good, and noble, and
trusting. He would have had you sent away, but like a foolish
woman I besought him to let you stay.' " (170)

Answer 2: " 'I always thought . . . that 'twas a pity to shut you out
from the world. You would but have pined and chafed at Castlewood, and 'tis better you should make a name for yourself. I
often said so to my dear lord. How he loved you! 'Twas my lord
that made you stay with us.' " (214)

Question 7: How long prior to his death did Francis Esmond know Henry
Esmond was the legitimate heir to the Castlewood titles?

Answer 1: A few months.

"The late lord, my dear patron, knew not the truth until a few
months before his death, when Father Holt brought the news to
him." (188)

Answer 2: Two years.

"It appeared from my poor lord's hurried confession that he had
been made acquainted with the real facts of the case only two
years since, when Mr. Holt visited him." (195)

Answer 3: One year.

Rachel quoting Isabella: " 'And a proof of this is that a year
before your husband's death, when he thought of taking a place
under the Prince of Orange, Mr. Holt went to him, and told him
what the state of the matter was.' " (331)

Answer 4: Four years.

According to one of Esmond's versions of Francis' dying confession (197), Father Holt's crucial visit was made at the time Sir
John Fenwick's conspiracy blew up, an event which occurred in
December 1696 (124, 125, 127). Francis Esmond died in October
1700 (155). Therefore, the period must have been almost exactly
four years.

Question 8: During which campaign did Esmond serve under General
Lumley?

Answer 1: Vigo Bay Campaign, 1702.

Describing the events immediately following the Vigo Bay Campaign, Esmond tells us: "And Esmond, giving up his post of secretary to General Lumley, whose command was over, and parting
with that officer with many kind expressions of goodwill on the
general's side, had leave to go to London to see if he could push
his fortunes any way further." (205)

Answer 2: Blenheim Campaign, 1704.

Describing the events immediately prior to the Blenheim campaign, Esmond tells us: "[Esmond] went immediately and paid his court to his new general, General Lumley, who received him graciously, having known his father, and also, he was pleased to say, having had the very best accounts of Mr. Esmond from the officer whose aide-de-camp he had been at Vigo." (234)

Question 9: After Francis Esmond dies, Rachel and Henry undergo a long period of estrangement, a period which begins with Esmond's imprisonment in Newgate and ends shortly after his participation in the Vigo expedition. An entire chapter, "The Twenty-Ninth December," is devoted to the day of their dramatic reconciliation at Winchester Cathedral. Both Rachel and Esmond find the timing of the event particularly significant. How many years have elapsed during their separation? What is the date on which the reconciliation takes place? At what time of day does it occur?

Part A: How many years have elapsed?

> Answer 1: According to the character's verbal statements, *one year* has elapsed. Esmond says, "The year of grief and estrangement was over" (213). Rachel says, "But last year we did not drink [to your birthday]—no, no. My lord was cold, and my Harry was likely to die, and my brain was in a fever, and we had no wine." (216)
>
> Answer 2: According to a comparison of the two dates on which the separation and reunion occur, *two years* have elapsed: Esmond was imprisoned in October 1700 (155), and it is presently December, 1702 (227).
>
> Answer 3: According to a comparison of Esmond's respective ages, *three years* have elapsed; when imprisoned Esmond was twenty-two (174); prior to his return to Rachel, he is twenty-five (209).

Part B: We know that the reconciliation itself occurs in December. According to Rachel, is it before or after Christmas?

> Answer 1: *After.*
>
> " 'Do you know what day it is?' [Rachel] continued. 'It is the twenty-ninth of December—it is your birthday!' " (216)
>
> Answer 2: *Before.*
>
> " 'I cannot follow [my children] into the great world, where their way lies—it scares me. They will come and visit me; and you will, sometimes, Henry—yes, sometimes, as now, in the Holy Advent season, when I have seen and blessed you once more.' " (217)[6]

Part C: At what time of day does their reconciliation occur?

Answers: Before Esmond even enters the cathedral, he tells us: "The

organ was playing, the winter's day was already growing grey, as
he passed under the street-arch into the cathedral-yard and made
his way into the ancient solemn edifice" (211). It is not until after
the evening prayers and a "rather long" anthem that Rachel looks
up and sees Esmond. Describing that moment later, Rachel says:
"I looked up from the book and saw you. I was not surprised
when I saw you. I knew you would come, my dear, and saw the
gold sunshine round your head" (216).

Question 10: How was Esmond's play, *The Faithful Fool*, received by
Rachel and its audience?

  Answer 1: "Mr. Henry Esmond remained in his sickroom, where he
  wrote a fine comedy that his mistress pronounced to be sublime
  and that was acted no less than three successive nights in London
  in the next year." (322)

  Answer 2: "But it must be owned that the audience yawned through
  the play and that it perished on the third night, with only half a
  dozen persons to behold its agonies. Esmond and his two mistresses came to the first night, and Miss Beatrix fell asleep, whilst
  her mother, who had not been to a play since King James the
  Second's time, thought the piece, though not brilliant, had a very
  pretty moral." (344)

Question 11: Was Frank Esmond wounded at Ramillies?

  Answer 1: "I remember at Ramillies, when [Frank] was hit and fell,
  a great big red-haired Scotch sergeant flung his halbert down, burst
  out a-crying like a woman, seizing him up as if he had been an
  infant and carrying him out of the fire." (225)

  Answer 2: In that part of Esmond's narrative specifically devoted to
  Ramillies, he tells us "if he had any anxiety about his boy 'twas
  relieved at once" (266) that evening, for he finds Frank singing,
  drinking, and enriched with booty looted during the day's battle.
  Esmond concludes, "Far more pleasant to him that the victory [of
  Ramillies], though for that too he may say *meminisse juvat*, it was
  to find that the day was over and his dear young Castlewood was
  unhurt" (267).

Question 12: Dick Steele was only four years old when his father died.
According to Steele, did he at that early age experience grief or was he
oblivious to the death?

  Answer 1: " 'That was the first sensation of grief,' Dick said, 'I ever
  knew. I remember I went into the room where his body lay and
  my mother sat weeping beside it. I had my battledore in my hand
  and fell a-beating the coffin and calling papa, on which my mother

caught me in her arms and told me in a flood of tears papa could
not hear me and would play with me no more, for they were
going to put him under ground, whence he could never come to us
again. And this,' said Dick kindly, 'has made me pity all children
ever since, and caused me to love thee, my poor fatherless,
motherless lad.' " (74)

Answer 2: " '... (grief touches the young but lightly, and I remember I beat a drum at the coffin of my own father) ...' " (181)

Question 13: According to Esmond, is a man's suffering greatest before,
during, or after the painful event? That is, is the anticipation of pain,
the immediate experience of pain, or the memory of pain the most
difficult to endure?

(Note: in all three quotations below, the painful event referred to is the
loss of a mistress.)

Answer 1: The memory of pain is more painful than the immediate
experience.
"You do not know how much you suffer in those critical maladies
of the heart until the disease is over and you look back on it
afterwards. During the time, the suffering is at least sufferable."
(176)

Answer 2: The immediate experience of pain is far more painful than
the memory.
"Wounds heal rapidly in a heart of two and twenty, hopes revive
daily, and courage rallies in spite of a man. Perhaps as Esmond
thought of his late despondency and melancholy and how irremediable it had seemed to him as he lay in his prison a few months
back, he was almost mortified in his secret mind at finding himself
so cheerful." (202)

Answer 3: The anticipation of pain is worse than the immediate
experience.
"From the loss of a tooth to that of a mistress there's no pang
that is not bearable. The apprehension is much more cruel than
the certainty; and we make up our mind to the misfortune when
'tis irremediable, part with the tormentor, and mumble our crust
on t'other side of the jaws." (361)

Question 14: Esmond never wins Beatrix. Does he ever outgrow his love
for her?

Answer 1: "Her cheek was desecrated, her beauty tarnished; shame
and honour stood between it and him. The love was dead within
him; had she a crown to bring him with her love, he felt that both
would degrade him." (454)

"As [Esmond] looked at her, he wondered that he could ever have loved her. His love of ten years was over; it fell down dead on the spot, at the Kensington Tavern, where Frank brought him the note out of *Eikun Basilikum*. The Prince blushed and bowed low, as she gazed at him, and quitted the chamber. I have never seen her from that day." (459)

Answer 2: "I invoke that beautiful spirit from the shades and love her still; or rather I should say such a past is always present to a man; such a passion once felt forms a part of his whole being and cannot be separated from it." (383)

Question 15: While it is difficult to know with any certainty whether or not Esmond's love for Beatrix dies when he reads her note contained in the *Eikun Basilikum*, we do at least know that he reads her note contained in the *Eikun Basilikum*. Where is Edmond when he receives and reads the note?

Answer 1: In that passage of the memoirs specifically devoted to a description of Frank's delivery of the note, Esmond twice tells us that the event occurs in a tavern called the King's Arms. (449, 451)

Answer 2: "[His love] fell down dead on the spot, at the Kensington Tavern, where Frank brought him the note out of *Eikun Basilikum*." (459)

Throughout the novel, a fact given is a fact that will be repeated, and repeated, contradicted.[7] Thackeray's technique, and its intended effect on the reader, are clarified when contrasted with the approach of Samuel Beckett, another writer who uses contradictions to make visible the instability of truth. Moran's narrative in *Molloy* begins: "It is midnight. The rain is beating on the windows." It ends: "Then I went back into the house and wrote, It is midnight. The rain is beating on the windows. It was not midnight. It was not raining."[8] The final sentence cancels out the first and, by implication, all that follows the first: the reader is given a simple instruction to erase from his mind all he has read. The life span of particular details is even shorter in *Texts for Nothing* where individual sentences are immediately self-cancelling: "Suddenly, no at last . . ." (I); "This evening, I say this evening, perhaps it's morning . . ." (IV); "Dry, it's possible, or wet . . ." (II).[9] For Beckett's narrators, the instability of truth is a self-evident given of reality; consequently, the contradictions are presented in overt declarations; they are made immediately accessible to the reader's attention.

The contradictions in *Henry Esmond* are not part of Esmond's overt, surface narrative but, rather, part of Thackeray's subversive counter-narrative. While Thackeray necessarily intends the reader to recognize them, the mode of recognition required is not the overt, self-conscious act expected of Beckett's reader; for they are carefully calculated to disorient and discomfort the reader without necessarily enabling him to specify the source of discomfort. Thackeray relies on two major factors to obscure the errors. The first is their location. As was evident in the series of quotations given above, the two terms of each contradiction are separated by anywhere from one to several hundred pages of intervening material, a separation which invariably interferes with our ability to recognize the error. A rare instance in which both terms of the contradiction occur within a single sentence will make visible two additional aspects of location that typically come into play. The contradicted fact is seldom the major clause of the sentence; it is usually a qualifying phrase embedded deep within the complex sentence structure of Esmond's prose:

The French began the action, as usual, with a cannonade which lasted three hours, when they made their attack, advancing in twelve lines, four of Foot and four of Horse, upon the Allied troops in the wood where we were posted. (290)

Obscured by its subordinate position in the sentence, the contradiction is further obscured by the nature of the surrounding subject matter: the sentence just cited occurs in the fourth of four successive, short paragraphs which contain a total of twenty-one numbers, numbers which blunt our sensitivity to Esmond's erroneous computation.[10] The oblique presentation of the contradiction, then, prevents it from being noticed by the reader; it does not, however, prevent it from affecting the reader. While we will probably not stop and consciously acknowledge the incompatibility of "twelve lines" and "four of Foot and four of Horse," neither will we have a visual image of the battle formation used in the French attack. While, in turn, we will probably not notice our inability to grasp this one isolated image, we will begin to notice that, despite the aura of precision in Esmond's descriptions, we have very few coherent impressions of the world he is describing. So much for logistics.

The second major factor which obscures the contradictions is their asymmetry. Beckett's contradictions are conspicuous not only because of their direct presentation but also because the contradictions themselves are symmetrical: they consist of antithetical pairs such as raining-not raining, evening-morning, suddenly-at last. A small percentage of Thackeray's are equally symmetrical—Frank is both wounded at Ramillies and not wounded at Ramillies (Question 11 above)—and are only made inconspicuous by the oblique mode of presentation. But the majority fall into two classes characterized by different degrees of asymmetry. Those in the first class consist of pairs whose terms, though not strict symmetrical opposites, are mutually exclusive: Esmond throughout his memoirs reckons his age on the birth year of 1679 (20, 138, *passim*) yet without hesitation or qualification relays to the reader Father Holt's description of his birth a few weeks after his parents' marriage in 1677 (197, 275, 276). The more the terms of a contradiction approximate each other while yet remaining contradictory, the more difficult it is to identify the contradictions. It is this phenomenon which makes the contradictions in the second group far more obscure than those in the first. They constitute a class exemplified by Beatrix's golden and chestnut hair (Question 5 above). The discrepancy between the two colors is too small to strike the reader as a contradiction; yet golden and chestnut, while neither symmetrical opposites (white and black) nor even mutually exclusive alternatives (golden and black), are facts which fail to coincide, reinforce, and substantiate each other and, therefore, facts which deprive us of a coherent visual image, facts which undermine our stable participation in the narrative.

The complexity of this second form of mutation is evident in Esmond's references to music:

1. "And Mr. Holt found that Harry could read and write and possessed the two languages of French and English very well; and when he asked Harry about singing, the lad broke out with a hymn to the tune of Dr. Martin Luther, which set [the Catholic] Mr. Holt a-laughing." (35)
2. "[Rachel's] songs did not amuse [her husband], and she hushed them and the children when in his presence. My lord sat silent at his dinner, drinking greatly, his lady opposite to him, looking furtively at his face, though also speechless." (97)
3. "[Beatrix] sang sweetly, but this was from her mother's teaching—not Harry Esmond's, who could scarce distinguish between 'Greensleeves' and 'Lillibullero.' " (102)
4. "Beatrix could sing and dance like a nymph. Her voice was her father's delight after dinner." (122)
5. "Why did [Beatrix's] voice thrill in his ear so? She could not sing near so well as Nicolini or Mrs. Tofts; nay, she sang out of tune, and yet he liked to hear her better than St. Cecilia." (301)
6. "The song yet lay on the harpsichord which Esmond had writ and [Beatrix and Esmond] had sung together." (313)
7. "Mr. Esmond whistled 'Lillibullero,' at which Teague's eyes began to twinkle." (325)

8. "[Beatrix] never at that time could be brought to think but of the
   world and her beauty, and seemed to have no more sense of devotion
   than some people have of music, that cannot distinguish one air from
   another." (338)
9. "[Beatrix] set up a school of children and taught singing to some of
   them. We had a pair of beautiful old organs in Castlewood Church, on
   which she played admirably, so that the music there became to be
   known in the country for many miles round, and no doubt people came
   to see the fair organist as well as to hear her." (395)

Each of these quotations either states or implies something about the
musical ability of Esmond or Beatrix. When read serially, they do not
appear strikingly incompatible. Each, however, is slightly out of phase with
those it follows, preventing the emergence of any single coherent picture.
The fifth reference, when read in isolation, suggests that Esmond's musical
acumen surpasses Beatrix's: she sings out of tune; his ear is sensitive
enough to detect her faulty intonation and to appraise her talent in relation to a second singer. The third reference is an inversion of the fifth:
here Esmond credits Beatrix with the ability to sing and confesses that he
himself is tone deaf. The fifth and third are, then, when each is read in
isolation, contradictory. When read in conjunction, however, they are
strangely compatible: the answer to Esmond's question "Why did her voice
thrill in his ear so?" is that an out-of-tune voice is resonating in a tone-deaf
ear. The third and the fifth references are, in turn, contradicted by the
sixth and the ninth: Esmond's formerly tone-deaf ear now enables him not
simply to sing but to compose music; Beatrix's formerly absent musical
talent now enables her to teach singing (the power of teaching is specifically denied to the tone deaf in the third) and endows her with a profi-
ciency on the organ admired "for many miles round." Even the more
neutral statements, those which neither credit nor discredit the characters,
lose their neutrality when juxtaposed with other statements: the seventh
reference, for example, would be simply a neutral description of an event
were it not that the anonymous Irish stranger immediately recognizes
Esmond's rendition of the very song Esmond has earlier named to illustrate
his inability to carry a tune. While the quotations collectively credit Beatrix
and Esmond with a spectrum of musical talent that ranges from poor to
distinguished, the mutation from one statement to the next is almost imperceptible. The method of contradiction is not, therefore, one which
invites us to keep tally of the inversions during the process of reading; it is,
however, one which ensures that we will emerge from the novel with little
or no idea of the characters' musical abilities.

The instability of Esmond's world, and the discomfort that instability instills in the reader, can not be demonstrated with any single instance of contradiction. Contradiction, in this novel, is never an instance, self-contained and isolated; it is a process, relentless and multi-dimensional. While all the aforementioned contradictions are occurring, the English victory at Lille, achieved over an enemy "six or seven times greater" (288), is achieved over an enemy "five times" greater (291); the estrangement of Strephon and Cloe, a psychological separation for which neither is exclusively to blame (97), is blamed exclusively on Strephon's physical brutality (119); Sir John Fenwick, executed for his participation in the conspiracy of 1691 (64), is executed for his participation in the conspiracy of 1695 (124); the memory of Nancy Sievewright, filling Esmond with gentle respect for the surprising strength of first love and its "magnetic attraction which draws people together from ever so far" (83, 84), provokes Esmond to an impatient dismissal of first love whose "passions . . . are mostly abortive and are dead almost before they are born" (94); and, far from finally, throughout all this, Esmond is faithfully served by his boyhood friend and lifelong manservant, Job Lockwood, Tom Lockwood, Jack Lockwood, and John Lockwood (49, 344, 357, 242).

While it would be neither possible nor enlightening to enumerate end-lessly all instances of contradiction, the discussion up to this point, confined to the narrative proper, has ignored a crucial part of the novel. Esmond's memoirs are accompanied by his daughter's introductory preface and footnotes appended by his wife, his daughter, and his grandsons. Esmond, as mentioned previously, conceives of the family as the unit of historical continuity: he not only wants to tell the truth about his past; he wants the truth told about his past to be understood by his family. The preface and footnotes provide a measure of the extent to which that desire is fulfilled. As the following examples will suggest, the family provides historical continuity only in perpetuating Esmond's custom of con-tradiction.

1. Despite Esmond's frequent references to his own act of narration, it is difficult to determine the precise time at which he is writing. Most of his comments suggest that he is elderly, so elderly that he considers death imminent: "Esmond could repeat to his last day . . ." (94); "To the very last hour of his life, Esmond remembered . . ." (21); "Now, at the close of his life . . ." (78). One particular statement, "My years are past the Hebrew poet's limit (375), an allusion to Psalm 90 where man's terminal age is given as three score and ten, reveals that *Esmond's age is at least 70 and the date, at least 1750.*

   A second set of comments, however, suggests that *Esmond is writing*

in his early 60's during the early 1740's; he tells us he is writing 40
years after the Vigo Campaign of 1702 (202); at a later point in the
memoirs, he tells us it is 40 years after the Blenheim Campaign of 1704
(383); and still later, he mentions that it is presently 27 years after the
political conspiracy of 1714 (402). (While all three comments refer to
the early 1740's, the sequence is disconcerting: as the memoirs progress,
the year progresses from 1742 to 1744 and then moves back to 1741.)

The contradiction is compounded rather than resolved by information provided in the preface and footnotes. According to Rachel Warrington's preface, Esmond's wife died in 1736 (viii). Presumably his wife
was alive during the writing of the memoirs since she has appended
footnotes (e.g., 315, 435). Consequently a third set of figures emerges:
Esmond is writing in the early 1730's and is in his early 50's.

2. According to the chronology given in Rachel Warrington's preface, her
   two sons were born either after their grandmother died or, at most, six
   months prior to her death (viii, ix). A footnote written by one of the
   grandsons, however, indicates that he and his brother were at least
   several years old before their grandmother died: "And our grandmother
   used to tell us children . . ." (296).

3. Esmond is, for Esmond, consistent in his condemnation of war's invariably base brutality (238, 266, 287, 321), a brutality so indiscriminate
   that it makes a mockery of victory celebrations, converts *Te Deum* into
   a "woeful and dreary satire" (321), and reduces "God is on our side"
   proclamations into revelations of fatuous ignorance. Yet when, lament-
   ing the continual deaths of young soldiers, Esmond exclaims, "What
   must have been the continued agonies of fears and apprehensions which
   racked the gentle breasts of wives and matrons in those dreadful days"
   (315), Rachel responds in an indignant footnote, "What indeed? Psm.
   XCI: 2, 3, 7" (315). The final verse of the reference reads, "A thousand
   shall fall at thy side, and ten thousand at thy right hand, *but* it shall
   not come nigh thee." Rachel has apparently missed the point of
   Esmond's arguments concerning the true nature of war.

4. Describing Rachel Esmond's complexion after the smallpox epidemic,
   Esmond writes, "When the marks of the disease cleared away, they did
   not, it is true, leave furrows or scars on her face (except one, perhaps,
   on her forehead over her left eyebrow); but the delicacy of her rosy
   colour and complexion were gone" (92). Rachel Warrington writes in
   her preface, "My dear mother possessed to the last an extraordinary
   brightness and freshness of complexion; nor would people believe that
   she did not wear rouge" (ix).

5. In one of Esmond's passages announcing his allegiance to truth he

writes that "he would have his grandsons believe or represent him to be not an inch taller than Nature has made him" (80). In compliance with the letter rather than the spirit of Esmond's words, Rachel Warrington notes in her preface that her father "was of rather low stature, not being above five feet seven inches in height" (viii). But she misunderstands the spirit of his request, for she goes on to speak of him in unmeasured praise: she says that he was unequalled in "grace and majesty of deportment" except by Washington (viii) and asks, "They say he liked to be first in his company, but what company was there in which he would not be first?" (x).

6. In describing the battle of Ramillies (1706), Esmond praises Marlborough's "intrepid skill" and calls him "the very genius of victory" (264). In describing the siege of Lille (1708) Esmond confesses his suspicion that Marlborough received a treasonous bribe immediately prior to the battle (287, 288). In a footnote, Esmond's grandson tells us of his grandfather's conviction that Marlborough received a treasonous bribe immediately prior to the battle of Ramillies (296).

One imagines Esmond's memoirs passed down endlessly from era to era, each generation appending its own footnotes, contributing its own layer of contradiction, compounding the confusion until the last semblance of stability disintegrates.

This sustained rhythm of statement and counter-statement systematically erodes the world Esmond is laboring to preserve. The following section will focus on Thackeray's precise use of language and demonstrate that the same instability characterizing sets of sentences is visible in individual words and images. Esmond can not, as he hopes, preserve his world by committing it to the written word, for the instability is inherent in the structure of language itself.

III

Typically when a writer reiterates a particular word or image throughout a work, he limits and controls its connotations, endowing it with a central core of meaning which, while gaining weight and resonance, remains essentially stable throughout successive repetitions. The image becomes not only a vehicle of meaning but a vehicle of stability: in the underlying coherence of its iterations, it functions as a structural or unifying element in the work. In *Henry Esmond* the opposite obtains. Denying the possibility that anything possesses an essential or fixed identity, Thackeray endows a given image with as many disparate connotations as possible, intentionally depriving it of a stable core of meaning. His imagery becomes a vehicle of instability, undermining rather than contributing to the structural coherence of Esmond's narrative.

Earlier this essay alluded to the incident in which a fire burns a sheaf of papers, leaving unburned a single passage warning of the disjunction between life and truth (66). Thackeray's treatment of fire is consonant with this message, for the image recurs incessantly, its meaning changing with each new appearance. In the following passage, for example, fire first embodies the idea of success and then the idea of failure:

[Addison] was bringing out his own play of *Cato* at the time, the *blaze* of which quite extinguished Esmond's farthing candle [his play, *The Faithful Fool*]; and his name was never put to the piece, which was printed as by a Person of Quality. Only nine copies were sold, though Mr. Dennis, the great critic, praised it and said 'twas a work of great merit; and Colonel Esmond had the whole impression *burned* one day in a rage, by Jack Lockwood, his man. (344, italics added)

Often, as in this instance, the connotations are paired by antithesis: the positive and the negative, here success and failure, cancel each other out. More often, however, even the logic of antithesis is abandoned: in the majority of passages Thackeray simply moves rapidly and arbitrarily from one connotation to a second to a third, allowing each to replace the one it follows until replaced by the one it precedes, thereby preventing the image from acquiring any solidarity of meaning:

"Fire! Fire!" cries out Father Holt, sending another shot after the trooper. . . . "The poor gentleman's horse was a better one than that I rode," Blaise continues. . . . He read that to himself, which only said, "Burn the papers in the cupboard, burn this. You know nothing about anything." (59)

"Here is a paper whereon his Majesty hath deigned to commence some verses in honour, or dishonour of Beatrix. Here is 'Madame' and 'Flamme,' 'Cruelle' and 'Rebelle,' and 'Amour' and 'Jour,' in the royal writing and spelling." . . . "Sir," says the Prince, burning with rage. . . . And taking the taper up and backing before the Prince with very great ceremony, Mr. Esmond passed into the little chaplain's room. . . . And as Esmond spoke he set the papers burning in the brazier. (457)

As these passages suggest, the creation of a self-effacing image requires that a given image be repeated as frequently as possible while any given meaning be repeated as infrequently as possible. This effect is most efficiently demonstrated with a catalogue enumerating the divergent meanings assigned to fire. It is not the particular meanings themselves, but their number and range which make visible the absence of a stable center in the connotative activity of the image:

1. Fire as success: " 'Tis not a masterpiece of wit, but Dick is a good fellow, though he doth not set the Thames on fire" (261, see 344).
   The expression, "set the Thames on fire," here used metaphorically, is later used in a strictly literal capacity (378).
2. Fire as failure: "Here it was her ladyship's turn to shriek, for the captain, with his fist shaking the pillows and bolsters, at last came to 'burn,' as they say in the play of forfeits" (63, see 344).
3. Fire revealing: "As characters written with a secret ink come out with the application of fire and disappear again and leave the paper white so soon as it is cool . . ." (445).
4. Fire concealing: The burning of conspiratorial notes, deathbed confessions, marriage certificates, birth certificates (50, 59, 165, 439, 457). Occasionally the same fire simultaneously reveals and conceals. The fire that burns Francis Esmond's dying confession simultaneously illuminates an allegorical mosaic over the fireplace. However, the revealed allegory returns us to the idea of concealing; for it pictures "Jacob in hairy gloves cheating Isaac of Esau's birthright" (166).
5. Fire as agent of illegality: The burning of documents, see above.
6. Fire as agent of legality: "The sentence, as we all know, in these cases is that the culprit lies a year in prison, or during the King's pleasure, and is burned in the hand" (173).
7. Fire coupled with genius: "The fire and genius, perhaps, he had not (that were given to baser men), but except these he had some of the best qualities of a leader" (401).
8. Fire as beauty: "Esmond looked at Beatrix, blazing with her jewels on her beautiful neck" (415, see 36).
9. Fire as disease: "The St. Anthony's fire broke out on the royal legs" (425). "Your lordship would be much better if you took off all that flannel—it only serves to inflame the toe" (147). While the passages coupling fire with disease focus on the feet, "the fire of the Foot" (288) refers to the gunfire of the infantry.
10. Fire as security: The domesticity and safety implicit in the fireside hearth (84, 85, 118, 140, 141). While the fireside hearth usually connotes comfort and safety, several incidents emphasize its perils: "I daren't leave the child lest he should fall into the fire" (378, see 126).
11. Fire as danger: The guns of war. Book II, *passim*.
    In contrast to the "seriousness" inherent in the destructive fires of war, there is also the destructive fire of caprice: among the schoolboy

pranks which eventually result in Frank's expulsion from Cambridge is his attempt to "set fire to Nevil's Court" (248).

12. Fire as mortal passion: Anger and desire: "With her illness and altered beauty my lord's fire for his wife disappeared" (121); "Hot as a flame at this salute" (369); "Cries the doctor in a great fume" (378); "A burning blush flushed over her whole face" (385); "Burning with rage" (457).

13. Fire as immortality: Fire as a test of sainthood (69).
Fire as punishment of hell (330).
Fire of sacred love: "From that day until now, and from now till death is past, and beyond it, he prays that sacred flame may ever burn" (234, see 120).

14. Fire as flame, the color: "Flame-coloured brocade" (38).
Fire as flame, a lamp: "There were flambeaux in the room lighting up the brilliant mistress of it" (385).

15. Fire in the names of unrelated people and places: Blaise, Tyburn, Ashburnam, Halifax, Firebrace, Boyle; and to add fuel to the fire, Castlewood, Lockwood, Marwood, Harwood, Rookwood, Woodstock, Holt, Berwick, Fenwick, Lodwick, Lowick, Warwick, and Hampton Wick.

This constant, deliberate mutation of meaning argues that truth, which posits the existence of a stable core of meaning, is an *ignis fatuus*.

Fire is not, of course, the sole instance of the self-effacing image. Equally unstable, for example, is the idea of the connective bond, its most positive connotations always threatening to collapse into its most negative. The dissonant images which spin forth from the idea include the household head's "purse strings" (31), the child's "lines for eels" (49), the coquet's "nets and baits" (341), the priest's "authority to bind and to loose" (218), the "mother's apron strings" (128), the domineering wife's "leading strings" (391), ornaments connoting love or attachment such as a "string of diamonds," a locket, a velvet bracelet, and a gold button from a military jacket (368, 164, 396, 463), "matrimonial chains" (399), an impotent religious medal (200), the honorable order of the "Garter" (361), the "garter" with which one hangs oneself (421), the rope with which one is hanged (20), colorful ribbons adorning a young girl's beauty (219), military ribbons connoting honor (359), military ribbons connoting dishonor (267), ribbons designating royalty (458), the silk-weaving profession of Henry's foster parents (277), beautiful tapestries (37), "spun smocks" as an image of demeaning servility (375), hair woven together as an image of family intimacy and affection (409), the "web" of bedding (409), the "web of coquetry" (351), the "snare" of deceit (456), Ealing, Bates, Knightsbridge,

Tunbridge, Brace, Bracegirdle, Armstrong, Cheyne, Lock, Lockit, Lockwood, Scurlock, Bullock, Button, and Webb.

In contrast to the complexity of these images, there are also much simpler manifestations of the instability of words.[11] The image of the rose is made an ineffective vehicle of meaning by its indiscriminate application to such diverse figures as Rachel (92, 181, 219, 355), Beatrix (136, 221, 454), Isabella (30, 306), Nancy Sievewright (93), Rosamond, the tipsy painted mistress of Francis (100), Rosaria, the "country lass endowed with every virtue" in Esmond's play (344), the "Rose," a London tavern (159, 209), and the *Rose*, a Spanish ship (226). Again, honorific titles such as "his Majesty," "my lord," "my mistress," and "our general" are deprived of single, stable referents: during the course of the narrative each is given so many antecedents that in any given instance it is often not immediately clear about whom Esmond is speaking. For example, describing the events which occur on the night Francis dies defending his wife's honor, Esmond writes, "My lord had a paper of oranges, which he ate and offered to the actresses, joking with them" (160). While "My lord" may refer to Francis Esmond, it may instead refer to "my lord the Earl of Warwick and Holland," mentioned in the sentence immediately preceding the sentence cited; then again, it may refer to "my Lord Mohun," mentioned in the sentence immediately following the sentence cited. At any rate, the reader will never know whether or not Frank busied himself flirting on the night of his fatal mission. In addition to single words, images, and titles, many multi-word expressions are also deprived of meaning by their occurrence in two or more dissonant contexts. At one point in the narrative, Esmond announces:

Now it was, after this, that Lord Castlewood *swore his great oath* that he would never, so help him Heaven, be engaged in any transaction against that brave and merciful man [King William]; and so he told Holt when the indefatigable priest visited him and would have had him engage in a farther conspiracy. (125, italics added)

When this sentence is read in isolation, "swore his great oath" seems a solemn expression: the weighty tone of the sentence implies that Frank's swearing of the oath is a singular event attended by significant political consequences. When the sentence is read in its narrative context, however, its potential impact is lost; for up to this point the expression "swore a great oath" has been consistently used to introduce the blasphemies accompanying Frank's frequent fits of merriment, impatience, or anger (87, 90, 96, 106, 122). Once more the ground suddenly shifts beneath the reader.[12]

In the midst of this constant verbal mutation there is one recurring image which has the semblance of stability. It is the image of Castlewood.

Esmond repeatedly prefaces his descriptions of the old estate with the insistence that Castlewood has a permanent hold on his memory. Furthermore, his new estate in America is named after the old, strengthening the impression that "Castlewood" is emblamatic of the underlying unity of experience. Critic John Loofbourow, one of Thackeray's most careful readers, claims that the image sustains "the novel's memory-motif," that its various "modalities are all aspects of permanence," and that "the persistent recurrence of the image is as timeless as memory itself."[13] Because the motif has this aura of permanence, it demands special attention here: as will be shown, Castlewood is an example of rather than an exception to Thackeray's reliance on disorienting imagery.

The Castlewood motif is in part a composite of several recurring images which, unlike the novel's other images, do not change when repeated. While, however, each remains stable from its first to its final occurrence, each from its first to its final occurrence connotes instability. At the heart of Castlewood, "plashing away in silence," is the fountain—a time-honored image of fluidity and flux (37, 40, 52, 152, 153, 392). Mentioned almost as frequently as the fountain is the "great army of rooks"—rooks that never fly unattended by connotations of deceit and fraud (23, 36, 37, 40, 453). Castlewood's sundial—time measured in the passing of a shadow, a shadow passing over the inscription *memento mori*—is a third image of the insubstantial and the transient (152, 394). Esmond's most vivid memories of Castlewood are typically of events occurring at dawn or dusk—moments, once more, of transition and flux (23, 36, 37, 40, 393, 453). Finally, in most instances three or four of these images occur simultaneously within a single passage: the idea of instability inherent in each is compounded and reinforced by the presence of the others.

Those aspects of the Castlewood motif which remain consistent throughout successive repetitions are, then, images in which the concept of instability is inherent. Conversely, those aspects of the Castlewood motif in which the concept of instability does not inhere are inconsistent in their repetitions: they are subjected to the contradiction and mutation elsewhere operative in the novel. If any aspect of Castlewood should convey stability and solidarity, it is the structure of the mansion itself, the fortress-like architecture with its ancient towers, gables, and buttresses. The locations of the buildings in relation to the surrounding land and the locations of particular rooms in relation to one another prove, however, to be as fluid as the fountain.

Esmond's descriptions confound the compass points. According to one passage, Castlewood is located on a hill and has two courts: the eastern court is the fountain court; the western court is the clock-tower court destroyed by the Roundheads in 1647. To the east lie the river, the road to London, and Castlewood village. To the west lie the hills from which enemy gunfire destroyed the western court (40). Approximately half of Esmond's other descriptions coincide with the description above, from which the other half depart. While, for example, it is reassuring that Esmond watches the dawn rise over Castlewood village (393), it is disconcerting that standing in the western court facing the sunset he sees Castlewood village (23). Again, when as a child Henry first comes to Castlewood with Father Holt, they are approaching from the east facing west; for they have come from London by the London road and enter by the front gate at the fountain court. Yet Esmond comments on the flaming reflection of the sunset in the windows, a reflection that he would only see if the sunset were behind him—if he were approaching from the west facing east (36). Again, throughout Book I of the memoirs, the woods where the rooks roost is located "behind" the house; that is, in the hills to the west of Castlewood (23, 37, 40). Returning to Castlewood in Book III, however, Esmond passes by the elms on the Castlewood village green and comments that "the rooks were still roosting" there (453).

Just as Castlewood's relation to the landscape shifts, so the rooms within Castlewood shift. The Queen Elizabeth room, with its tapestries and stained glass windows, is occupied first by Isabella and years later by Beatrix. While the room is usually located in the western or clock-tower court (23, 455) on at least one occasion it is located immediately above Holt's and Harry's rooms (37), rooms which are consistently situated in the eastern court. While Harry's bedchamber and Holt's bedchamber and study are consistently located near one another in the eastern court, the precise arrangement of the three rooms peridically shifts: on one occasion, Harry's sleeping closet is within Holt's study (44); on another occasion, Harry's room and Holt's study are separate but adjoining chambers (392); on a third occasion, Harry's room and Holt's study face each other on opposite sides of a corridor (50). Again, the terrace-walk is usually located in the western court (23, 40, 41, 394). Yet one day when Rachel faints on the terrace, she is quickly revived with water from the fountain—which is in the fountain court, half a mile away (151, 453). The sundial, too, roams from the eastern (152) to the western court (394). Finally, Esmond tells us that on his penultimate visit to Castlewood, he lay awake "for many hours as the clock kept tolling (in tones so well remembered)" (392). The tones so well remembered may well not be remembered by the reader, for while we have heard the cawing of the rooks, the tolling of the church bells, and the babbling of the fountain, we have never heard a sound from the clock-tower, which was partially destroyed by the Roundheads in 1647 and never restored (23, 40). Esmond's vividly remembered Castlewood, the bastion of stability and tribute to the power of memory, seems at times to be located on a rotating hill and to have migrating rooms and a clock that re-materializes during the sleepless nights of sentimental visitors. The Castlewood motif, like the novel's other images and idioms, seems intended to disorient rather than orient the reader.

The instability introduced into the narrative by these disorienting images and rapid shifts in word meanings is compounded by one additional factor, the intentional inconsistencies in grammar. There is, for example, no coherent logic underlying Esmond's rapid alternations between first and third person:

Now, at the close of *his* life, as *he* sits and recalls in tranquillity the happy and busy scenes of it, *he* can think, not ungratefully, that *he* has been faithful to that early vow. . . . But few men's life-voyages are destined to be all prosperous, and this calm of which *we* are speaking was soon to come to an end. (78, italics added)

Prometheus *I* saw, but when first *I* ever had any words with him . . . *I* disliked this Mr. Swift, and heard many a story about him, of his conduct to men and his words to women. He could flatter the great as much as he could bully the weak; and *Mr. Esmond*, being younger and hotter in that day than now, was determined, should he ever meet this dragon, not to run away from his teeth and his fire. (374, 375, italics added)

Esmond desired *my* landlord not to acquaint Mistress Beatrix with *his* coming. (437, italics added)

We travelled through the night, *Esmond* discoursing to *his* mistress of the events of the last twenty-four hours. (460, italics added)

Finally, even that part of grammar devoted to the external form of words is subjected to mutation. In Esmond's imitation *Spectator* paper, Jocasta's trick to elicit her suitor's name springs out of her complaint about the absence of consistent rules in English orthography, the arbitrary relation between sound and spelling (347). On another occasion, Esmond remarks that "spelling was not an article of general commodity in the world then" (185); and periodically, with bemused detachment, he comments on the poor spelling abilities of Isabella (185), Marlborough (185), the Chevalier (457), young Frank Castlewood (334), and Frank's wife, Clotilda (334). Esmond himself, however, is also victimized by the instability of English orthography. Although Thackeray's modern editors, mistaking strategy for carelessness, have "corrected" many of the original inconsistencies in spelling, a few have survived: there is Sieveright (49) and Sievewright (83),

Hexton Castle (70) and Hexham Castle (393), Brussels (280) and Bruxelles (403), Marshal (324) and Mareschal (324), Montagu (83) and Montague (308) and Aimes (164) and Aymé (438).

The instability of grammar, the instability of spelling, and, above all, the instability of imagery and word meaning conspire to create a language which is often as much a barrier between Esmond and the reader as it is a vehicle of communication, a language in which both meaning and tone repeatedly shift, rapidly alternating between coherence and incoherence. While it is not possible to chart the disruptive effect of this linguistic instability, a brief examination of one passage will begin to suggest the dislocation and discomfort it generates. Book III focuses on Esmond's attempt to win Beatrix's love by his participation in a political conspiracy. After recounting the failure of the conspiracy and his loss of Beatrix, Esmond summarizes the remainder of his life story with three concluding paragraphs in which he announces his marriage to his beloved mistress, Rachel. The overt tone of this final passage is one of serenity and joy: Esmond calls his marriage "the great joy of my life" (462) and describes their life together in America as one of sustained tranquillity (463). Many nineteenth- and twentieth-century readers, however, have found themselves unable to share Esmond's attitude toward his fate. Their dissatisfaction is in part attributable to the language itself, for the passage is a paradigm of the many modes of ambivalence examined in this section of the discussion. An analysis of a few representative sentences will suggest how consistently and artfully Thackeray operates on his reader in these final moments.

Esmond makes his transition from Beatrix and his past aspirations to Rachel and his future reality in a startlingly abrupt summation:

With the sound of King George's trumpets, all the vain hopes of the weak and foolish young Pretender were blown away; and with that music too, I may say, the drama of my own life was ended. That happiness which hath subsequently crowned it cannot be written in words; 'tis of its nature sacred and secret, and not to be spoken of, though the heart be ever so full of thankfulness, save to Heaven and the One Ear alone—to one fond being, the truest and tenderest and purest wife ever man was blessed with. (461, 462)

The first sentence provides a curious opening for a passage in which Esmond will describe his fate as one enriched with gifts from God, for it is suffused with the sense of loss: the expression "the drama of my own life was ended" is almost funereal. On the surface, the tone of the second sentence immediately redeems the first; for if Esmond has died, he has also gone to heaven. However, the sentence contains several disconcerting elements. Attempting to describe his happiness in the superlative mode, he uses the word "crowned." This word, like many others in the passage, is an example of the unstable image. Throughout Book III it continually occurs in conjunction with the Chevalier's aspirations to the English throne and with Esmond's longing for the queenly Beatrix. In this final passage, then, the word is more. likely to evoke the name of Beatrix than that of her mother. Furthermore, by this point in the narrative the word has acquired perjorative connotations. Rejected by Beatrix, Esmond has bitterly rejected the concept of the crown. In the passage immediately preceding the final passage, Esmond, anxious to show Rachel's otherworldly superiority to the worldly Beatrix, praises her disdain for crowns: "*She* wasn't thinking of queens and crowns" (460). After asserting that the remainder of his life has been "crowned" with great happiness, he must explain why, in that case, he is ending the memoirs now, why he will not share the story of that happiness with the reader: it is, he tells us, too "sacred and secret." Both adjectives are troubling. While Esmond has previously argued that the proper subject of a history is the personal, the familiar, the intimate, here intimacy becomes a reason for silence. In addition, as was shown earlier (see above, pages 5, 6) the religious vocabulary, used not only in this sentence but throughout the entire passage, is a discredited idiom. The focus of our discomfort is the grammatical ambiguity at the end of the sentence. No longer satisfied to designate Rachel a mere saint, goddess, or angel, Esmond here comes perilously close to identifying her with God, for the two are placed in apposition: his story is not to be spoken of "save to Heaven and the One Ear alone—to one fond being, the truest and tenderest and purest wife."[14]

The instability of these complex sentences is equally visible in far simpler statements. Toward the end of this first paragraph, Esmond writes:

In the name of my wife I write the completion of hope, and the summit of happiness. (462)

"In the name of my wife" is a figurative expression which does not necessarily demand that Esmond utter Rachel's name. Figurative language, however, derives its stability from its basis in or compatibility with the literal fact. The occurrence of this expression in a passage from which Rachel's name is conspicuously absent is, consequently, troubling: the presence of the expression heightens our awareness of the absence of her name, heightens our awareness of Esmond's reliance on titles such as "my mistress," titles which have not, during the course of the narrative, been exclusively reserved for Rachel. Furthermore, while the phrase "the completion of hope" means "the fulfillment of hope," it is similar to "the drama of my own life was ended," for it carries with it the faint suggestion of "the end of hope."

In the second paragraph of this passage, Esmond confides to the reader:

We had been so accustomed to an extreme intimacy and confidence, and had lived so long and tenderly together, that we might have gone on to the end without thinking of a closer tie; but circumstances brought about that event which so prodigiously multiplied my happiness and hers (for which I humbly thank Heaven), although a calamity befell us which, I blush to think, hath occurred more than once in our house. (462)

In the first half of the sentence Esmond asserts that he had not previously considered marrying Rachel and in making that assertion, reminds the reader that he had, in fact, previously proposed to Rachel: Esmond has apparently forgotten that when he returned to England after the Vigo Bay expedition, he asked her to leave Europe and live with him in America until death (217). The first half of the sentence, then, describes an event, overtly denies the existence of an historical antecedent, and thereby reminds the reader that such an antecedent exists. Conversely, the second half of the sentence alludes to an unspecified event, asserts that the event has antecedents in the Castlewood family history, and wrongly assumes that the reader will remember those antecedents. Unless Esmond is suggesting that he and Rachel—like Henry's own parents (see above, page 17) and like young Frank and Clotilda (327, 328)—have conceived a child out of wedlock, it is not clear what he means by "the calamity . . . which, I blush to think, hath occurred more than once in our house." Esmond's "blush" of shame is also disconcerting. Six sentences later he will use the expression "blushes of love" to describe the way in which Rachel accepted his marriage proposal. The one disrupts our reading of the other: the shame of the first intrudes upon the tenderness of the second.

Later in the same paragraph, Esmond writes of Beatrix:

I know not what infatuation of ambition urged the beautiful and wayward woman whose name hath occupied so many of these pages and who was served by me with ten years of such a constant fidelity and passion, but ever after that day at Castlewood when we rescued her, she persisted in holding all her family as her enemies, and left us, and escaped to France, to what a fate I disdain to tell.

The most disturbing element in this sentence is the phrase, "who was *served* by me with ten years of such a *constant fidelity*." Three sentences later, describing Rachel's situation immediately prior to their marriage, Esmond tells us she was "alone but for one *constant servant* on whose *fidelity*, praised be Heaven, she could count." The asserted fidelity to Rachel is undermined by the assertion of fidelity to Beatrix. Throughout the passage, he describes Rachel in the language of superlatives, creating the surface illusion that she is above and apart from all other humanity. For Rachel to share any given vocabulary with Beatrix would disrupt this illusion, but the repetition of this particular vocabulary is especially troubling since "fidelity" itself contains the concept of exclusiveness. Furthermore, our discomfort is compounded by the sentence which immediately follows the repetition. Up to this point, the repetition has contained one potentially positive idea: Esmond's fidelity to the Castlewood family as a whole supersedes his devotion to any one woman in the family. The next sentence, however, dismisses as merely pathetic such family allegiance: " 'Twas after a scene of ignoble quarrel on the part of Frank's wife and mother (for the poor lad had been made to marry the whole of that German family with whom he had connected himself) that I . . ." (463). The parallel between Frank's situation and Henry's is unmistakable. There is one additional reason why Esmond's description of the heartless Beatrix is troubling. In specifying the length of his devotion as "ten years," his complaint recalls an almost identical complaint made against Rachel during his imprisonment: "Not that [Esmond's] fidelity was recompensed by any answering kindness, or show of relenting even, on the part of a mistress obdurate now after ten years of love and benefactions" (179). While, then, Esmond devotes much of the energy of his final passage to praising Rachel's virtue, the complaint against Beatrix reminds us of that long period of time in which Rachel seemed most cruel. Finally, the conclusion to the sentence, "to what fate I disdain to tell," recalls to the reader one of Esmond's major criticisms of historical works, their artificial propriety: in his introduction to the memoirs, he protests, "The Historical Muse turns away shamefaced from the vulgar scene and closes the door" (19). The dignity of "to what fate I disdain to tell" carries with it the indignity of a shamefaced retreat from the vulgar scene.

Toward the end of the passage, Esmond presents a brief picture of his life with Rachel in America:

In our transatlantic country we have a season, the calmest and most delightful of the year, which we call the Indian summer; I often say the autumn of our life resembles that happy and serene weather, and am thankful for its rest and its sweet sunshine. (463)

When read in isolation, this is surely one of the most beautiful sentences in the novel. But its aura of tranquillity and fulfillment, largely generated by the controlling image of "Indian summer," is subverted by the presence of the word "Indian," which is, as a brief review of its antecedent uses will show, an explosive image. In the preface to the memoirs, we learn that Rachel dies of a nervous breakdown following a violent attack on their home by the Indians (ix). Equally untranquil is the second reference. Describing the suffering he endures at the hands of Rachel while in prison, Esmond writes: "Esmond thought of his early time as a novitiate and of this past trial as an initiation before entering into life—as our young Indians undergo tortures silently before they pass to the rank of warriors in the tribe" (176). On another occasion, Esmond confesses to Beatrix his inability to withstand the longing he experiences while in her presence and the consequent necessity of his separation from her: "I am thinking of retiring into the plantations, and building myself a wigwam in the woods, and perhaps, if I want company, suiting myself with a squaw" (358). Finally, in the paragraph which immediately precedes this concluding passage, Indians appear in conjunction with Father Holt, the character in the memoirs most explicitly associated with unintentional inaccuracy as well as intentional disguise and deception: "I am not sure that he did not assume the hatchet and moccasins [in America], and attired in a blanket and war-paint, skulk about a missionary amongst the Indians" (461). The Indian image, then, is associated with violent death, with torture, with the reluctant desire for companionship amidst the isolation of unrequited love, and with semi-comic attempts at deception—associations which make it difficult for the image to function in this final passage as a vehicle of serenity and purity.

Finally, there is the concluding sentence of the passage, the climactic statement of the memoirs:

Our diamonds are turned into ploughs and axes for our plantations, and into Negroes, the happiest and merriest, I think, in all this country; and the only jewel by which my wife sets any store, and from which she hath never parted, is that gold button she took from my arm on the day when she visited me in prison, and which she wore ever after, as she told me, on the tenderest heart in the world. (463)

Throughout Book III, diamonds are associated with Esmond's futile longing for Beatrix. The underlying movement of this final sentence is its transition from the image of the diamonds to that of the gold button—on the surface, a graceful emblematic statement of the difference between Beatrix and Rachel, between the compelling worldly splendor of the first and the unworldly simplicity and virtue of the second. Several factors, however, conspire to discomfort the reader. The phrase "I think" by this point in the narrative discredits rather than makes creditable the assertion in which the phrase is embedded. The phrase "as she told me" is grammatically unstable. Its position in the sentence fosters two interpretations: the dominant reading, "She told me she wore it ever after on her heart," is unavoidably attended by a second, slightly embarrassing reading, "She told me hers was the tenderest heart in the world." But the major souce of instability is the image of the gold button itself. There is only one previous occasion on which the button is mentioned. While Harry is in prison, the keeper's wife visits him and relates to him the news of Francis Esmond's funeral and Rachel's interview with the King. Esmond then writes:

Such were the news, coupled with assertions about her own honesty and that of Molly, her maid, who would never have stolen a certain trumpery gold sleeve-button of Mr. Esmond's that was missing after his fainting fit, that the keeper's wife brought to her lodger. (172)

Far from suggesting simplicity and virtue, the "trumpery" button is here surrounded with connotations of deceit. Even the grammatical structure of the sentence is deceitful, for it may easily mislead the reader into thinking that the keeper's wife returns the missing button. The word "that" in the final phrase, "that the keeper's wife brought to her lodger," is unstable in its antecedent. It may either be read as "the news that the keeper's wife brought" or as "the button that the keeper's wife brought." The reader who emerges from this complex sentence believing that the button has been restored to Henry will, of course, be troubled by the final sentence of his memoirs.

The final image of the button, then, acquires its most disturbing associations from the specific sentence in which it is originally mentioned. But it is also troubling in its evocation of the more general context, its evocation of the prison incident as a whole. Here, in the climactic statement, we are not only reminded of Rachel's former cruelty, we are reminded that the ostensible cause of that cruelty was illusory. Her grief and rage had appeared to be˙ inspired by her love for her dead husband. Instead, as the final passage makes emphatic, she was obsessed with love not for Francis but for Harry. The reversal is charted in the displacement of one icon by another. Shortly before dying, the repentant Francis asks Harry to carry a small, heart-shaped locket to his wife. It is as Francis reaches into his breast for the locket that he falls unconscious from the wound he has just received (164). The concluding sentence of the narrative informs us that during that prison meeting between Henry and Rachel immediately following Francis' death, Rachel takes and begins to wear on her heart not Francis' locket but Henry's button. The charm of the button is tarnished by the poignancy of the forgotten locket. It is not, however, the morality of the reversal but the simple fact of the reversal that is most troubling— not the displacement of Francis by Harry in Rachel's heart but the displacement of Francis by Harry in our understanding of Rachel's love motives during the prison incident. This reversal, like the hundreds of similar reversals, makes visible the continual confusion and uncertainty that surround human thoughts and affections, the human thoughts and affections that Esmond believes "divine and immortal." Nor does the uncertainty ever resolve itself into any final certainty. It was Rachel who during the prison incident tells Henry that she is grief-stricken by her love for her lost lord. Now it is Rachel who tells Henry about the button and its significance. Given the instability of her previous "telling," there is perhaps no reason to trust her final words.

Esmond intends this final passage to be unequivocal in its praise of Rachel and of the happiness she bestows on him: "Let the last words I write thank her, and bless her who hath blessed [my home]" (463). On the surface his language is characterized by its conviction and its commitment to the superlative mode, but its primary characteristic is its instability, an instability unable to accommodate unequivocal superlatives, an instability which converts single-minded conviction into half-hearted assertion. By the time the reader emerges from the final passage, he feels uncertain whether the grace with which Esmond abandons Beatrix and embraces Rachel reflects the serenity of a newly matured man or only the fatalistic stoicism of one whose repertoire of maxims includes, "If the palace burns down, you take shelter in the barn" (98) and "I can't but accept the world as I find it, including a rope's end, as long as it is in fashion" (20) and "There is no fortune that a philosopher cannot endure" (261). In the end, it is the insistent survival of the two incompatible possibilities that is so troubling. If there were only the surface serenity, the reader would simply share Esmond's serenity; if the underlying despair were wholly able to eclipse the surface serenity, the reader would simply feel despair. As it is, the reader feels neither serenity nor despair but discomfort.

The instability found in the final passage is present throughout the memoirs. The reader consistently encounters the language of dislocation, a language in which it is difficult to ascertain the narrator's meaning and tone, a language in which the denotative and connotative activities of a given word are so unrestricted that its possible sphere of meaning expands to accommodate polar opposites. At one point, in the midst of a conversation with Beatrix, Esmond perceives and consciously exploits the instability of language to extricate himself from an embarrassing moment: as he confesses to the reader, he tells Beatrix "a truth which [is] nevertheless an entire falsehood" (354). Esmond's confession, while immediately descriptive of a single statement made to Beatrix, is also descriptive of Thackeray's entire narrative.

IV

These covert events of Thackeray's counternarrative, these embedded patterns of verbal manipulation, alert the reader to the instability of the narrator's facts, feelings, thoughts, and language. But the same instability of truth evident in these complex patterns of verbal manipulation is also evident in the novel's larger, more immediately visible structural elements.

By locating its source of stability in the subject rather than the object of perception, subjective truth credits the concept of identity, assumes in the individual an underlying unity of self. This assumption, the implicit premise of any autobiography, is made explicit in the motto Esmond affixes to his memoirs: *"Servetur ad imum / Qualis ab incepto processerit, et sibi constet."* Esmond's life story, however, is dominated by events which continually call into question the validity of this premise. A simple enumeration of incidents will recall to the reader the extent to which the overt plot, in both its general outlines and its details, is saturated with confusions in identity.

Esmond lived in a period of English history notable for sustained confusion in both its international and domestic policies. Internationally, England was engaged in the War of the Spanish Succession: the unnecessary length of the war—it lasted from 1701 to 1713—is usually attributed to the fact that its participants had a stable definition of neither the issues nor the lines of allegiance. The instability generated by England's foreign policy was amplified by the confusion in its internal affairs, a confusion which centered on the dissension over the identity of the proper heir to the English throne.

Just as England's history in both its international and domestic dimensions is dominated by confusions in identity, so Esmond's life story in both its public and private dimensions is dominated by such confusion. His public identity—as revealed in the relation between his religious, military, and political careers (Books I, II, and III respectively)—is a composite of incompatible allegiances. His military ambition, for example, is dedicated to England's triumph over France; yet a major cause of England's animosity toward France is the latter's support of the Stuart claim to the English throne, a claim which Esmond himself actively supports. In turn, his support of the Stuart claim is incompatible with his religious and social sympathies, which are Anglican rather than Catholic, republican rather than divine-right authoritarian. Esmond's personal identity is equally unstable: until the end of the memoirs, the identity of his parents, the legitimacy of his birth, and his status within the Castlewood family hierarchy are questions continually asked and unanswered.

In its most general outlines, then, *Henry Esmond* consists of two spheres, a historical background and an autobiographical foreground, each dominated by its confrontation with the undefined. But it is in the novel's details even more than in its general outlines that its obsessive concern with identity is made visible.

The relevant details occur in conjunction with major characters and incidents as well as with characters and incidents so minor and isolated that they appear to exist almost solely to reinforce the theme of identity. In addition to the sustained counterpoint of disguise and counterfeit dress surrounding both Father Holt (Holtz, von Holtz, Holton) and the Chevalier in his attempt to establish his "true" identity as James III, the novel contains such isolated fragments of masquerade as Esmond's encounter with "Captain James," a disguised Duke of Berwick (124, 401); his meeting at Cambridge with a Jesuit priest who presents himself as a French Protestant refugee (116); and his contact in France with a deserter from the Irish army masquerading as a French soldier, a masquerade whose transparency Esmond finds "infinitely amusing" (325). Again, in addition to the psychological resonance of the episode in which Rachel mistakes Harry Mohun for Harry Esmond (80, 151) and the complexity of confusion arising from the affinity between young Frank Castlewood and Henry Esmond, there are such brief incidents as that in which Esmond, delirious with smallpox, is unable to recognize Rachel (170) and that in which Esmond, delirious with a wound received at Blenheim, mistakes a surgeon's assistant for Beatrix (242). At times the confusion in identity results from a conscious act of deception that carries with it the moral disapproval of the narrator: it is uncertain whether Marlborough's primary efforts are committed to England or to England's enemy, France (287, 288); Thomas Esmond conceals his true identity from his first wife, Gertrude Maes, and, by abandoning her and marrying Isabella, virtually denies her existence and that of her son (278). But for the most part such acts seem so omnipresent that they appear a given of reality, whether presented humorously, as in Isabella's attempt to obscure her physical identity with paints and wigs (45); painfully, as in Trix's constant play of deceptive coquetry; or compassionately, as in the description of Rachel, who "amongst her other feminine qualities had that of being a perfect dissembler" (398).

Almost without exception, the letters and other written articles which Esmond records in his memoirs use language to disguise their writer's meaning. There are, for example, three conspiratorial notes whose messages are embedded in code, intended to be comprehensible to a few, incomprehensible to most. The degree of obscurity ranges from the naïve transparency of Thomas Esmond's code in which the Prince of Orange is designated as

"the P. of O." and King James as "the K." or *"you know who"* (65) to
Father Holt's more sophisticated code in which the political idiom is replaced by an economic idiom (64) and finally, to Henry Esmond's code in
which the key is so deeply concealed that the reader can only take
Esmond's word that one exists (405). Equally, if not intentionally, obscure
is a letter Esmond receives from Isabella written in a "strange barbarous
French" that converts "Mohun" to "M. de Moon" and "Warwick" to "M.
le Compte de Varique": as is clear to any reader who has worked his way
through that barbarous French, Esmond's comments following the letter
reveal that he himself has misunderstood its meaning, that he has misread
her reference to Lord Blanford, Lady Marlborough's son, as a reference to
Prince James (185, 186). Again in Esmond's imitation *Spectator* paper
(345-349), duplicity is visible on three levels: first, its subject is deception,
the deception in Beatrix's coquetry; second, that subject is obscured,
embedded in a parable rather than presented overtly; third and most importantly, the presentation of the paper itself is deceptive, for its effect on
Beatrix requires her ignorance of the author's true identity. Many additional pieces of writing which Esmond describes but does not record *verbatim*
also demonstrate the failure of language to act as a vehicle of honest
communication: Mohun's seductive notes to Rachel (157), Beatrix's deceptive note to her mother at Kensington (452), Frank's untruthful letters to
his mother (322), Rachel's letters to Esmond lost or stolen by a privateer
(317), Esmond's play to which, when published, he refuses to sign his
name (344), and the Gazette that credits Cadogan rather than Webb for the
English victory at Wynendael (294).

Such confusions in identity, generated both by conscious acts of deception and by mere chance, penetrate every dimension of Esmond's life
story.[15] *Henry Esmond*, however, is not only a life story but a love story;
and in one sense, all the random instances of confusion enumerated above
are tangential to the overriding complexities of the central love triangle, or
what would be a triangle were it not too insistently equivocal to be defined
by geometric design. While Esmond's two mistresses are on the surface
polar opposites—one dark, the other fair; one tall, the other short; one
worldly, the other unworldly—their two identities repeatedly merge, emerge
and separate, only to merge once more. The intricacies of this sustained
confusion, too familiar to warrant detailed examination, ultimately involve
a mother-mistress interchange whose incestuous implications have been immediately apparent to both nineteenth- and twentieth-century readers. Only
two points, obvious but unacknowledged, need be emphasized here.

The first involves the relationship between Esmond's autobiography and
his daughter's preface. In the autobiography proper, the theme of incest

occurs only on the psychological plane, never the physical: while Rachel is emphatically a mother figure, she is not Esmond's biological mother. Even the smaller manifestations of the incest theme stay safely within the realm of the non-physical. Sometimes it emerges as metaphor: it is in the guise of Beatrix's brother that the Chevalier attempts to seduce Beatrix. At other times, its appearance is reduced to mere mistake: Esmond at one point incorrectly identifies Isabella as "his father's wife and . . . his grandfather's daughter" (187); depending on whether one reads the antecedent of the second "his" as Henry or Thomas, Isabella has married either her brother, her nephew, or her son. If, however, in the autobiography proper the incestuous implications are confined to the psychological, metaphorical, and mistaken, they are solidly grounded in biological reality in Rachel Warrington's preface. We there learn that she and her father, Henry Esmond, became widow and widower in the same year (ix), after which they shared a happy and intimate life-long union. More importantly, we learn that Warrington's death occurred prior to the birth of his wife's children (viii, ix). These factual details do not, of course, rule out the probability that Warrington did beget his wife's sons; they merely invite the possibility that he did not. Thackeray has selected details consciously calculated to arouse for a moment the suspicion that Esmond, fulfilling his desire to "found a family" in the new world (358), fathered his own grandsons. This suspicion is amplified by Rachel Warrington's impassioned descriptions of her father: they convey an intensity of affection and admiration that makes even her simplest assertions vulnerable to *double entendre*:

I am sure that [my sons] love me, and one another, and him above all, my father and theirs, the dearest friend of their childhood, the noble gentleman who bred them from their infancy in the practice and knowledge of Truth, and Love, and Honour. (viii)

I know that, before [my mother], my dear father did not show the love which he had for his daughter; and in her last and most sacred moments this dear and tender parent owned to me her repentance that she had not loved me enough, her jealousy even that my father should give his affection to any but herself; and in the most fond and beautiful words of affection and admonition she bade me never to leave him and to supply the place which she was quitting. With a clear conscience and a heart inexpressibly thankful, I think I can say that I fulfilled those dying commands . . . (ix)

The presence of these implications of physical incest in the preface emphasizes the importance of the theme in the autobiography itself.

The second point which warrants attention is the reason for Thackeray's inclusion of the incest theme in the novel. While he, like his readers and critics, may have found the subject fascinating in and of itself, it seems certain that he selected the theme for its participation in the larger theme of identity. Esmond's autobiography is a sustained attempt at self-definition, an attempt in which he relies heavily on relational terms. As the memoirs progress, these terms undergo rapid, unpredictable changes: Rachel is Beatrix's mother, Rachel is Beatrix's elder sister (328), Beatrix is Rachel's elder sister (303), Esmond is Isabella's son (317), Esmond is Isabella's son-in-law (187), Esmond is Rachel's son (251, 252, 315), Esmond is Beatrix's brother (385), Esmond is Rachel's brother (386), Esmond is elder brother and father of Rachel, Frank, and Beatrix (358, 359). The very fluidity of the terms reveals their instability, an instability made more emphatic by the presence of the incest theme. A recognition of the incestuous impulse in humanity requires a rejection of the concept of fixed, relational identities: the familial is no longer exclusive of the sexually intimate; mother-son, father-daughter, and brother-sister are no longer stable, definitive terms.

Esmond's surface narrative, then, in its major outlines as well as its details, its historical background as well as its personal foreground, is saturated with confusions in identity. The dominance of such confusions in the overt events of the story is twofold in its purpose. First, it announces the novel's central concern, designates as a major problem Esmond's belief in subjective truth. Second, and more importantly, after designating the problem, it dismisses the problem, creates the illusion that the problem does not exist. Despite the onslaught of confusions in identity, despite the fact that Esmond himself is often their temporary victim, he ultimately appears to be in control of those confusions by virtue of the very fact that he is writing about them. If he is a participant he is also the narrator: his act of describing an instance of identity interchange necessarily entails the act of differentiating an erroneous perception from its accurate counterpart, an act which carries with it the assurance that the dislocated can be relocated, that the confusion can be clarified, that ignorance finally yields to the perception of a stable, knowable reality. Within the overt surface of the story, then, Esmond's concept of subjective truth is threatened but simultaneously salvaged—only to be obliterated on a second, deeper level where, as shown earlier, Esmond's narrative, and with it his identity, are subjected to a sustained and systematic process of erosion. While Esmond is calmly assuring us that physical disguises can be penetrated, psychological interchanges explained, people's identities identified, Thackeray is busy demonstrating the ultimate inaccessibility of personal identity: by the end of the novel, we do not know the first thing about our autobiographer, not the simplest fact, the date of his birth, not the simplest thought, his ideas about pain, not the simplest emotion, his feeling for Rachel.

Thackeray's act of refuting on a second level what he has superficially affirmed on the first is not simply a gratuitous act of irony at Esmond's expense. Although ultimately illusory, the surface affirmation is crucial to the author's central argument. He is trying to show that subjective truth—a stable core of facts, feelings, and thoughts—is an impossibility *per se*, not merely an impossibility for Esmond. If the disintegration of subjective truth is to be attributed to an instability inherent in the concept itself rather than to an instability peculiar to a particular character, Thackeray must absolve his hero of personal responsibility by convincing us that were reliability possible, Esmond would be reliable; were there a truth to be told, Esmond would tell it.

Four major factors contribute to Esmond's absolution. The most important is his rejection of objective truth, a rejection which makes his acceptance of subjective truth appear more trustworthy, less capricious: it assures us that he is not an eager idealist randomly affirming all dimensions of all possible realities; he is, instead, one who has tested reality before becoming the exponent of the single realm his testing proved sound. Secondly, not only is objective truth rejected but, as this section of the discussion has shown, subjective truth is itself tested on the surface of the story: the narrator proves himself both interested in and capable of disentangling the ordinary confusions arising from physical disguise and psychological affinity. As important as these two factors which encourage us to trust Esmond are two other factors which, once we realize the failure of Esmond's narrative to substantiate our trust, assure us that the failure was not Esmond's to avert. While he is devastatingly unreliable, it is notable that nowhere in the novel is the possibility of reliability affirmed: as was suggested in the second section of this discussion, all the characters in the narrative as well as those who supplement the narrative with preface and footnotes share the hero's habit of contradiction. Esmond's final absolution resides in that factor examined in the third section of the discussion, the structure of language itself. The instability characterizing the narrator's assertions is equally characteristic of much smaller grammatical units such as individual words and images. As a result, the problem of instability is dissociated from Esmond: it penetrates language so deeply that it appears to be beyond his control, out of his hands. In his espousal of subjective truth, then, Esmond is the dupe of dreams, but he is not the agent of the dream's disintegration. While he is assuredly the victim of Thackeray's irony, he is also the victim of a larger irony in which Thackeray, too, plays victim.

V

The overall structure of *Henry Esmond* is based on an ironic formula familiar to readers of *Vanity Fair*. In both novels, the surface narrative poses a question and offers the illusion of two alternative answers, one of which is made to appear strong, the other, weak. In both novels the argument presented in the surface narrative is refuted by a counter-narrative in which the antithesis is proved illusory, the two alternatives equally inviable. On the surface, *Vanity Fair* questions the source of value and virtue and proposes, in response, the Amelia life style against the Becky life style, an opposition obliterated on a second level where the polar life styles collapse and merge in their shared absence of value. On the surface, *Henry Esmond* questions the source of truth and proposes, in response, the subjective realm of existence against the objective, an opposition obliterated on a second level where the first disintegrates into the instability of the second.

Although *Vanity Fair* is more overtly cynical in tone, the transition from the earlier novel to the later represents a movement toward a deeper pessimism, for the focus shifts from the ethical to the epistemological, from the impotence of the distinction between "good and bad" to the impotence of the distinction between "true and false." While the first questions the validity of assigning moral labels to facts, the second denies our ability even to know the facts to which we cannot assign the labels. But if Thackeray's pessimism deepened, so did the artistry of the techniques he used to present the surface alternatives in the two novels. In *Vanity Fair*, he explores the resources of plot, dramatizing the opposition in life styles by simply doubling the plot-line. In *Henry Esmond*, he explores not plot but genre, converting the two spheres implicit in "historical-romance," the public and the private, into the two spheres where the potential existence of truth might be examined. In rejecting both spheres he calls into question major assumptions the nineteenth century held about the distinction between history and fiction.

The essential dynamic of *Henry Esmond*, however, resides not in the relationship between the novel and the author's earlier works, nor in the relationship between the novel and its genre, nor in the relationship between the novel and nineteenth-century assumptions, but in the relationship between the novel's author and its hero, a relationship epitomized in a single sentence describing Esmond's portrait:

[Dowager Isabella] must have his picture taken; and accordingly he was painted by Mr. Jervas, in his red coat, and smiling upon a bomb-shell, which was bursting at the corner of the piece. (300)

Despite the brevity of its description, Esmond's portrait is emblematic of his entire life story: Esmond's surface narrative is dominated by the tone of serene conviction, but immediately beneath this glacine surface is the restless energy of Thackeray, ever threatening to explode in the smiling face of the self-assured narrator.

HAWTHORNE AND MELVILLE:
AN INQUIRY INTO THEIR ART
AND THE MYSTERY OF THEIR FRIENDSHIP

Sidney Moss

For William Simeone, wise in the ways of art and friendship

The questions which interest me most when reading a poem are two. The first is technical: "Here is a verbal contraption. How does it work?" The second is, in the broadest sense, moral: "What kind of a guy inhabits this poem? What is his notion of the good life or the good place? His notion of the Evil One? What does he conceal from his reader? What does he conceal even from himself?"

W. H. Auden, *The Dyer's Hand*

Melville and Hawthorne were so polarized in temperament, moral vision, literary execution, and in their sense of life that one has reason to be nonplussed that they became friends at all, let alone that the friendship proved rapturous on both sides and supposedly effected an artistic conversion in Melville. Whatever Henry James meant by calling him a man of fancy, Hawthorne's best work is the result of the *I* in profound conflict with the *Me*, of the superego with the id. At his best he projected his psychic preoccupations in his fiction and masked his psychological difficulties in his personae. In this way he exercised, to quote Freud, the "discretion one owes to oneself." At the same time, suffering from incurable dividedness, he judged his psychic problems harshly. For this reason Hawthorne, when writing to James T. Fields, his publisher, to explain why he could not write "a sunshiny book," said: "The Devil himself always seems to get into my inkstand...."[1] That is why there was "something preternatural" in his "reluctance to begin," to enter the house of fiction. "I linger at the threshold, and have a perception of very disagreeable phantasms to be encountered if I enter."[2] That is why he told George B. Loring that "his work grew in his brain as it went on, and was beyond his control or direction...."[3] As in dreams, the stuff of his fiction, when it surfaced from psychic depths, was concerned with self-

47

experience, not with actual or imagined experiences. That is why Emerson said of Hawthorne, "He holds a dark steed hard."[4] That is why Hawthorne could say when he reread *Mosses from an Old Manse* three years after its publication: "Upon my honor, I am not quite sure that I comprehend my own meaning, in some of these blasted allegories. . . . To tell you the truth, my past self is not very much to my taste, as I see myself in this book."[5] That too is why Edwin P. Whipple, whom Hawthorne respected above all other contemporary critics, was able to say of his admirer: "Hawthorne cannot . . . use his genius; his genius always uses him. . . . His great books appear not so much created by him as through him."[6] And that is why Hawthorne pronounced Whipple's study, when it appeared in 1860, "a really keen and profound article."[7]

Melville, however, was a man of imagination. At his best, he was undivided; he wrote from his entire being. The world he drew upon was the world of actuality; and when he turned inward, in a way as profound as Hawthorne's, it was in an effort to fathom the implications of experience as they were felt by his baffled tragic heroes. If, as Flannery O'Connor has said, "the main concern of a fiction writer is with mystery as it is incarnated in human life," Melville's fiction is incomparably richer in complexity, denser in detail, more powerfully and compellingly rendered than Hawthorne's, whose preoccupations on the whole were limited to exploring his misery-ridden soul in disguised, dream-like, and somewhat self-therapeutic ways, locked as he was in the cage of narcissism.

Apart from a few tales and *The Confidence Man*, Melville was an "ambiguist" in the sense that Hawthorne never was, for he had no certainties concerning the world within and without. His major works represent a questioning and even an abandonment of the so-called pieties and verities. Pierre's statements in the book pointedly subtitled "The Ambiguities" are typical: "The world seems to lie saturated and soaking with lies. . . . Henceforth I will know nothing but Truth. . . . I strike through thy helm, and will see thy face, be it Gorgon! . . . All piety leave me;—I will be impious, for piety hath juggled me, and taught me to revere, where I should spurn. From all idols, I tear all veils. . . ." And Pierre comes, as Melville early did, to reject in fiction as in life those "false, inverted attempts at systematizing eternally unsystemizable elements . . . which make up the complex web of life. . . ."[8]

Hawthorne, known as an ambiguist too, is by no means morally ambiguous in his fiction, however concerned he is to depict the moral and psychological ambiguities of his anti-heroes. If the world does seem morally ambiguous or evil in his fiction, it is only as his characters perceive it to be so. That is their delusion; that is at once the sign and price of their moral failure. The reason for Hawthorne's being morally unambiguous is that he believed with perfect certitude in the traditional moral order and in "divine Providence." "... All things perish from the instant when they cease to answer some divine purpose," he wrote in his *English Notebooks*, and, in applying this principle in his *Life of Franklin Pierce*, he observed that slavery is "one of those evils which divine Providence does not leave to be remedied by human contrivances, but which, in its own good time, ... when all its uses shall have been fulfilled, it causes to vanish like a dream."[9] He thus regards his anti-heroes, from the unnamed woman of "The Hollow of the Three Hills" to Hollingsworth of *The Blithedale Romance*, from a number of points of view, all of which finally fuse into one. Psychologically, they are narcissists, acting out of self-love. Theologically, they are prideful, enacting the deadliest sin. Philosophically, if loosely speaking, they are solipsists in that they consider their own selves as of highest importance and their own views of reality as paramount. Socially, they are individualists imposing their own contracted values and narrow visions upon the community. Regarding these antinomian, Romantic, subjectivist anti-heroes of his as moral deviates and holding them in profoundest contempt, Hawthorne feels no compassion for them (except as, like Hester Prynne, they return to the fold), any more than Dante comes to feel for the damned in Hell. But Dante, given his plot, is forced to see his characters *sub specie aeternatatis*. They are stripped of human circumstances, removed from the human condition; their very presence in the Inferno is proof of their sinfulness; and in hardening his heart to them, Dante is only seconding God's judgment. Given *his* plots, however, Hawthorne can only see his characters *sub specie temporis*, yet he has no difficulty in judging them in what seem to him absolute moral terms. His difficulty, in fact, is entirely the other way. Speaking of an ill-fated politician in his campaign biography, he approves Pierce's public repudiation of him, though the man was "unfortunate" and a "personal friend," for anything else "would have been fatal" to Pierce's "sense of right." John Ciardi in a gloss to his translation of *The Inferno* tells us that "the souls of the damned are locked so blindly into their own guilt that none can feel sympathy for another, or find any pleasure in the presence of another." We shall see, if we do not now, that Hawthorne was damned in this sense to his private psychological hell.

Given the literary situation, Hawthorne is, if not anti-tragic, at least untragic. For the tragic vision minimally involves the sense that evil is metaphysical, inherent in the very scheme of things, and that people at best are only nominally in control of their destinies. That is the tragic vision we find in *Moby-Dick, Pierre*, "Benito Cereno," and *Billy Budd*.

Hawthorne, on the other hand, *seems* to conceive of evil as morally and individually willed, something that can also be counteracted to a degree by exercise of the moral will. All of Hawthorne's narratives, then, with such rare exceptions as "The Canterbury Pilgrims," are cautionary tales, negative examples of how one may become alienated by abandoning traditional moral codes (like the Man of Adamant) or by violating them and floundering in psychological ambiguities (like Giovanni in "Rappaccini's Daughter"). In short, apart from a few tales like "My Kinsman, Major Molineux," Hawthorne's stories are written from a position of moral absolutism, a position that elicits his condemnation rather than his sympathy for those characters who prove derelict vis-à-vis the moral standards.

I say that Hawthorne *seems* to conceive of evil as morally and individually willed because free will is more illusory than real in his fiction. His protagonists do not define the situations in which they appear; rather, the situations define them, and that in narrow, morbid, psychological terms, by arousing their latent anxieties and guilt-feelings. Some of Hawthorne's best tales, "Young Goodman Brown," "Rappaccini's Daughter," and "Roger Malvin's Burial," exemplify the point. While this kind of character definition constrains Hawthorne to probe what Henry James in *Hawthorne* calls the "deeper psychology," it is a far cry from James's own practice, let alone Melville's. In James, the "sensibility" of the protagonist defines the situation, and that sensibility is not so much psychological as it is moral. For what James's heroes come to be all but exclusively concerned with is moral values, and they regard their predicaments in moral terms. In "The Pupil," "The Birthplace," and "The Jolly Corner," for instance, not to mention such large works as *The Wings of the Dove*, monetary gain becomes to the protagonists of far less consequence than moral gain. The point is that typical Jamesian protagonists really have free will; and if at times they seem to be victimized by a situation, it is only as we mistakenly judge them by worldly and, to James, meretricious standards. Melville's protagonists likewise define their situations—for instance, the narrators of *Moby-Dick*, "Bartleby," "The Two Temples," "Poor Man's Pudding and Rich Man's Crumbs," "The Paradise of Bachelors and The Tartarus of Maids," and "Benito Cereno"—though Melville has much less confidence than James in the efficacy of moral exercise. Hawthorne's protagonists, to repeat, have only the semblance of free will, for they are the victims of their psychological perturbations, perturbations that the situations arouse and exacerbate and that Hawthorne broods upon to the virtual exclusion of their other human qualities.

Hawthorne differs radically from Melville in still another respect. Given his absolutist moral position, Hawthorne is not concerned with the value of ethical exploration, with what, in other words, might be gained from questioning or defying the moral system, for he knows a priori where such antinomianism leads: to some form of self-damnation, whether in monomania, anxiety, guilt, or heartsickness. *The Scarlet Letter*, apart from being his most compassionate work, as well as a brilliant recreation of the Puritan past, pictorially in a class with the work of such Dutch painters as Vermeer and Frans Hals, is in great measure an exhaustive clinical account of Arthur Dimmesdale's psychic misery on the one hand and a depiction of Hester Prynne's reacceptance and revitalization of the community's values on the other. Though Hawthorne recognizes those values to be flawed and uncharitable, he feels that such values are better than those we each of us might improvisationally and anarchically create for ourselves. And, admittedly, he felt charitable to the lovers (even at the end to Roger Chillingworth), but no more than Dante did for Paola and Francesca.

Typically, then, Hawthorne presents us with three ethical stages in his fiction. In the first, we generally see the moral ground which the protagonist occupies (Goodman Brown, for instance, who has recently married Faith, or Reuben Bourne who acts with all good intention in leaving the wounded Roger Malvin to seek help). In the second stage we see the protagonist slipping away from that moral ground (Brown keeps his covenant with the Devil; Bourne fails to speak the truth about leaving Malvin). In the final stage we see either the character failing (like Brown) or succeeding (like Bourne) in recovering his moral ground. Whatever the variations of this formula, and however artfully Hawthorne plays the changes, there is a moral vacuum so far as ethical exploration is concerned, as there is not, say, in *Moby-Dick* or *Pierre*, not to mention the diptychs such as "The Two Temples" or "Bartleby" and "Cock-a-Doodle-Doo!"—the diptych, perhaps derived from the form of the debate, being a fictional invention uniquely Melville's own in his continual struggle to find a moral center. The moral vacuum created by Hawthorne is filled with the psychological data of anxiety, guilt, despair, or compulsion. In such tales as "Rappaccini's Daughter" and "My Kinsman, Major Molineux," to make the proper qualification, these data are both necessary and sufficient. But in most of the other stories, such as "Ethan Brand" and "Wakefield," not to mention his novels, these data, while essential, are decidedly inadequate, for they supplant the moral inquest these narratives require in their own terms.

Reduced to its ultimate banality, the message that Hawthorne repeatedly stresses in almost all his work is that anyone who disturbs the status quo does so at the risk of his psychological undoing. Given this fixed position, Hawthorne was seldom at liberty to use his art to derive the implications of his starting-points, except in psychological terms. The self is explored to the virtual exclusion of the ethical problem. His characters, as well as the severely limited conditions in which he places them, are so predetermined and the results so foreknown that his art, far from being organic and self-developing, tends to be mechanical. The tales incline to be moral diagrams rather than moral investigations, the characters moral personifications rather than persons, and the symbols, like the stone hearts of the Man of Adamant and Ethan Brand, tend to be mechanical too, to reinforce the moral. His narratives for these reasons contain few characters (where, one wonders, are the other members of the Blithedale Community?); they dramatize no real opposition of character; they do not grant to opposing moral positions equal, let alone equally blazing, conviction; and they draw the conditions of human life to the point of impoverishment. Nothing, in short, is permitted to qualify the desired results and obscure the moral point. For this reason Hawthorne's narratives tend to be variations on a theme; and for this reason there is little felt life in his work, except as it derives from the profound tension of his own psychic disturbance. If the art of literature lies ultimately in its power to convert moral knowledge into emotional terms, Hawthorne, with the marvelous exception of *The Scarlet Letter*, is seldom artistically successful.

If the unexamined life is not worth living, one wonders what can be said about an unexamined value system in literature. R. J. Kaufman observes in "Tragedy and Its Validating Conditions":

Tragedy may be understood as an inquest into traditional ethical stipulations by subjecting these—and the putative virtues they designate—to pragmatic scrutiny. The tragic form gives animated embodiment to otherwise bodiless abstractions and thereby provides contextual texts for the social utility of traditional virtues. . . . Tragic artists challenge the permanence of the "fabric of imperatives" which governs their epoch's notions of human resolution and human obligation. . . . Tragic heroes tend to be those for whom common sense is either a foreign idiom or only a beginning step on the road. Think of a society which has never had any Cordelias, any Antigones, any Hamlets, any Oedipuses, any Medeas—the vision is depressing, for tragic heroes exist to raise the ceiling of possibility, to widen the margins of our imaginative tolerance. . . . We need acquaintance with someone who shouts "No!" to expediency and has the spiritual obstinacy to hold out against common sense. Spiritual obstinacy makes for that uncomfortable virtue called nobility. . . . Tragedy is a form of artificial respiration for some of the higher virtues.[10]

Or, as Emerson says in "Self-Reliance": "He who would gather immortal palms must not be hindered by the name of goodness, but must explore if it be goodness. Nothing is at last sacred but the integrity of your own mind." While such statements could only gall Hawthorne, they elicited Melville's whole-hearted approbation. Though there is no evidence that he read "Self-Reliance," Melville did read Emerson's "Illusions." Of the following passage he wrote, "True & admirable! Bravo!": "I look upon the . . . virtues of veracity and honesty as the root of all that is sublime in character. Speak as you think, be what you are. . . . This reality is the foundation of friendship, religion, poetry and art." Similarly, of this passage in Emerson's "Heroism" he said, "This is noble again": "Self-trust is the essence of heroism. It is the state of the soul at war, and its ultimate objects are the last defiance of falsehood and wrong. . . ."[11]

Another significant way that Hawthorne differs from Melville lies in his tendency to work within traditional rather than modern allegory. This observation calls for explanation. We must recognize, if we are not to be slaves to the tyranny of terms, that the last great traditional allegory was written by John Bunyan, the kind that establishes an invariable one-to-one correspondence between literal events (such as Christian's physical journey to the Celestial City) and figurative events (his spiritual pilgrimage to Heaven), in the process of which sloughs are metaphorized into Despair and a state of mind personified as Hope. This is not to say there have been no reversions to the form, though Hawthorne's "Great Carbuncle" and "Celestial Railroad" may well represent its last gasp. Yet, though its traditional devices have been dropped by modern authors as being too mechanical, allegory is still a useful term in that it suggests a sustained metaphoric intention. What other term proves so serviceable in describing the fourth book of *Gulliver's Travels*, Genet's *The Balcony*, Weiss's *Marat/Sade*, Camus's *The Plague*, Vercors' *You Shall Know Them*, Graham Greene's *A Burnt-Out Case*, or Beckett's *Waiting for Godot*? Allegorically, are not the two tramps in *Godot* Bunyan's pilgrims in modern guise who, though beggared by the world and fallen by the wayside, are still wanting to journey to the Celestial City, except that they do not know where it lies, what direction to take, or even if it exists, and are waiting for a word or sign that never comes?

This comparison suggests another significant difference between traditional and modern allegory and, of course, between Hawthorne and Melville, a difference apart from literary devices and metaphoric intention. The difference lies in moral outlook, something I touched upon in discussing Hawthorne's value system and his refusal or psychological inability to question or explore it. Where traditional allegory is hopeful because it is certain of its moral reference points, modern allegory runs only the range from despair to stoicism. For traditional allegory, given its unerring moral compass, heads with certitude toward known harbors; modern allegory, uncertain of its destination, flounders in seas of uncertainty. Whatever sense traditional allegory may have made in the past by reducing life's mysteries to a set of abstractions, in Hawthorne it tends to falsify experience by the process of banalizing it. Too, in terms of meaning and moral significance, traditional allegory is dependent upon universal myths and a frame of moral reference antecedent to the work, like Bunyan's dependence on the Bible. One does not have to interpret *Pilgrim's Progress*: it would be an act of supererogation, for Bunyan's allegory contains only a two-value system, the one holy way and the variety of wicked ways. Modern allegory, however, generates its own "myths," which is to say it creates its own accreted images that, when successful, penetrate the collective consciousness and come to assume, almost, the status of myths, like Melville's Albino Whale. Not only that: by refusing to occlude the middle, the *viae mediae*, the moral space human beings habitually occupy, modern allegory creates and explores a multi-value system, and tests that system, however inconclusively, by the interaction of multi-dimensioned characters in dense, life-like situations, and such allegory does require interpretation, just as the life it reflects does. No one who reads *Pilgrim's Progress* can mistake its moral, for the medium is indeed the message. In *Waiting for Godot*, however, the moral, programmed into the drama by all sorts of suggestive devices, comes as an aftermath to our reading or seeing it, when the play resonates in the heart and brain; and even then the interpretations are as various as those who have experienced the play. Where, then, a modern allegorist is forced to be original in terms of myth, value system, and vision of life, a traditional allegorist is finally derivative. More, he tends to subordinate life to art and in the process exhibits a questionable virtuosity in overcoming the allegorical problem he set himself. That is why Poe—and he was discussing Hawthorne's art at the time—could scarcely say one respectable word in defense of allegory. Though he failed to make the proper distinctions and is somewhat confusing on that account, he was speaking of traditional as opposed to modern allegory. Its best appeals, he wrote, are made to the fancy, not the imagination, in that allegory deals "not of matters proper, but of matters improper. . . . The deepest emotion aroused within us by the happiest allegory, *as* allegory"—and here, I would insist, he is distinguishing between allegorical devices and allegorical intention—"is a very, very imperfectly satisfied sense of the writer's ingenuity in overcoming a difficulty we should have preferred his not having attempted to overcome." However, "to allegory properly handled, judiciously subdued, seen only as a shadow or by suggestive glimpses"—surely a description of allegorical intention—Poe had no objection whatever.[12]

Henry James also had very little respect for traditional allegory. "Hawthorne, in his metaphysical moods," he wrote, "is nothing if not allegorical, and allegory, to my sense, is quite one of the lighter exercises of the imagination. ... It is apt to spoil two good things—a story and a moral, a meaning and a form...." Having a sense too of the two-value system of traditional allegory, though James nowhere mentions it, he noticed that Hawthorne "is neither bitter nor cynical—he is rarely even what I should call tragical. ... There has rarely been an observer more serene [in his fiction], less agitated by what he sees, and less disposed to call things deeply into question." James, I hazard, would have qualified this statement had he not stopped with recognizing Hawthorne's "deeper psychology," but gone on to investigate its source in the man himself. Similarly, concerning the *Notebooks*, James observed that Hawthorne held "no general views that were in the least uncomfortable. They are the exhibition of an unperplexed intellect."[13] Here again the statement should be qualified, for Hawthorne's *Notebooks* at times reveal a man profoundly uncomfortable *with himself*, deeply perplexed *about himself*. T. S. Eliot, borrowing a page from James, also noticed that Hawthorne "was forever tailing off into the fanciful, even the allegorical, which is a lazy substitute for profundity."[14] If this is so, it may be that the pleasure we take in Hawthorne's work is in some measure the "intellectual" one of de-allegorizing his allegorical devices and characters. We say, for instance, that the "evil" Goodman Brown sees in the woods and later in the community is visionary, self-induced, in that as soon as he calls upon Faith to "resist the wicked one," the scene instantly vanishes and he finds himself alone "amid calm night and solitude...." We say that Donatello in *The Marble Faun* relives in his own person the Etruscan, Roman, and Christian phases of Italy's development and, by extension, reenacts the "progress" of human history on earth. But one has reason to wonder if such a pleasure is not a secondary one, after all. The pleasures we derive from making sense of the allegorical code and from our equating, as we must, the appropriate emotional associations with that code—may we not be confusing those pleasures with the primary pleasure we derive from a fully rendered work such as "Benito Cereno" or *Moby-Dick*? Much as Poe admired Hawthorne's tales, he felt, apart from their "sameness, or monotone," that Hawthorne would do doubly well if he got "a bottle of visible ink" and wrote of "honest, upright, sensible, prehensible and comprehensible things."

For a time Melville was confused about allegory, thinking, perhaps, that allegory, to be allegory, had to be written in the traditional mode. He had, of course, attempted a kind of old-fashioned allegory in *Mardi*, a venture that proved a literary and commercial fiasco, and he would tend to lapse into traditional allegory again in "The Bell-Tower" and "The Lightning-Rod

Man," as he did in *Moby-Dick* to the extent of creating allegorical figures in Fedallah and his crew. But in "The Affidavit" chapter, convinced that *Moby-Dick* was no allegory as he understood the term, he bluntly interrupted his narrative to insist "in all respects [upon] the reasonableness of the whole story of the White Whale," as well as to scoff at anyone who considered "Moby Dick as a monstrous fable, or still worse and more detestable, a hideous and intolerable allegory." The light may have struck him when he read the Hawthornes' letters about *Moby-Dick*. For in answer to Sophia's letter, contrary to what he had maintained in "The Affidavit" chapter, he was now able to say: "I had some vague idea while writing it, that the whole book was susceptible of an allegorical construction, & also that *parts* of it were," and that Hawthorne—that allegorist *par excellence*—had intimated to him "the part-&-parcel allegoricalness of the whole."[15] At any rate, once he began his next novel, he devoted himself entirely to modern allegory, so much so that *Pierre* can easily be read as a modern-day *Pilgrim's Progress*, as ironic in its way as *Waiting for Godot*. Lawrance Thompson, for example, wrote that Pierre "is a genuinely devout idealist whose name might literally be the same as that of Bunyan's hero. At the end of the story, however, Pierre has become convinced"—and no doubt the reader too—"that he has been awarded an unearned damnation, rather than salvation; that he has been betrayed, disowned, abandoned, by man and God."[16]

Clarification of this problem involving the two kinds of allegory was crucial for Melville, as it enabled him to grasp consciously what he had apparently only intuited even as late as *Moby-Dick*. The clarification was that a literary construct, an author's way of subsuming, understanding, and rendering experience, could be employed without critical loss either to artistic form or to experience; that a literary construct is a way of suggesting the universal implications in particular experiences without stripping experience of its essential density and richness. Thus, by the time Melville wrote *Pierre*, a work that, like his review of "Hawthorne and His Mosses," is electric with literary discoveries, he was able to say: Pierre "was not merely a reader of poets and other fine writers," but a "thorough allegorical understander of them."

There were at least two reasons for Hawthorne's habitually adopting the traditional allegorical mode, intermixed, to be sure, with fairy-tale elements, which caused James Russell Lowell in *A Fable for Critics* to label him a "John Bunyan Fouqué, a Puritan Tieck." Having, Hawthorne confessed in a letter to Longfellow, "seen so little of the world ... I have nothing but thin air to concoct my stories of, and it is not easy to give a lifelike semblance to such shadowy stuff."[17] Secondly, old-fashioned allegory was compatible with his temperament which, by his own repeated self-recognitions, was inhibited and conservative, quite unlike Melville's, which was open, anti-authoritarian, and defiant. Given the two-value system of traditional allegory, the problem of ethical analysis, which in fiction as in life is accomplished by the tests of action, could be set aside as pre-solved. He did not in this respect have to draw upon his intellectual and emotional resources. Instead, he could devote his creative faculties to conceiving the framework and images of his morality tales ("A man to swallow a small snake—and it to be a symbol of a cherished sin"; "A physician for the cure of moral diseases"[18]), and he could apply his creative energies to the "deeper psychology," in respect to which his authority and authenticity cannot be questioned. As his friend George S. Hillard said upon reading *The Scarlet Letter*: "You are . . . quite a puzzle to me. How comes it that with so thoroughly healthy an organization as you have, you have such a taste for the morbid anatomy of the human heart, and such knowledge of it, too? I should fancy from your books that you were burdened with secret sorrow; that you had some blue chamber in your soul, into which you hardly dared to enter yourself. . . ."[19] In this regard one can begin to see why Frederick Crews called Hawthorne a "self-examining neurotic,"[20] though the stricture is too harsh, for Hawthorne, after all, did project his neurosis in his fiction. But nevertheless, where in the entire Hawthorne canon is there a sign that he could transcend his psychological problems? Where is his "Tartarus of Maids," his "I and My Chimney," his "Cock-a-Doodle-Doo!" or even his *Typee*?

Hawthorne was aware of the limitations of his allegorical mode and of his censoring of his psychic resources that prevented him so often from creating felt life in his fiction. In fact, he is almost compulsively plain-spoken on these scores. In his otherwise playful introduction to "Rappaccini's Daughter," he tells us he had "an inveterate love of allegory, which is apt to invest his plots and characters with the aspect of scenery and people in the clouds, and to steal away the human warmth out of his conceptions." And he knowingly adds that the reader must take the tales "in precisely the proper point of view" if he is to be amused; "otherwise, they can hardly fail to look excessively like nonsense." In another Preface he concedes the obvious, that if *The Blithedale Romance* is put side by side with nature," the comparison would make its "paint and pasteboard . . . but too painfully discernible," though he does not tell us that for the first and last time in his fiction (sketches aside), he adopted a first-person narrator as a way of being evasive about the Brook Farm experiment. In still another Preface (to the 1851 edition of *Twice-Told Tales*), Hawthorne says: "Instead of passion" in his tales, "there is sentiment; and, even in what purport to be pictures of actual life, we have allegory. . . . Whether from lack of power, or an unconquerable reserve, the Author's touches often have an effect of tameness. . . ."

"Lack of power" and "unconquerable reserve" are, of course, effect and cause. "So far as I am a man of really individual attributes," he writes in "The Old Manse," "I veil my face; nor am I, nor have I ever been," he adds defensively, "one of those supremely hospitable people who serve up their own hearts, delicately fried, with brain sauce, as a tidbit for their beloved public." In "The Custom-House" we hear the same self-assessments. He cannot "indulge" himself in "confidential depths of revelation"; he must keep the "inmost Me behind its veil." Yet he does reveal his true moral character in passages that at first glance seem only self-mockery. For with whatever contempt he imagines his "stern and black-browed" Puritan grandsires would regard his "business in life," he discloses that "strong traits of their nature have intertwined themselves with mine." Those traits, as he obliquely suggests, condensed into "the persecuting spirit," a spirit that, deprived of the instrumentalities of church and state, was attenuated in him into mere moral righteousness. To be sure, there were no Roger Williamses to deport or witches to condemn, but there were the Abolitionists like John Brown ("Nobody was ever more justly hanged"[21]) and his sister-in-law Elizabeth Peabody ("like every other Abolitionist, you look at matters with an awful squint"[22]); there were the reformers and intellectuals (better that "the world . . . be . . . rendered immovable in precisely the worst moral and physical state . . . than be benefited by such schemes of such philosophers"[23]); and there were the world's failures ("The fault of a failure is attributable—in a great degree at least—to the man who fails. . . . Nobody has a right to live in the world unless he be strong and able, and applies his ability to good purpose";[24] "For it is my creed . . . that a man has no claim upon his fellow-creatures, beyond bread and water, and a grave, unless he win it by his own strength or skill"[25]). Thus, when Hawthorne imagines his ancestors asking these questions about him: "A writer of story-books! . . . what mode of glorifying God, or being serviceable to mankind in his day and generation,— may that be?" we—and assuredly Hawthorne—know the answer. James again, with his remarkable acuity, recognized Hawthorne to be "morally, in an appreciable degree, a chip of the old block," for there was in him "an element of simplicity and rigidity . . . which might have kept his black-browed grandsires on better terms with him than he admits to be possible."[26]

"The Old Manse" further bears out the point. In that sketch Hawthorne plainly wished that the human race might be restored to "the simple perception of what is right, and the single-hearted desire to achieve it, both of which have been lost in consequence of this weary activity of brain and torpor or passion of the heart that now afflict the universe." To be sure, he did not wish this statement ever to be quoted against him, but the entire body of his fiction is an exemplification of this principle—namely, that the exercise of brain and heart can only lead to ambiguity and contention, and that somehow the human race can find a resting-point in Victorian or consensual morality—a principle, one need hardly say, that leads to a kind of moral fascism. The only vital thing that Hawthorne does not identify in these and various other self-criticisms is the fixity of his moral position, let alone his desperate psychological need for rigidity. Apparently it never occurred to him ever to question it. The more incoherence there was within, the more coherence there had to be without. Whatever the wide range of reference Melville intended in *Pierre* by the "guild of self-imposters," among them "Muggletonian Scots and Yankees," we must include Hawthorne, for as author he was certainly a "chronometric" man, one who always knew the exact moral time wherever he went. It was Hawthorne who all but declared in his fiction that he had found the "Talismanic Secret" to the bewildering complexities of experience, though assuredly he failed to find it in his own life.

From this position of pietistic conservatism, Hawthorne wrote of *Typee* in his short, unsigned *Salem Advertiser* review, his first acknowledgment of Melville's existence. Had he not been doing a favor for Evert Duyckinck, not to mention himself, he might have spoken with less leniency. For Duyckinck, as editor of Wiley and Putnam's Library of American Books, had not only published *Typee* in the series, but Hawthorne's reworking of Horatio Bridge's *Journal of an African Cruiser* (for which Hawthorne received the royalties), and was in the process of bringing out *Mosses from an Old Manse*. Without mentioning Melville by name, though his name appeared on the title page, Hawthorne wrote that the author "has that freedom of view—it would be too harsh to call it laxity of principle—which renders him tolerant of codes of morals that may be little in accordance with our own." To be sure, Hawthorne found a pretext to forgive him: the author is "a young and adventurous sailor" and the book may be "wholesome to our staid landsmen."[27] From the selfsame position Hawthorne made his final statement about Melville in his *English Notebooks*, though Melville was no longer the "young and adventurous sailor," but a poor, ailing, overworked author who had "pretty much made up his mind to be annihilated" (did Melville give Hawthorne to understand that he was about to give up writing fiction, as he in fact did, or something more dreadful?). Desperately needing encouragement, Melville had gone out of his way to visit Hawthorne in Liverpool; yet, judging from the available evidence, Hawthorne on the whole merely sat in judgment of him: "It is strange how he persists—and has persisted ever since I knew him, and probably long before—in wandering to-and-fro over these [intellectual and emotional] deserts. . . ." Remembering the days of their friendship in the Berkshires, Hawthorne added, ". . . He has a very high and noble nature, and [is] better worth immortality than most of us." As it was, however, Melville's "writings, for a long while past," writings that include *The Piazza Tales, Pierre,,* and very likely even *Moby-Dick*, "have indicated a morbid state of mind."[2][8]

If it is true that a good fiction "mystifies" life—that is, presents man and his condition in proper complexity and puzzlement, Hawthorne's art, so unlike Melville's in this crucial respect, falls short of the mark. Such a vision, that life is dense, uncertain, mysterious, forces the fiction into paradox, implication, connotation, allusion, irony, and the other literary devices designed to render the felt difficulties of the human situation. Poor fiction "de-mystifies" man and his condition by explanation, suppression, and evasion, and this process cannot draw upon the significant and essentially dramatic devices just specified, except, as Hawthorne too often does, by literary contrivance and manipulation. I am not suggesting, as Poe seems to suggest on occasion, that the vague, the indefinite, the unrealized in fiction is to be taken as a means of adumbrating the essential mystery of life. Such "methods" can only be considered strategies of evasion. What I *am* suggesting is that the constant and crucial struggle of every author must be to harmonize art with experience, form with formlessness. Victory of one over the other can only be a grievous defeat. Shakespeare is the model in this in that his art seldom trivialized, falsified, or vulgarized the richness and truths of experience in the process of subsuming experience under a literary construct, nor did experience overpower his art and make his dramas mere slices of life. But Shakespeare represents literary perfection. If, then, imbalance must occur, it is better that experience predominate somewhat over art, lest the art prove too reductive of experience. Hawthorne's art, to which merely as "art," much devotion has been paid, was characteristically achieved at the cost of curtailed and devitalized experience. True, according to his own statements, a journal of his "whole external life" from dawn to night would be a "dry, dull history"; true, living an "inward life" ("Nobody would think," he confesses, "that the same man could live two such different lives simultaneously"[2][9]), he was unable to be enriched by the experiences he had ("The fault was mine," he acknowledges in "The Custom-House": "The page of life . . . spread out before me seemed dull and commonplace, only because I had not fathomed its deeper import. A better book than I shall ever write was there. . . .

These perceptions have come too late"); true, he was the son of his grand-sires. But if only, like Melville's Pierre, he could have been able to act upon the principle that "the visible world of experience" is that "procreative thing that impregnates the muses"; if he had been able "with the soul of an Atheist" to write down "the godliest things"; if the "crowning curse" of his narratives (to borrow Melville's phrase from "The Encantadas") was not "their drudging impulse to straightforwardness in a belittered world," one might be tempted to believe that he might have outdone Melville.

> ... When the big hearts strike together, the concussion is a little stunning.
> Melville in a letter to Hawthorne

The mystery is how these two writers, so polarized in temperament, moral vision, literary execution, and sense of life, became such great friends and how Hawthorne, if at all, effected an artistic conversion in Melville. As friendship is not one-sided but mutual, we must also try to discover, in penetrating this mystery, what Melville did or, better, tried to do for Hawthorne. The answers to these riddles lie deeply buried in the familiar facts. By chance, they became neighbors in the Berkshires, living six miles apart from each other, one near Lenox, the other near Pittsfield. Melville was then thirty-one years old; immensely productive, having published five books in four years; and blessed with literary reputation ever since *Typee* had appeared in England and America. Hawthorne was forty-six at the time and remarkably unproductive, considering he had labored as an author for a quarter of a century and had produced only four books for the American market. Indeed, he had good reason to consider himself the obscurest man of letters in America, but the recent publication of *The Scarlet Letter* (March 1850) was now beginning to earn him a wide and very rich reputation. These men first met in early August 1850 and continued to meet, sometimes for extended visits, over a period of sixteen months, until the Hawthornes left the Berkshires for West Newton in late November 1851. Melville made two more visits to Hawthorne, one to Concord in 1852, the other to Liverpool in 1856.

Typee was evidently the only book of Melville's Hawthorne had read before they met; in fact, as was noticed earlier, he had reviewed it for the *Salem Advertiser* of 25 March 1846. Now, interested at once in the young author, he apparently asked Evert Duyckinck, their mutual friend and "patron," for the rest of his works. Duyckinck, in the middle of August 1850, sent the parcel of books to Melville for delivery to Hawthorne without disclosing the nature of the contents. On August 29 Hawthorne wrote his impressions to Duyckinck, and no doubt discussed those impressions with Melville himself: "I have read Melville's works with a progressive appreciation of the author. No writer ever put the reality before his reader more unflinchingly than he does in 'Redburn,' and 'White Jacket.' 'Mardi' is a rich book, with depths here and there that compel a reader to swim for his life. It is so good that one scarcely pardons the writer for not having brooded long over it, so as to make it a great deal better."[30] For his part, though his Aunt Mary had given him a copy of *Mosses from an Old Manse* a month before their first meeting, Melville seems to have read nothing of Hawthorne's until after they met, with the exception of a few stories in *Twice-Told Tales.*[31] In *White-Jacket,* referring to "A Rill from the Town Pump," a very popular sketch widely copied in the magazines, Melville wished that "my fine countryman, Hawthorne of Salem, had but served on board a man-of-war in his time, that he might give us a reading of a 'rill' from the scuttlebutt."

These facts would be trivial indeed, mere literary gossip, if Melville had not felt overpoweringly compelled to rewrite a novel that was almost ready for publication in August 1850 ("Melville," Evert Duyckinck wrote to his brother, "has a new book mostly done . . ."[32]). For Hawthorne had somehow enlarged him, made him feel full of possibility. As Melville confessed in his essay, "Hawthorne and His Mosses" (published in Duyckinck's *Literary World* on 17 and 24 August 1850): ". . . This Hawthorne has dropped germinous seeds into my soul. He expands and deepens down, the more I contemplate him." Hawthorne also seems to have roused in Melville the courage to act on the deep-seated conviction he expressed to Judge Lemuel Shaw, his father-in-law, in a letter written in the fall of 1849, a time before he had met Hawthorne. That conviction arose from his *"jobs"* on *Redburn* and *White-Jacket,* which, he said, "I have done for money—being forced to it, as other men are to sawing wood. . . . So far as I am individually concerned, & independent of my pocket, it is my earnest desire to write those sort of books which are said to 'fail.' "[33] To quote from his triumph-sounding *Mosses* review again, Melville now felt it "better to fail in originality than to succeed in imitation," imitation either of others or of himself, one supposes. He now wanted to probe "at the very axis of reality"; like Lear, he wanted to tear off "the mask, and speak the sane madness of vital truth."

In its original form the manuscript was described by Melville as a "whaling voyage"[34] and as a "romance of adventure, founded upon certain wild legends in the Southern Sperm Whale Fisheries,"[35] and by Duyckinck as "a romantic, fanciful & literal & most enjoyable presentment of the Whale Fishery,—something quite new"[36] —hardly the way he would view the published version in his magazine, the *Literary World*. No reference to the *ur*-manuscript hints at a tragic hero whose name would be that of the Biblical king who "did evil in the sight of the Lord above all that were before him"; nor of an inscrutable and invincible Albino Whale whose legendary name would become the title of the book, though the English publisher may have received the new title too late to make the change. Nor were there in those earlier references any mention of allegorical intention (".... We ... must," Melville wrote to Hawthorne after *Moby-Dick* was published, "be content to have our paper allegories but ill comprehended").[37] The reworking of the book—"ditcher's work," Melville called it—took the better part of a year, a long time for a man who could dash off a work like *Redburn* or *White-Jacket* in a season; who had recently suffered a commercial disaster with *Mardi* (1849), his only other attempt at allegory; who had an extended family to support, his own and his mother's; and who, failing to meet his publishing schedule and being refused further advances from his publishers, was forced to borrow $2,050 at nine percent interest.[38] Yet the "fit" was on him, less to become the American Shakespeare than to achieve self-realization, though the two, of course, are not incompatible, and he substantially, even transubstantially, changed the book from a fact-ridden *White-Jacket* into the metaphysical *Moby-Dick*. And in recognition of the effect Hawthorne had on him, he dedicated the novel to him "In Token of My Appreciation for His Genius. . . ." Hawthorne was impressed with the book and in November offered to review it, despite its being dedicated to him, if only to repay Melville for his incandescent review of the *Mosses* volume, a review, as Mrs. Hawthorne wrote to Duyckinck, that rang with "such a generous, noble enthusiasm as I have not before found in any critic of any writer,"[39] though no doubt he had begun to feel great affection for Melville too. But Melville demurred: "Don't write a word about the book. . . . I am heartily sorry I ever wrote anything about you—it was paltry."[40] In December, from West Newton, Hawthorne wrote to Duyckinck: "What a book Melville has written! It gives me an idea of much greater power than his preceding ones." And he took occasion in that letter to add: "It hardly seemed to me that the review of it, in the *Literary World*, did justice to its best points."[41] If this were not Hawthorne writing, the demurrer might be considered mild indeed, for though the *Literary World* had found *Moby-Dick* "a most remarkable sea-dish," it had been "compelled to object" to the book on the grounds that Ishmael prays with "a cannibal to a piece of wood," that he speaks disrespectfully of the Archangel Gabriel and of priestcraft, and that the novel as a whole is rashly "daring in speculation, reckless at times of taste and propriety. . . . This piratical running down of creeds and opinions ... is out of place and uncomfortable. We do not like to see what, under any view, must be to the world the most sacred associations of life violated and defaced."[42]

During this time of friendship with Hawthorne, Melville's genius came to its full power. It would explode again in *Pierre*, a work as experimental in its way as *Moby-Dick* and even, one may insist, a realistic and inverted version of *Moby-Dick*: realistic in that Melville abandoned all allegorical devices; inverted in that he adopted as his tragic hero, not an egoist but an altruist, not a man seeking to revenge the random injustice done him by the White Whale, but a man intent upon righting the random injustice done Isabel. And despite its many gaucheries, not the least of which is Melville's mockery of Pierre in the chapter "Young America in Literature," and despite its rather melodramatic plot rendered in an unfortunate Elizabethan linguistic mode (for *Hamlet* was as much on his mind in writing this work as *King Lear* and *Tamburlaine II* were in the creation of *Moby-Dick*[43]), the book remains a powerful, if badly underrated, achievement. Melville's genius would shine too in subsequent work, in the brilliant and beautifully controlled "Bartleby," "The Tartarus of Maids," "The Encantadas," and especially "Benito Cereno," until it would dissolve into the blank nihilism of *The Confidence-Man*. One pauses to ask what sense it makes to conjecture that the Confidence Man is Christ, the Devil, or some other representation, or to distinguish Thoreau, Emerson, or even Poe among the characters, when everyone in the book is cast into the selfsame indistinguishable moral blackness. For whatever the ambiguity of Melville's technique in that work, there is no ambiguity whatever about his misanthropy or about the nihilism of his one-value system that flattens humanity to the single level of swindler and swindled and that makes moral discriminations impossible. Melville's vision of man as a species of Yahoo is profoundly blacker here than Swift's, for Swift provided a moral standard in the Houyhnhnms. In eliminating all moral ambiguity by leveling all values, a device more reductive, not to say destructive, than the two-value system of traditional allegory, how could he not write a plodding, joyless, circular work that can only be likened to a treadmill? His genius, to be sure, would gleam again fitfully in *Billy Budd*, but that work needed greater artistic will toward *finish*, in both senses of the word, than Melville at the time could muster. Billy and Claggart remain thin Hawthornian characters belonging to the world of allegory; significant scenes, such as the "closeted interview" when Captain Vere "communicated the finding of the court to the prisoner," as they remain undramatized, are artistically evasive; and Captain Vere himself, though the very center of the narrative, lacks personhood. He is defined only by the moral dilemma in which he is helplessly implicated.

Nevertheless, the unarguable point is that during the time Hawthorne lived in the Berkshires, Melville passed through an artistic conversion. Precisely what role Hawthorne played in that conversion has yet to be investigated, but there is a prior question that presses for attention—namely, the nature of that conversion. The answer seems to be that, sometime during his reworking of *Moby-Dick*, Melville was struck by a conviction throughout his entire being, the way Ahab was struck by lightning from crown to sole in his "sacramental act" of fire-worship. What seems more probable is that his being struck by this conviction was the very reason for his rewriting *Moby-Dick* in the first place. For he now came to feel in his soul what spasmodically and rather intellectually he had recognized in his earlier fiction, that evil was not social in origin, a condition that could be ameliorated and, conceivably, extirpated by social criticism, personal valor, and reform. Now he became certain in the depths of his being that the taint in the universe and in man was universal, metaphysical, and incurable. He now felt that starvation in a Liverpool slum, flogging aboard naval vessels, the inhumanity of whaling masters and missionaries, the incursions of French militarists in the Marquesas—all those abominations, in short, that call upon us "to civilize civilization and christianize Christendom"—were only social outcroppings of the "organic ill" that permeates creation. Melville, to repeat, had intellectual glimmerings of this view before, but he had not synthesized them, nor felt them so profoundly, nor sustained them so protractedly as he did in *Moby-Dick*. In *Mardi*, for instance, he had "the voice of the gods" proclaim: "And though all evils may be assuaged, all evils cannot be done away. For evil is the chronic malady of the universe, and checked in one place, breaks forth in another." Likewise in *White-Jacket* he expressed awareness of the "heartless necessities of the predestination of things; some sin under which the sinner sank in sinless woe." And in that novel too he also discerned that "the best wisdom that has ever in any way been revealed to our man-of-war world—is but a slough and a mire, with a few tufts of good footing here and there." But these are isolated passages. The works in which they occur and the rhetoric in which they are couched do not testify to the fullness, the passion, and the certitude of the conviction that possessed him in the rewriting of *Moby-Dick*.[44] And the strange thing is that Hawthorne, far from approving this view, would pronounce it "morbid," if his statement made on 20 November 1856 applies to *Moby-Dick* (". . . his writings, for a long while past, have indicated a morbid state of mind"). If that was indeed Hawthorne's reconsideration of *Moby-Dick*, especially in the wave of reaction to it and particularly to *Pierre*,[45] there was reason for it. For if there was a single credo in Aristotle's *Poetics* that Hawthorne endorsed above all others and adopted in his own fiction, it was that tragedy "is the result . . . of some great error or frailty" in man and man alone, not in the universe, for "divine Providence," however inexplicably, makes the world unquestionably ordered and good. He is not plainer on this score than in his *Life of Franklin Pierce* when he equates the "evil fate" of a politician with "the natural infirmity of his character. . . ."[46]

The signs of this conversion experience appear in Melville's review of Hawthorne's *Mosses*, an essay that, judged in terms of conscious deception and of unconscious self-deception, falls into a class with Poe's "Philosophy of Composition." Duyckinck, under whose auspices the *Mosses* volume had appeared, was, of course, happy to have a puff for his *Literary World*, but why was the essay written and published in such haste? After all, Melville had first met Hawthorne on August 5 and the review, in all likelihood, was written on August 11.[47] It is hardly surprising that Melville, when he received the *Literary World* containing the first installment of his two-part review, should be pleased to remark: "Under the circumstances the printing is far more correct than I expected; but there are one or two ugly errors [*the same madness of truth* for *the sane madness of truth* was the worst]. . . . Send me the other proof [of the second installment], if you can. . . ."[48]

The anonymous essay, of course, was intended as a tribute to Hawthorne, who had aroused great admiration in him, but some readers, including Sophia Hawthorne's mother, were annoyed that the reviewer had been carried away, "had injured the subject by saying too much. 'No man of common-sense,' " Mrs. Peabody added, quoting Aunt Rawlins, " 'would seriously name Mr. Hawthorne . . . in the same day with Shakespeare. . . .' " To Hawthorne himself, she continued, "the idea must have appeared too absurdly monstrous to be understood otherwise than as covert satire, or at least as the ravings of well-meaning imbecility."[49] But Hawthorne's own reaction was quite different when he wrote to Duyckinck on 29 August 1850: ". . . Next to deserving his praise, it is good to have beguiled or bewitched such a man into praising and more than I deserve," adding, ". . . Nor do I think it necessary to appropriate the whole magnificence of his encomium. . . ."[50]

As conscious deception, the essay was sheer fiction, even to persona (a Virginian), to locale (Vermont), to dissimulation that the "Virginian" had not met Hawthorne and that he had previously read *Twice-Told Tales* and *The Scarlet Letter*. (Afterward he wrote to Duyckinck, referring to the stories in *Twice-Told Tales*: "I hadnt read but a few of them before";[51] and he did not acquire a copy of *The Scarlet Letter* until 1870.[52]) As unconscious self-deception, which is more to the purpose, the *Mosses* volume represented the first opportunity Melville had to formulate his new literary convictions, particularly his conviction concerning the nature of evil, and he pounced upon it eagerly. Another way of putting the matter is that the essay represents Melville's projection of his newly discovered self-image upon Hawthorne, who had somehow, in a "shock of recognition," become in his mind an *alter ego*. Only in terms of self-revelation does the essay make sense, for what he says of Hawthorne's fiction applies only to his own preoccupations. Since he evidently began writing the review just less than a week after meeting Hawthorne, it certainly seems that the *Mosses* was only an occasion, hardly the cause, for Melville's formulating the new views that were tumultuously calling for expression in him. The very tumultuousness of his ideas and the need to express them constitute the explanation, in my judgment, for his great haste in writing the essay. In the essay itself, he quickly turned aside from the "harmless Hawthorne" to speak of "a great deep intellect which drops down into the universe like a plummet"; of "a blackness, ten times black"; of the "great power of blackness that derives its force from . . . that Calvinistic sense of Innate Depravity and Original Sin"; of "probings at the very axis of reality"; of tearing "off the mask" to speak "the sane madness of vital truth"; and of the "blackness . . . that so fixes and fascinates me." And he also speaks of a fiction "immeasurably deeper than the plummet of a mere critic," a fiction that can be tested only by the heart and not the brain—the kind of fiction that would engross him now for most of his literary life.

Caught in this process of projection whereby he saw Hawthorne as a mirror-image of his new-found artistic self, Melville wrote a curious statement to Hawthorne on 16(?) April 1851 after he received a presentation copy of *The House of the Seven Gables*. Though wishing, he said, "to devote an elaborate and careful paper to the full consideration . . . of the purport and significance of what so strongly characterizes all of this author's [Hawthorne's] writings," he lapsed at once into an analysis of himself, or at least the self he had projected in Captain Ahab—precisely the same curious trick of mind that occurred when he wrote the *Mosses* review:

We think that into no recorded mind has the intense feeling of the visable truth ever entered more deeply than into this man's [Hawthorne's]. By visable truth, we mean the apprehension of the absolute condition of present things as they strike the eye of the man who fears them not, though they do their worst to him,—the man who, like Russia or the British Empire, declares himself a sovereign nature [nation?] (in himself), amid the powers of heaven, hell, and earth. He may perish; but so long as

he exists he insists upon treating with all Powers upon an equal basis. If
any of those other Powers choose to withhold certain secrets, let them;
that does not impair my sovereignty in myself; that does not make me
tributary. And perhaps, after all, there is *no* secret.

In the same letter too, by the same process of self-projection, he said what
was only true about himself now, never about Hawthorne: "There is the
grand truth about Nathaniel Hawthorne. He says NO! in thunder; but the
Devil himself cannot make him say *yes*"—yes, that is, to the pieties of the
age. "For all men who say *yes*, lie. . . ."[53]

Yet if Melville learned nothing from Hawthorne about the nature of evil,
except as he distortedly read the tales in the *Mosses*, it is possible that he
may have learned a great deal from him about literary technique, though
he says nothing on this score in the essay. For deeply concerned as he now
was with the paradoxes one encounters in the world and within oneself, he
must surely have been concerned with the literary strategies by which those
paradoxes are rendered. The methodology most characteristic of Hawthorne
involves the problem of perception—call it phenomenology—as is perhaps
readily illustrated by the Rorschach-like reactions of Reverend Hooper's
parishioners to his black veil. Whatever the source—and one cannot discount the possibility that it could have originated in Melville himself—this
technique is what he had in mind in writing "The Whiteness of the Whale"
and "The Doubloon" chapters of *Moby-Dick*.

This methodology of Hawthorne's is worth some elaboration, as it
figures so largely in Melville's major fiction. Perhaps the best example is
"Rappaccini's Daughter," a tale that appeared in the *Mosses* volume. In
that narrative Hawthorne, concerned with the deceptiveness of human
motive and experience, makes it possible and even necessary for us to take
almost every detail in two ways. The garden, for instance, is an Eden to
Dr. Rappaccini and an anti-Eden to Beatrice; Rappaccini is a marvelous
doctor to Dame Lisabetta, but a charlatan to Baglioni. To create such
ambiguities, Hawthorne continually makes use of subjunctives; of double
explanations; of doubt-creating words such as *perhaps, ostensibly,
suspicion*; of doubt-creating questions ("Was this garden . . . the Eden of
the present world? And this man . . . was he the Adam?"); and, of course,
of such symbols as Beatrice's poison, which is, from one point of view,
destructive, yet, from another, efficacious in that it makes her and eventually Giovanni "redundant with life, health, and energy." Too, since the
reader experiences the events of the tale largely through Giovanni's consciousness, the youth is continually shown to be confused by wine, rumor,
fantasy, and self-doubt. Even in his supposedly corrective authorial voice,
Hawthorne deceives us by denying the accuracy of Giovanni's perceptions

("... There could be no possibility of distinguishing a faded flower from a fresh one at so great a distance").

One wonders, then, at the following "coincidences": that Captain Delano in "Benito Cereno" is very much like Robin in "My Kinsman, Major Molineux" in that both are taken in by a charade—the one enacted aboard the *San Dominick*, the other in Boston; and that both systematically misinterpret the data of their experience until the denouement. That Ahab is like Goodman Brown in that one projects his own sense of evil upon the White Whale, the other upon his townspeople; and that both participate in the black mass. That Pierre is like Reuben Bourne of "Roger Malvin's Burial" in that both suffer from ambiguous motives. (Melville says of Pierre: "womanly beauty" in the form of Isabel "... invited him to champion the right.... How, if accosted in some squalid lane, a humped, and crippled, hideous girl should have snatched his garment's hem with—'Save me, Pierre—love me, own me, brother; I am thy sister!'" Similarly, Hawthorne says that Bourne's decision to champion the right—to find someone to rescue Malvin—"was aided ... by the hidden strength of many another motive," among them his desire "for his own happiness and that of Dorcas.") One wonders too about Ahab's fire-worship, especially as Melville selected Hawthorne's "Fire-Worship" for special commendation in the *Mosses* essay; or about the similarity of "I and My Chimney" and *The House of the Seven Gables*, for both feature a house as a symbol of tradition vs. modernism. And, finally, one wonders if it is accident that *Pierre* and *The Blithedale Romance*, both published in 1852, should both feature altruists who botch their own lives and those of others. Though our puzzlement cannot be resolved, such "identities" enable us, perhaps, to glimpse another reason why Melville was so excited by the *Mosses* and why Hawthorne was so enthusiastic about *Moby-Dick*. Whatever the case, "Ripeness is all," and Melville was ready to emerge from his dormancy, like the bug in his "Apple-Tree Table."

We can now explore the friendship that was rapturous on both sides, a rapture that no other man roused in them and which they roused in no other man. Sophia, surely aware of how Melville was drawing her husband out, wrote to her mother on 4 September 1850: Melville is a "man with a true, warm heart, and a soul and an intellect,—with life to his finger-tips; earnest, sincere, and reverent; very tender and *modest*.... He has very keen perceptive power...."[54] The Hawthorne children loved him too; Julian, according to Hawthorne, said he "loved Mr Melville as well as me, and as mamma, and as Una."[55] We recall that Hawthorne, after he met Melville for the last time in Liverpool, wrote: "... He has a very high and noble nature, and better worth immortality than most of us." And Melville,

though "generally silent and incommunicative," according to Mrs. Hawthorne, was able to pour "out the rich floods of his mind and experience"
to Hawthorne, so sure was he "of apprehension, so sure of a large and
generous interpretation, and of the most delicate and fine judgment."[56] So
intense became Melville's sense of spiritual brotherhood with Hawthorne
that he could write in response to that man's admiration of *Moby-Dick*:
". . . I felt pantheistic then—your heart beat in my ribs and mine in yours,
and both in God's. . . . I feel that the Godhead is broken up like the bread
at the Supper, and that we are the pieces. . . . Knowing you persuades me
more than the Bible of our immortality."[57]

This was not the Hawthorne who arrived in the Berkshires in 1850, "the
hidden spirit," to quote Austin Warren, "who never appeared in company
or even revealed himself to wife and children. . . ."[58] The testimony on
this score is plentiful, but a little will suffice. Sophia wrote a poem called
"The Seraph and the Dove" (the "Seraph" being her husband and the
"Dove" herself), which delineates Hawthorne's essential relations with his
"friends" and wife:

> He was alone; he stood apart from men:
> His simple nature could not solve their ways. . . .
> So mused he on the visions of his mind. . . .
> Then lo! came fluttering to his arms a Dove, . . .
> And as he felt the brooding warmth, he conscious, smiled and said,
> "Yes, Father! Heaven can only be where kindred spirits wed!"[59]

Similarly, in a typical confession of estrangement from others, Hawthorne
wrote to Sophia after leaving Brook Farm: "The real Me was never an
associate of the community; there has been a spectral Appearance
there, . . . doing me the honor to assume my name. . . . This Spectre was
not thy husband."[60] His daughter Rose acknowledged what is undeniable,
that he was considered "shy and reticent to the verge of morbidness,"
though she explained his withdrawnness in terms of "dignity" and
"gentlemanliness."[61] And William Dean Howells, toward the end of Hawthorne's life, provides us with a more extended view to the same import. A
newcomer to Boston, he tells us in *Literary Friends and Acquaintance*, he
was having dinner with three of Hawthorne's long-time "friends," Oliver
Wendell Holmes, James Russell Lowell, and James T. Fields, the publisher,
when he ventured to remark that he had not yet met Mr. Hawthorne. "Ah,
well!" Dr. Holmes caught him up, "I don't know that you will ever feel
you have really met him. He is like a dim room with a little taper of
personality burning on the corner of the mantle." The three men, Howells
recalled, all spoke of Hawthorne "with the same affection, but [with] the
same sense of something mystical and remote in him. . . ." When Howells

finally visited Hawthorne, he found him to be as cordial "as so shy a man could show himself," but "there was a great deal of silence in it all, and, at times, in spite of his shadowy kindness, I felt my spirits sink." That was the Hawthorne who appeared in the Berkshires in 1850, the Hawthorne of whom Sophia herself wrote to her sister Elizabeth on 4 July 1851: "....He has but just stepped over the threshold of a hermitage. He is but just *not* a hermit still."[62] And "hermit" was the word Melville would use in a poem on Hawthorne.

Yet, incredibly, this reclusive man was able to write to Horatio Bridge only two days after meeting Melville: "I met Melville, the other day, and like him so much that I have asked him to spend a few days with me . . ."; and later to Duyckinck: "If you were to see how snug and comfortable Melville makes himself and friends, I think you would not fail [to visit us again in the Berkshires]"; and still later to George W. Curtis: "Herman Melville . . . is an admirable fellow"; not to mention that within two weeks of his meeting Melville, he had sent for and read all his novels.[63] It was also this withdrawn man who made a point of giving Melville the thoughtful gift of the four-volume *Mariner's Chronicle*; who permitted his wife to present him with an engraving of himself; who celebrated Melville's birthday, talking volubly about "all sorts of things," and who did the forbidden thing—"smoked cigars even within the sacred precincts of the sitting room"; who planned a trip with him to New York; who, when he moved back to Concord, invited Melville to his home ("I greatly enjoyed my visit to you," Melville wrote, "and hope that you reaped some corresponding pleasure"); who engaged with Melville in exchanging presentation copies of their works as they appeared from the press; who sought determinedly, if unsuccessfully, to secure Melville a foreign consulship; and who acted as his literary agent, at least to the extent of signing the contract for the English publication of *The Confidence Man*.[64]

What was there in Melville that so appealed to Hawthorne and drew him out? They had much in common, to be sure: they both enjoyed brandy, champagne, and cigars; their wives were pregnant at roughly the same time (Rose was born in May, Stanwix in October 1851); they were both professional writers and deeply concerned about literary matters (they had, along with their other literary projects, discussed *Moby-Dick* at length while Melville was rewriting it, for Hawthorne in his *Wonder-Book* wrote: "On the hither side of Pittsfield sits Herman Melville, shaping out the gigantic conception of his 'White Whale' . . ."). And obviously, with their many differences of conviction, they often engaged in heated, if friendly, dispute. On 1(?) June 1851, for instance, Melville, having read "The Unpardonable Sin" ("Ethan Brand") in the *Dollar Magazine*, took issue

with Hawthorne's "frightful poetical creed that the cultivation of the brain
eats out the heart." It was his "*prose* opinion that in most cases, in those
men who have fine brains and work them well, the heart extends down to
hams. And though you smoke them with the fire of tribulation, yet, like
veritable hams, the head only gives the richer and the better flavor."[65]

But, to come to the heart of the matter, the thing that roused such
friendship in Hawthorne was Melville's absolute candor, and decency, and
great generosity of character. Echoing her husband's sentiment, as she
usually did, Sophia wrote to Duyckinck: "....The freshness of primeval
nature is in that man." When Duyckinck sent the letter to Melville's sister
Augusta, she replied on 30 September 1850: "She has offered a beautiful
tribute to my noble-souled brother.... Of him, no truer words were ever
written than those...."[66] Julian Hawthorne likewise noted: "...There
were few honester or more lovable men than Herman Melville."[67] And
Melville himself wrote to Hawthorne: "With no son of man do I stand
upon any etiquette or ceremony, except the Christian ones of charity and
honesty."[68] It was these great-hearted qualities in Melville that won Hawthorne over. But there is more: in his capacity as friend, Melville acted as a
lay psychotherapist. In the words of "Ethan Brand," he was "a
brother-man, opening the chambers or the dungeons of our common nature
by the key of holy sympathy...." He urged Hawthorne to "let us speak,
though we show all our faults and weaknesses,—for it is a sign of strength
to be weak, to know it, and out with it...."[69] He assured him that there
are "certain crotchetty and over doleful chimearas, the like of which men
like you and me and some others, forming a chain of God's posts round
the world, must be content to encounter now and then, and fight them the
best way we can." He offered him diversion by "some little bit of
vagabondism," suggesting that "ere we start, we must dig a deep hole, and
bury all Blue Devils...." He told him not to stand on "punctilios. You
may do what you please—say or say *not* what you please." He explained
that he understood "how a man of superior mind can ... by intense cultivation" become "exceedingly nice and fastidious," and how, "when you
see ... my ruthless democracy ..., you may possibly feel a touch of a
shrink...." He insisted that he would continue to visit him "until," he
added with humorous redundancy, "you tell me that my visits are both
supererogatory and superfluous." And when unable to visit him, he would
write him thick, discursive letters rich with grand conceits and good humor
("If ever, my dear Hawthorne, ... you and I shall sit down in Paradise, in
some little shady corner by ourselves; and if we shall by any means be able
to smuggle a basket of champagne there ..., and if we shall then cross our
celestial legs in the celestial grass that is forever tropical, and strike our

glasses and our heads together, till both musically ring in concert,–then . . . how shall we pleasantly discourse of all the things manifold which now so distress us . . .").[70]

What Hawthorne's friendship meant to Melville in the way of inspiration and reinforcement has already been indicated. Before he had been damned by dollars; now, prepared to say dollars be damned, he resolved once and for all to write the books he wanted to write, books that would proclaim the "sane madness of vital truth" and say "NO! in thunder. . . ." He recognized, even while reworking *Moby-Dick*, that no one gets a living by telling "the Truth"–he wrote as much to Hawthorne. "Let any clergyman try to preach the Truth from its very stronghold, the pulpit, and they would ride him out of his church on his own pulpit bannister." But tell "the Truth" he was now determined to do, though "the gutter" and the "Soup Kitchens" awaited him.[71] But as it was a time of great unfolding for Melville, so it was for Hawthorne too. In the Preface to the 1851 edition of *Twice-Told Tales*, both by implication and plain statement, Hawthorne reveals what the time he spent in the Berkshires meant to him. He was no longer "the obscurest man of letters in America"; in fact, though he was too modest to say so, the literary and commercial success of *The Scarlet Letter* was beginning to make him the most respected and eminent author in the United States. Now at last he had "an incitement to literary effort in a reasonable prospect of reputation or profit," a stimulation that, not to dwell on the reinvigoration he drew from Melville, impelled him to his period of greatest productivity. In quick succession in 1851 he published *The House of the Seven Gables, The Snow-Image,* and *A Wonder-Book.* In 1852 he published *The Blithedale Romance* and *The Life of Franklin Pierce,* the book that would earn him the very lucrative consulship at Liverpool. In terms of mere numbers, he turned out more books in these two years than he had in twenty-five years of literary activity. No wonder Melville remarked to Hawthorne on 17 July 1852: "This name of '*Hawthorne*' seems to be ubiquitous."[72] Hawthorne also tells us in the 1851 Preface to *Twice-Told Tales* that he had been a "person in retirement" whose stories were "attempts . . . to open an intercourse with the world." True, "on the internal evidence of the sketches," he "came to be regarded as a mild, shy, gentle, melancholic, exceedingly sensitive, and not very forcible man"; and perhaps, he adds with some bitterness, he was influenced "to fill up so amiable an outline, and to act in consonance with the character assigned him." But now, he says, he is prepared to "forfeit" all that, which he did to the extent of emerging into the more or less contemporary worlds represented by *The House of the Seven Gables, The Blithedale Romance,* and the campaign biography of

Pierce. He concludes by saying, with a sweep of reference that must include Melville, if it is to include anyone, that *Twice-Told Tales* had opened the way "to the formation of imperishable friendships" and that such friendships are "far better than fame."

There is another indication of how Hawthorne's stay in the Berkshires roused his creative energies, for once he left, those energies began to fail, the sign of which is that, from the time he left the Berkshires until his death twelve years later, he published only three more books. These were the *Tanglewood Tales* (1853), a retelling of the Greek myths that could little have engaged his imagination; *Our Old Home* (1863), a reworking of his *English Notebooks* that was seldom fictionized; and *The Marble Faun* (1860), a work that, one-part allegory and two-thirds guide-book material, was derived verbatim at times from his *Italian Notebooks*. There were also, of course, the four unpublished Romances, but, abortive as they were, they only reinforce the point that his creative energies were in decline.

But to plumb the mystery of their friendship to its bottom-most depths, we must take a cue from Melville and dive still deeper, even if we come up with bloodshot eyes. In 1839, whether as an idea for a story, or as a form of self-analysis, Hawthorne recorded this phrase in his *American Notebooks*: "To have ice in one's blood."[73] That was Hawthorne's condition at the time, a condition that would be interrupted only twice in his life, once when he met and married Sophia Peabody, the other when he met and became friends with Herman Melville. Emotionally frozen, he simultaneously feared thawing and dreaded remaining frozen. As he wrote to Longfellow in 1837, changing the figure of ice to self-imprisonment: "I have made a captive of myself, and put me into a dungeon, and now I cannot find the key to let myself out—and if the door were open, I should be almost afraid to come out."[74]

In *Our Old Home*, published in 1863, Hawthorne reverts to the image of "ice in one's blood." The phrase recurs when he tells us about a member of his party visiting a workhouse, a workhouse being, according to Taine's *Notes on England*, "a sort of asylum with something of a prison about it." This "gentleman" Hawthorne describes as "burthened with more than an Englishman's customary reserve, shy of actual contact with human beings, afflicted with a peculiar distaste for whatever was ugly, and, furthermore, accustomed to that habit of observation from an insulated stand-point which is said (but, I hope, erroneously) to have the tendency of putting ice into the blood." During the tour they enter the children's ward. A child of about six, whose sex is indeterminate, it is so "sickly, wretched, [and] humor-eaten," at once takes a fancy for the fastidious gentleman. Prowling about him, rubbing against his legs, following everywhere at his heels, the child finally positions itself directly before him and holds out its arms, mutely insisting on being taken up. It says not a word, being underwitted, perhaps, and incapable of speech. But it smiles up into the gentleman's face in such perfect confidence that it is going to be fondled and made much of, that "there was no possibility in a human heart of baulking its expection. It was as if God had promised the poor child this favor on behalf of that individual, and he was bound to fulfil the contract, or else no longer call himself a man among men." But having ice in the blood, the man struggles with himself.

"So," Hawthorne says, "I watched the struggle in his mind with a good deal of interest, and am seriously of opinion that he did an heroic act, and effected more than he dreamed of towards his final salvation, when he took up the loathsome child and caressed it as tenderly as if he had been its father." The squeamish gentleman, Hawthorne tells us, holds the child for "a considerable time," and when he puts it down, it continues to follow him, "keeping fast hold of his forefinger. . . ." When the party returns to the children's ward after a further tour of the workhouse, "here again was this same little Wretchedness waiting for its victim." "No doubt," Hawthorne concludes, "the child's mission in reference to our friend was to remind him that he was responsible, in his degree, for all the sufferings and misdemeanors of the world in which he lived, and was not entitled to look upon a particle of its dark calamity as if it were none of his concern; the offspring of a brother's iniquity being his own blood-relation, and the guilt, likewise, a burthen on him, unless he expiated it by better deeds."[75]

When we turn to the *English Notebooks*, the workbooks for *Our Old Home*, we find what we suspect, that the squeamish gentleman is Hawthorne himself. But more: we find a Hawthorne who really has ice in the blood. "I never saw . . . a child," he writes, more honestly than he did in *Our Old Home*, "that I should feel less inclined to fondle." But the "imp" made its mute appeal, as no doubt (though Hawthorne does not speak of this) did the "persons of eminent station . . . of both sexes in the party," and he found it "impossible" not to hold his "undesirable burden." Full of disturbed feelings, Hawthorne says: "It was as if God had promised the child this favor on my behalf, (but I wish He had not!) and that I must needs fulfil the contract." He held the child, not for "a considerable time," as he tells us in *Our Old Home*, but for "a little while"; and when he set the child down, it held two of his fingers—"luckily the glove was on"—"just as if (God save us!) it were a child of my own." And instead of the child's reminding him of his implication in the sufferings and crimes of the world, Hawthorne says: ". . . I cannot conceive of any greater remorse than a parent must feel, if he could see such a result of his illegitimate embraces. I wish I had not touched the imp; and yet I never should have forgiven myself if I had repelled its advances."[76]

This episode enables us to peer into the murky depths of the man and of his art, for this is conscious, not unconscious, manipulation of materials. His art, I have been suggesting, is psychologically autobiographical. Just as he projected his own conflicting sensations upon an imagined character, so, operating from behind "the Veil," he projected upon the personae of his fiction the guilt, fears, and anxieties of his profoundly troubled psyche, those psychic afflictions that put ice in the blood and emotionally freeze his characters, as they did himself. It is this kind of projection that gives his narratives their haunted and haunting quality, for it is the "heart's truth," as Faulkner says in "The Bear," that is written "out of the heart's driving complexity, for all . . . complex and troubled hearts. . . ." But there is also his fear of ice in the blood, and it is this which creates the tension in his fiction, the tension between self-expression and self-repression. That is why Hawthorne, with his Dimmesdale-like compulsion to confess, said about himself in the Preface to The Snow-Image: "You must . . . look through the whole range of his fictitious characters, good and evil, in order to detect any of his essential traits." These two psychic conditions, at truceless war with each other, energized his genius and serve to define his literary power. They also suggest his severe limitations, however willing we may be to overlook them in the light of what he did achieve: the narcissism of his preoccupations; the narrowness of his vision; the repetitiousness of his themes; the claustrophobia of his fictional worlds; and the barrenness of his ideas, except the moralistic ones, which he continually reiterated. It is this moralistic insistence that marks the point where Melville and Hawthorne part company, the insistence upon imposing Victorian "truths" on the truths of the heart. We see it in the episode in which Hawthorne masks his honest, if baffled, responses to the child in the workhouse with sentimentality and moralizing to provide himself and his public with an aseptic version of his true self. We can see in that episode too, not only the hollowness, but the heartlessness, of the Victorian shibboleths he endorsed. Can one, for instance, say of that child in the workhouse, as Hawthorne did in other contexts: "The fault of a failure is attributable—in a great degree at least—to the man who fails"? Is one prepared to say of such a child: "Nobody has a right to live in the world unless he be strong and able, and applies his ability to good purpose"? Indeed, Hawthorne, as he revealed himself in the English Notebooks, was even more pitiless than this toward the workhouse children: "It would be a blessing to the world," he wrote, "—a blessing to the human race, which they will contribute to vitiate and enervate—a blessing to themselves, who inherit nothing but disease and vice—if every one of them could be drowned to-night, instead of being put to bed. If there be a spark of God's life in them, this seems the only chance of preserving it."[77] Though he expressed the same sentiment in a somewhat gentler form in *Our Old Home*, if such a Dachau-type of sentiment can ever be expressed gently, he added: "This heroic method of treating human maladies, moral and material, is certainly beyond the scope of man's discretionary rights...."[78]

This episode, together with some profound self-revelations made in a letter to Sophia, enable us to penetrate the mystery of the friendship, for we can now surmise with some assurance just how Hawthorne responded to Melville's "divine magnanimities" that were so "spontaneous and instantaneous...."[79] We can only surmise because Hawthorne is usually so tight-lipped in his correspondence and notebooks, and his letters to Melville have vanished. That revelatory letter was written from his "haunted chamber" in his thirty-sixth year. In this letter he harks back to the image of ice in the blood: "... Sometimes ... it seemed as if I were already in the grave, with only life enough to be chilled and benumbed." When fame "with a still, small voice" called him out of that chamber, "forth I went, but found nothing in the world that I thought preferable to my old solitude," until he found Sophia, who had dwelt "in the shadow of a seclusion as deep as my own had been." The ice thawed when he became "mingled with another's being!"—a being who kept "my heart warm" and renewed "my life with her own." For, he explains:

Thou only hast taught me that I have a heart—thou only hast thrown a deep light downward, and upward, into my soul. Thou only hast revealed me to myself; for without thy aid, my best knowledge of myself would have been merely to know my own shadow.... Indeed, we are but shadows—we are not endowed with real life, and all that seems most real about us is but the thinnest substance of a dream—till the heart is touched. That touch creates us—then we begin to be—thereby we are beings of reality, and inheritors of eternity.

Without her, he concludes, "I ... never should [have] been created at all!"[80]

It now seems evident that Hawthorne's heart, "masking in visible ice," as his son said,[81] was touched by Melville, as once before, if more lastingly, it had been touched by Sophia Peabody; and, like his own Feathertop, he for a time vindicated "his claims to be reckoned human." For a time he was unafraid of, even welcomed, human contact; for a time he was drawn out of his "habit of observation from an insulated stand-point"; for a time he allowed the ice in his blood to melt. The veil behind which he hid dropped away to disclose his true self; and he became "mingled with another's being!" The words, of course, are those Hawthorne addressed to Sophia, but the feeling is Melville's too, if sounded more resonantly in his letters to Hawthorne. How else can we account for Melville's spontaneity and love and his grand assumption that Hawthorne would understand and return his feelings, if this is not the case? "The divine magnet is on you," Melville wrote him, "and my magnet responds. Which is the biggest? A foolish question—they are *One*."[82] How else can we account for Hawthorne, always shy and very often silent with strangers, talking with Melville, as he himself says, "about time and eternity, things of this world and of the next, and books, and publishers, and all possible and impossible matters, that lasted pretty deep into the night"?[83] How else can we account for Hawthorne saying of their last reunion in Liverpool: ". . . We soon found ourselves on pretty much our former terms of sociability and confidence,"[84] when almost any intimacy aroused in him anxiety about self-exposure?

In short, the mystery of their friendship dissolves when we understand that the Hawthorne we know, and the Hawthorne that Bridge, Emerson, Thoreau, Alcott, Duyckinck, Holmes, Lowell, Fields, and the others knew, and that even his wife and children knew, was not the Hawthorne that Melville knew. *That* Hawthorne to our loss we shall never know, except in glimpses, such as we catch here, and in his fiction, and in Melville's "Monody." The first stanza of that two-stanza poem seems to have been written much earlier than the second, perhaps soon after Hawthorne's death on 19 May 1864, and constitutes Melville's unmistakable lament for his loss of Hawthorne, not only in death but in life:[85]

> To have known him, to have loved him
>   After loneness long;
> And then to be estranged in life,
>   And neither in the wrong;
> And now for death to set his seal—
>   Ease me, a little ease, my song!

The second stanza, abandoning the flatness of the first, suggests Melville's sense of Hawthorne by images, including the ice and veil images. Hawthorne in death is hidden in his "hermit-mound," as in life he was hidden behind his "cloistral vine"; and the reason given for his reclusion is his great shyness:

> By wintry hills his hermit-mound
>   The sheeted snow-drifts drape,
> And houseless there the snow-bird flits
>   Beneath the fir-trees' crape;

> Glazed now with ice the cloistral vine
> That hid the shyest grape.

Later, in 1884, Melville explained in two interviews with Julian Hawthorne
that he had "a deep affection" for Hawthorne, but was convinced, not
only that "some secret in my father's life ... accounted for the gloomy
passages in his books," but that "some great secret" had caused Hawthorne
to estrange himself.[86] For estranged they had remained, even after Hawthorne returned to the States in June 1860. Neither man made an effort to
meet the other again, though separated by no greater physical distance than
that between Concord and Pittsfield or New York. The psychological distance between them had become too great.

We have arrived at a point where we can say that during the Berkshire
interlude, Melville and Hawthorne experienced a great rapport in their
friendship; that they found sounding boards in each other for their deepest
feelings and ideas; and that Melville brought Hawthorne out of his self-
seclusion, even as Hawthorne reinforced Melville's courage to write books,
not for "my pocket" but "from my heart."[87] Melville's review of the
Mosses volume was at once a sign of and spur to that friendship, for did he
not in that essay make the annunciatory statement that Hawthorne was all
but Shakespeare? Melville encouraged his friend, too, to write the "Agatha
story,"[88] even to visiting him in Concord for that purpose, though, very
likely, he also wanted to quicken a friendship that for Hawthorne, perhaps,
had already begun to flicker. We cannot know the reason why Melville kept
urging Hawthorne to write the "Agatha story," but we can hazard the
guess that he wanted to draw his friend out of his narcissistic preoccupations and shadowy allegories by forcing him into the world of actuality—to
deal with the rigors of real people caught in real human problems rather
than project, however disguisedly, his own psychic ones. If this was so, the
enterprise was doomed, as Melville soon discovered; and though he toyed
with the idea of writing the "Agatha story" himself, he dropped the entire
project, possibly because it had soured. Possibly too, since we are guessing,
Melville might have suggested to Hawthorne that he move from the fixed
moral position he had assumed in his fiction. For Melville's view, as expressed in *Pierre*, is that "in a world so full of all dubieties as this, one can
never be entirely certain whether [one] has acted in all respects conceiv-
able for the very best." Perhaps this is what he had in mind when he wrote
in the *Mosses* review that Hawthorne is "a seeker, not a finder yet," or in a
letter to Hawthorne that "He says NO! in thunder. . . ." But whatever else
Melville did, it is certain that, by letters, by visits, by sheer abounding good

nature, honesty, and charity, he tried and for a time succeeded in breathing life into a man in whom, even in the heyday of their friendship, he found "a good deal lacking";[89] a man who, at the peak of his fame and prosperity, could write of himself in the same year Melville visited him in Liverpool: "Really, I have no pleasure in anything; . . . a weight is always upon me. Nothing gives me any joy. . . . 'Remote, unfriended, melancholy, slow—' I can perfectly appreciate that line of Goldsmith; for it well expresses my own torpid, unenterprising, joyless state of mind and heart. . . . Life seems so purposeless as not to be worth the trouble of carrying it on any further."[90] Melville's effect on Hawthorne's psychological condition was temporary and negligible. Hawthorne felt too vulnerable to long expose himself to anyone, and he withdrew into his dark self again, the self that Samuel G. Goodrich in 1856 called "cold, moody, distrustful," that "stood aloof, and surveyed the world from shy and sheltered positions."[91]

The friendship, though the warmest that either man enjoyed, was never perfect. Near "the close of 1851" Hawthorne complained to Fields, without an oblique reference to the pleasure he and his family were taking in Melville: "To tell you a secret, I am sick to death of Berkshire, and hate to think of spending another winter here. But I must. The air and climate do not agree with my health at all; and"—an obvious piece of deception or self-deception, for languid and dispirited he felt all his life—"for the first time since I was a boy, I have felt languid and dispirited during almost my whole residence here."[92] Too, Hawthorne, like his own Ethan Brand, exemplified "the sin of an intellect that triumphed over the sense of brotherhood with man and reverence for God, and sacrificed everything to its own mighty claims!" For despite Melville's feeling "such a love & reverence & admiration for M[r] Hawthorne as is really beautiful to witness—& without [Hawthorne's] doing anything on his own part, except merely *being*," Hawthorne, it would appear, could not help feeling superior to Melville, entrenched as he was in his moral and psychological positions. Sophia, in worshipful regard of her husband, said that Melville was "a boy in opinion—having settled nothing yet"; that, in fact, "this growing man" would be "considered perhaps impious, if one did not take in the whole scope of the case," a strange echo indeed of Hawthorne's 1846 review of *Typee*. And for all Melville's candor in expressing his "tumultuous" and "innermost" thoughts "about GOD, the Devil, & Life . . . so . . . he can get at the Truth," she disapproved of him too for there being no "concession" in him when out of "M[r] Hawthorne's great, genial, comprehending silences" would come "a wonderful smile, or one powerful word. . . ." Indeed, all she seems to have approved in Melville was his "love & reverence & admiration for M[r] Hawthorne. . . ." Sophia said all this in a letter

written to her sister Elizabeth some two months before they left the Berkshires, not knowing what Melville meant—or had meant—to her husband as
a person.[93] Yet the evidence indicates she was only reflecting Hawthorne's
essential judgment of the man; and judgmental—the thing that destroys
"I-Thou" relationships—they both were of him. For five years later Hawthorne made like observations of Melville when they met for the last time
in Liverpool, except, unlike Sophia, he concluded that Melville is "better
worth immortality than most of us":

. . . We took a pretty long walk together, and sat down in a hollow among
the sand hills . . . and smoked a cigar. Melville, as he always does, began to
reason of Providence and futurity, and of everything that lies beyond
human ken . . . ; and, I think, [he] will never rest until he gets hold of a
definite belief. It is strange how he persists—and has persisted ever since I
knew him, and probably long before—in wandering to-and-fro over these
deserts, as dismal and monotonous as the sand hills amid which we were
sitting. He can neither believe, nor be comfortable in his unbelief; and he is
too honest and courageous not to try to do one or the other. If he were a
religious man, he would be one of the most truly religious and reverential.
He has a very high and noble nature, and better worth immortality than
most of us.[94]

Hawthorne had forgotten what he had written in the Preface to *Twice-Told
Tales* about "imperishable friendships," though he ought to have remembered that ideology kills love, for he stressed the idea so often in his
fiction. But he had little capacity for love, being, as he says, torpid. But
one now sees why a weight was always on him; why little gave him joy;
why he suffered from a recurring dream "these twenty or thirty years," the
"same dream of life hopelessly a failure," a dream he recalled in curious
juxtaposition with mention of Melville, whom he had recommended to
Commodore Perry as an editor for his book on Japan.[95] And one can see
why life seemed so purposeless to him as not to be worth the trouble of
carrying it on. For, as Archibald MacLeish said, the "crime against life, the
worst of all crimes, is *not* to feel." That crime, "the crime of torpor, of
lethargy, of apathy, the snake-like sin of coldness-at-the-heart," to quote
MacLeish again, Hawthorne committed, to none more maimingly than himself. The only time he overcame his "own adamant," he confessed on 14
September 1855, was when he read the "last scene" of *The Scarlet Letter*
to his wife.[96] In writing this, he had apparently repressed the memory of
his reaction to his mother's dying in 1849, for he had overcome his
adamant then too. The reaction he experienced at his mother's deathbed
had surprised him, for, as he said, "there has been, ever since my boyhood,
a sort of coldness of intercourse between us. . . . I did not expect to be

much moved at the time—that is to say, not to feel any overpowering emotion struggling, just then—though I knew that I should deeply remember and regret her." What made the tears gather in his eyes and caused him to shake "with sobs" was his mother's "few indistinct words—among which I understood an injunction to take care of my sisters."[97] It was an injunction that would have broken anyone's heart; for he who had never had a mother, let alone a father, to care for his emotional needs, was now enjoined to care for his sisters, and that by the very woman who, through sheer neurotic incapacity, had starved him into emotional shadowhood.

It is curious at first, but obvious upon reflection, why on the two occasions Hawthorne overcame his "own adamant," a mother-figure was involved, for his own mother had never been more to him than that. In the last chapter of *The Scarlet Letter* he had written that the townspeople came to Hester Prynne with their "sorrows and perplexities," including "the dreary burden of a heart unyielded, because unvalued and unsought . . . , demanding why they were so wretched, and what the remedy! Hester," he added, "comforted and counselled them as best she might. She assured them, too, of her firm belief, that, at some brighter period, . . . sacred love should make us happy. . . ." No wonder in trying to read that passage to his wife, "just after writing it," his "voice swelled and heaved," as if he "were tossed up and down on an ocean. . . ."[98] For surely in that passage he was alluding to the burden of his own unyielded heart; surely he sensed in the depths of his being that his own heart had gone unyielded because it had been "unvalued and unsought" in the years of his emotional formation; and surely he must have recognized that the "sacred love" Hester practiced and saw as coming, "not through dusky grief, but the ethereal medium of joy," had been denied him in his most critical years. No wonder, too, that he wrote to Sophia in his thirty-sixth year that "we are but shadows" until we are loved, and that he turned to her, the only woman who had loved him, with such trust and devotion. The one "significant other" in his life, she gave him the courage to be, as Paul Tillich put it, or, as Hawthorne expressed it, she "only has revealed me to myself. . . ." And no wonder that the *American Notebooks* of the Concord period again and again reiterate the names of Adam and Eve, "those two progenitors of our race," as Austin Warren stated it, "who found each a world in the other."[99] The tragedy is that the effect did not last. Having received little love, Hawthorne had little to give; and great as Sophia's love for him was, he lapsed into his deadly habit of psychological hiding, with the inevitable consequence of self-alienation. If this was so, as the evidence indeed confirms, Emerson, who knew the man many years, was right in suggesting that Hawthorne had committed the ultimate crime against life. On 24 May 1864, the day after serving as pallbearer at Hawthorne's funeral, he took exception in his *Journals* to the service read by James Freeman Clarke. Clarke, he wrote, "said that Hawthorne had ... shown a sympathy with the crime in our nature, and, like Jesus, was the friend of sinners." Emerson, who had never, as he said, been able "to conquer a friendship" with Hawthorne, "thought there was a tragic element [in the man's life] ... that might be more fully rendered [than Clarke had]." That tragic element was "the painful solitude of the man, which ... could not longer be endured, and he died of it."

Nothing I have written is intended to suggest that Hawthorne failed to recognize his psychological problem or that he made no effort to rid himself of it. He knew as well as W. H. Auden—he indicated as much in such fiction as "Rappaccini's Daughter" and "The Canterbury Pilgrims"—that there "is no joy or success without risk and suffering, and those who try to avoid suffering fail to obtain the joy, but get the suffering anyway."[100] Emotionally, however, he was so self-protective that he built a wall to shut out suffering, in the process of which he shut out joy. He also knew the values of self-disclosure, a disclosure that enables us to resolve ambiguous feelings that otherwise produce an harassing sense of anxiety, guilt, and self-abasement, for he had shown the dangers of self-concealment in such characters as Reuben Bourne and Arthur Dimmesdale. In fact, the only moral he wished to draw from Dimmesdale's "miserable experience" was this: "Be true! Be true! Be true! Show freely to the world, if not your worst, yet some trait whereby the worst may be inferred!" Yet emotionally, except for the interval when Sophia was his "significant other," he could not disclose himself and remained, instead, the sealed self that so many of his friends recognized him to be. Hawthorne knew too that those who have sealed selves suffer intellectual arrest and emotional paralysis— such characters as Chillingworth and Hollingsworth demonstrate as much; for by closing our hearts and minds, we permit the world to disclose to us only stereotypically. Hawthorne also knew that a person feels alive only to the extent that he feels, and that his "own torpid ... state of mind and heart," as he described his condition in the *English Notebooks*, made him feel that life seemed "so purposeless as not to be worth the trouble of carrying it on any further." He also knew that psychological redemption comes only through love, a love that breaks through self-alienation and its self-condemning symptoms into "I-Thou" relations that restore one's sense of community, self-worth, and gladness with life. Harassed by these irresolutions and unable to resolve them, he turned to Victorian pieties and ethics for help, but those neurotic standards, if they did not aggravate his own neuroticism by making him judgmental and thereby insulating him all the more, did nothing to relieve him. The only relief he seems to have found was in his fiction, though even there, as he said, there were "very disagreeable phantasms to be encountered. . . ." But confessing one's problems obliquely to a spectral audience is not the same as discussing them with one's wife and intimate friends, and the relief, therefore, was temporary at best.[101]

The unexamined life, we are told, is not worth living, but Hawthorne discovered to his misery that even the compulsively reexamined life, the life he projected in his fiction, was not worth living either. For principle must be enacted in behavior if self-reintegration is to occur, and Hawthorne, emotionally unwilling to engage in such behavior, except for short intervals as with Sophia and Melville, doomed himself to self-alienation. Nevertheless, to his credit, he resolved, not once but hundreds of times no doubt, to reunite his head and heart, for his fiction is a testament to that resolution. Tragically, he failed, and one cannot help wondering what he might have been as man and artist had he been able to embrace life. Yet, if fiction is to be valued for its penetration into the misery-burdened heart and for suggesting ways to alleviate, if not rid, the heart of that burden, Hawthorne's fiction is invaluable.

DREISER'S *STOIC*:
A STUDY IN LITERARY FRUSTRATION

Philip L. Gerber

I hate to leave a piece of work undone.
Theodore Dreiser, 1912

I

*B*ecause August 27 would be Theodore Dreiser's sixty-fifth birthday, reporters from The New York *Herald Tribune*, jumping the gun by a week, sought him out at his Westchester estate, Iroki. They found the white-haired author in splendid health, tanned from the hot summer sun of 1936, in an amiable mood to answer questions. Yes, it was his view that England persisted as the chief devil spoiling world affairs; yes, the interference of Italy and Germany and the Church in Spain was a damned outrage; and yes, it was true that while he had supported the Communist ticket in 1932, he just might cast a vote for Roosevelt in the fall. The President's programs, while not going halfway far enough to suit Dreiser, at least had opened the nation's eyes. Except for the decisive actions of an aggressive centralized government, what hope did the people have for riding out the Depression? Without the recent socio-economic reforms, the country would long since have been swallowed whole by the whales of finance.

The interview[1] took place on the screened porch of a tiny clapboard cabin, Dreiser's main house being leased and himself legally a California resident, back east only temporarily. He had been working at a flimsy card table, a mound of yellow paper and pile of soft lead pencils evidence of slow, steady composition in his old manner. A peek was enough to see that he appeared to get something like twenty-five words to the page. How was the writing going? Very nicely, with the inspiration of outdoor living. Would he care to comment on his project? He would not, except that it was a novel, a fat one, about 120,000 words, due at his publishers in the autumn.

87

Some twenty miles away, at the Simon and Schuster Manhattan office, the interview was read with guarded optimism. The new novel could only be *The Stoic*, imminent ever since the house had signed Dreiser in 1934, but never delivered. Author-publisher relations were not good, communication in fact almost at a halt for some time now, and M. Lincoln Schuster seized this opportunity to rush birthday greetings from himself and Richard Simon and say, "We were immensely interested to learn . . . that the new novel is making such notable progress." Receiving only silence in return and being too proud—or perhaps, with much justification, too infuriated—to continue playing this one-sided game, Schuster turned the correspondence over to Simon, who wrote a month later ostensibly to enclose an advance order from a book dealer for seventeen copies of *The Stoic*. How fine it would be to have the book for the company's Spring 1937 list. Did Dreiser think he might be ready to deliver it in time?[2]

There was no reply. The truth was that Dreiser had used a generous S & S advance to attempt a complicated philosophical tome, which also was bogged down. He was not working on *The Stoic* and had no immediate intention of working on it. He had lost interest.

If interest ebbed in 1936, it had run at high tide in 1913 when Dreiser first announced *The Stoic* as the title for the final volume of his trilogy concerning the financial wizard Frank Cowperwood, a translation into fiction of the streetcar king, Charles T. Yerkes, Jr., builder of the Chicago "Loop," donor of the Yerkes Observatory. Volume One, *The Financier*, recounting Yerkes-Cowperwood's activities in Philadelphia up to 1880, had been published in 1912 by Harper. Volume Two, *The Titan*, following the hero to his Chicago traction monopoly during the Eighties and Nineties, was written and on the verge of publication by the same house. Dreiser's progress had been good, if not as rapid as his tight personal schedule called for, and he was preparing to plunge into the composition of Volume Three, Cowperwood's venture in the London Underground, at once. Physically and mentally a big man, standing over six feet, not overly handsome, to be sure, but possessed of a healthy stride, Dreiser impressed newsmen with his vigor:

His hair is sprinkled with gray, and he has gray eyes behind gold rimmed glasses. He wears gray clothes and gray ties—not a gentle gray, but a massive steel gray that makes you think of strength and power.[3]

The same descriptives—massive, strength, power—were commonly used to cite characteristics of Dreiser's published novels also, and at the end of 1913, at forty-two, he seemed unstoppable. With research for his Cowperwood books practically finished, there seemed no reason at all why *The Stoic* should not follow its predecessors within a year, ending what Dreiser called *A Trilogy of Desire* on a note borrowed from Herbert Spencer, the inevitable dissolution which ends all evolutionary cycles, in this instance the death of Cowperwood and the dispersal of his properties and his millions. The finale was critical; the idea of Cowperwood had begun there, in December 1905, with the death of millionaire Yerkes, and lacking such a conclusion the trilogy sat like a drama without a third act. With it, the story would climax, Dreiser predicted, in an illumination of "the inscrutable forces of life as they shift and play—marring what they do not glorify—pagan, fortuitous, inalienably artistic."[4] A grand plan, supplied to him by life itself and tallying with the only philosophy of human existence Dreiser had been able to patch together.

"I need a large canvas [and] a huge enthusiasm," said Dreiser.[5] Early in 1914, *The Titan* on its way to press and he on his way to Chicago for final research, he had both of these. The Yerkes story encompassed decades of financial chicanery in Philadelphia, Chicago and London, an ideal opportunity for representing the world as he knew it, manipulated by money lords practicing the Triumphant Capitalism of Andrew Carnegie almost without let or hindrance. Hewing closely to the actualities of the Yerkes story—it had more than enough drama to suffice—he saw himself author of "a book of life as it really is," uncolored by elusive imaginings or romanticism, so unflinchingly honest that its writer must be a man possessed, daring to "look with his eyes right into the sun, even though he knows it may blind him."[6]

In the beginning no trilogy was imagined, only a single massive novel which would carry Yerkes-Cowperwood from cradle to tomb, one life so representative of its time as to summarize the entire gilded era of laissez faire industrialism, a definitive work. Had he been more prescient, Dreiser would have pushed his story through to its finish in 1912 rather than acquiescing in its dismemberment. But Harper, faced with the probability that the manuscript would total 500,000 words and more, could not face the horrendous problems involved in getting such a behemoth between covers, and Dreiser, always in need of royalties, equally hungry for critical notice, was impatient to have a novel on the stalls. Why not make a trilogy out of the story? It was big enough, and its triple environments would provide a unity of ambience for each separate volume. Dreiser agreed. So the single book he had conceived was broken up—with consequences that made it the most drastic judgmental error of his literary career. That error committed, his enthusiasm for the project was sustained by the encouragement of H. L. Mencken, his friend and principal booster. Dreiser, almost alone among current writers, seemed to evince the promise Mencken demanded, particularly in opposing the Puritan tradition already identified as his whipping boy. With Dreiser to strike out on bold, unconventional paths and Mencken to ballyhoo his work, they complemented each other ideally, both profiting, and Mencken fed him continually, one cheery letter upon another, urging him on, assuring him that however good his *Financier* had been, his *Titan* promised to be great, a commercial and artistic success. He was already, in Mencken's opinion, the writer against whom would-be authors now must be judged, but he must produce many books, and soon, without any long intervals between. "You ought to have seven or eight volumes on the shelves," he wrote, "instead of only three."[7]

Dreiser was happy to oblige, considering a book every six months not too heavy a demand to make upon his own resources. With book four going to press and book five imminent, he boarded the train for Chicago to be lionized, his expanded reputation having preceded him. To have The *Journal* headline him was flattering even if with more error than truth, their impression being that the new Dreiser novel would center upon former Illinois Governor John P. Altgeld.[8] While in Chicago he was dealt the first of the blows which ultimately doomed *The Stoic*, devastating news that Harper was backing out of its agreement for *The Titan*. With 8500 sets of pages already run, the company refused to publish. There had been no inkling of trouble, and the fact that full-page advertisements in the current *Harper's Monthly* announced release of the novel was indication enough that the decision had come late. What reconsiderations motivated the Harper retreat were never made public, of course, but Dreiser was convinced that his realism was too uncompromising for the policy of this timid house. His aide Anna Tatum, who had remained in New York, sent news that the firm was shaky financially and therefore susceptible to pressure from backers: "*Too much truth told about the high financiers. Do you get it?*"[9]

He got it, yes, and also the story that his depiction of Berenice Fleming had become a point of contention. Berenice, the last mistress of Frank Cowperwood, became important in *The Titan* as the romantic rival of Aileen Cowperwood. Her prototype, Emilie Grigsby, the third point in the Yerkes marital triangle, was the only one of the three alive as Dreiser wrote. Still in the public eye, she was wealthy, a result of lavish gifts from Yerkes, and her influential friends in America and abroad were suspected of having pressured the publishers to quash the novel, so closely patterned after actual events that her portrait was unmistakable.[10] Although John Lane, newly established in America and delighted to have a major writer fall like a ripe plum into its lap, liking Dreiser's novel not only for its own sake but because it was to be followed soon by *The Stoic*, bought *The Titan* from Harper and published it in May 1914, Dreiser was not eased, for Berenice was to be even more prominent in *The Stoic*, for which his files were filled with newspaper clippings disclosing the details of her extended affair with Yerkes. Pressures against publication promised to be severe.

Reviews of *The Titan* helped little, for despite praise from many quarters Mencken's thundering chorus of acclaim failed to materialize. If the book was said to be wonderfully complete, big and terrible in its effects, and more urbane than Dreiser's previous books, it was also called offensive, nasty, and loathsome. Its hero was labeled an animal, the book itself worse than pornography. Sales were discouraging. The first flurry of interest sold 6600 copies by June 30, but Dreiser's royalties scarcely covered his advances, and then sales declined precipitously.

In the autumn Mencken wrote Ellery Sedgwick to say that Dreiser, mired "in the dumps," talked of giving up the writing game entirely, as he had threatened to do in 1912 if it did not become a paying concern for him within a reasonable time. Now if ever seemed the psychological moment, while sales lagged and disappointing notices continued to depress him. From England, Ford Madox Heuffer [Ford] called *The Titan* "a running sore," its hero devoid of ethics in business or in love. Before abandoning the novel in disgust, he had tallied eleven seductions; a fast check in later chapters revealed more. It made him sick, it was revolting, the most horrible, demoralizing, immoral chunk of trash he had ever encountered, misrepresenting the entirety of American life. What was worse, Dreiser appeared to approve fully of his hero's methods.[11]

To rescue his protégé, Mencken proposed "a careful article" for Sedgwick's *Atlantic Monthly*, basing his suggestion on a current *Yale Review* essay in which Bliss Perry decried the national timidity in attempting serious appraisals of living writers. That current authors deserved "really trenchant and exhaustive" analyses was something Mencken could agree with wholeheartedly, and an interpretive piece in the *Atlantic* might work wonders. He had studied nearly one hundred reviews without coming across even one which offered helpful criticism, let alone "any coherent account" of what Dreiser was up to, and he was as depressed as the author himself. "It seems to me," he told Sedgwick, "that so honest and talented an artist has a right to expect something better." Sedgwick was unimpressed. To sum Dreiser up in mid-career seemed inappropriate, besides which *The Titan* was anathema to him personally; he wanted no part of the proposal. Mencken was forced to withdraw, more apprehensive than before that the discouraged novelist might well abandon fiction altogether.[12]

Despite his threats, however, Dreiser was irrevocably committed to writing, and the years ahead, his most productive decade, saw a remarkable outpouring of plays, poems, short stories, autobiography, essays, and travel accounts, a shelf of books—everything but novels. The novel was a question mark, not only because of his personal difficulties with publication, but because the form itself seemed in jeopardy. The kind of extremely realistic reflection of experience toward which his own work gravitated might easily be supplanted by something else. Balzac had written forty or fifty novels in the old manner about as well as might ever be done; after such a performance, what was to be gained by perpetuating established patterns? What would succeed realism, he wasn't sure; perhaps something more highly informed by poetic intuitions than by scientific research. The suggestion of a literature paralleling the post-impressionist revolution in painting seemed to be a possibility, if a somewhat remote one, but it was certain that some turning would occur. He was appalled to learn that the printing presses had spewed out over twelve hundred novels in 1912; far too many, even of a good thing. Life, always tiring of excess, would change, and literature must adapt. "Perhaps," he speculated, "the mammoth of realism will finally sink into the mud by its own weight, to be superseded by the five-toed horse of symbolism," much as the behemoths of the paleozoic era were succeeded by smaller, more useful animals. Spencer had proved to him that evolution would have its way. What then might succeed the novel? "If I knew, I would write it." Whatever it was, he was certain a new genre could succeed only by abandoning past tradition to make an attempt at illuminating the facts of life in full spectrum, "not only the concentrated filth at the bottom but the wonder and mystery of the ideals at the top,"[13] and many of his forthcoming books would be attempts either to master new forms or to capture the elusive quality of life as it actually is, stripped clean of its heavily-sugared romantic coating.

Meanwhile, he was not swearing off the novel entirely. More than once the public had been informed that *The Stoic* would be forthcoming, and both he and Mencken had asked openly that judgment on *A Trilogy of Desire* be suspended until the story was finished. Whatever his doubts about the survival of the novel or of his own capacity for producing a commercial success, he understood the crucial importance of seeing this concluding volume published. Yet, even before *The Titan* had reached the bookstores, Dreiser had come to a momentous decision, however casual it may have seemed when he confided it to Mencken. "I haven't done with the trilogy yet," he promised; "one more volume—but not immediately."[14]

Dreiser was captivated by his vision of life as an inexplicable welter of forces which reduced individual ambition to mincemeat; this was central to the trilogy, and now it was as if his own life were to serve as an example, for his supposedly momentary pause was to compound itself into a delay of years and then decades, *The Stoic* not appearing during his lifetime at all, but posthumously, and even then uncompleted, its import turned awry.

II

Dreiser had more than enough subsidiary projects to engage him. On hand already was his endless, much-circulated manuscript of *The "Genius"*, which needed a new ending, something like the final scenes he had added to *Jennie Gerhardt*, to underscore the grim nature of its truth. John Lane's eagerness to publish this story and to purchase from Harper all remaining sheets and bound stock of Dreiser's novels, together with the plates for *Jennie Gerhardt* and *The Financier*, gave the author's morale a boost, his lifelong dream of his works in a uniform edition seeming possible now. And the physical act of putting words on paper seemed to buoy up his spirits. Unlike literary men who confess to agony in recording their thoughts and feelings, Dreiser looked forward to getting at his daily stint of three thousand words; it kept him from being unhappy with himself. Above all, he told George Jean Nathan, he was a writer, with all that implied; he liked to write, and he was wretched when he did not.[15]

The "Genius" ran into censorship, was banned by the New York Society for the Suppression of Vice, and was withdrawn by John Lane. The entire incident, including years of litigation, impressed Dreiser with his precarious position anent the novel, and he turned in other directions. Autobiography proved a satisfactory outlet, and as might be expected, he planned a multi-volume tome, the first of which was *Dawn*; because of its frankness concerning his family, it remained in manuscript until 1930, preceded in publication by the second volume, *A Book About Myself*. Numerous shorter works were under way, stories, philosophical essays intended for publication under the iconoclastic title *The King is Naked,** a set of impressionistic one-act plays, some of which Mencken took for his *Smart Set*. During the 1915 summer John Lane subsidized an auto trip which took Dreiser back to Indiana and served as the basis for his travel/reminiscence *A Hoosier Holiday*. He tried his hand at the free verse made respectable by the Chicago renaissance of 1912, and as always, his plans included labor on *The Bulwark*, a novel destined like *The Stoic* to periodic death and resurrection.

In these troubled but productive years the Dreiser reputation was established. *The Nation* for December 1915 carried the first sustained critical

*Published (1920) as *Hey Rub-A-Dub-Dub*.

essay on his work, and it was not a flattering appraisal. Mencken must have been chagrined at having allowed Sedgwick to influence him in putting off his own projected article, which would have been laudatory, because the writer for *The Nation* was Stuart Pratt Sherman, his essay a savage attack which in book form bore the descriptive title, "The Barbaric Naturalism of Mr. Dreiser." Perhaps without being fully aware of it, Sherman put his critical axe to the Spencerian concepts underlying all of Dreiser's novels. The notion of human beings helpless under the control of inscrutable forces, whether physical, chemical, or otherwise, and therefore mere pawns of an amoral Nature, was repulsive to Sherman. Strong Darwinistic strains were readily apparent, and these Sherman bludgeoned, berating the jungle-motives and the disregard for conventional morality he equated with Dreiser himself, whom he considered a subversive wrapped in the realist mantle—a naturalist. And to Sherman the term "naturalist," suit Zola as it might, was a most un-American term. Under his own definition of the naturalistic novel as "a representation based upon a theory of animal behavior," which theory he considered to be manifestly inadequate for describing life on these shores, Sherman could state categorically that if Dreiser's novels concerned life anywhere at all on this globe, then they must concern existence in some alien sphere "curiously outside American society." Where that might be, Sherman was not able to speculate.[16]

This charge of selling America down the river was not easy to counter-act, particularly in the heat of wartime emotions, with the Germanic Dreiser being labeled a "literary Prussian." But Mencken, the logical defender, accepted the challenge, his stinging rebuttal, "The Dreiser Bugaboo," appearing in *The Seven Arts* in 1917. Taking on not only Sherman and "his pompous syllogisms," but the whole of the genteel tradition or that remnant of it not already moribund, he pointed out that Dreiser had never announced himself as either realist or naturalist, and that in matter of fact he was something aside from either, his aim being not merely to record, but to translate and understand: "The thing he exposes is not the empty event and act, but the endless mystery out of which it springs." In his themes, Dreiser might be compared to the Greeks, being inspired with the same vision of mankind moving through the confusion of life into nothingness characteristic of works like "Oedipus Rex."[17]

In this manner, by 1917 the poles from which Dreiser might be approached were clarified. As it became mandatory to ally oneself either with Sherman or with Mencken, and thus to picture Dreiser either as the Neanderthal savage of American letters or as its fearless Prometheus, a tradition was formed. To Helen and Wilson Follett, writing in 1918, Dreiser was an unfortunate influence misleading the younger generation of writers into brutal naturalistic biologizing. His characters, be they men or women, were infra-human, enslaved to predacious individualism; the telling image in his fiction became that scene from *The Financier* in which the lobster devours his natural victim the squid. For Dreiser, it seemed, life stalled on the plane of the beasts.[18] To present a contrary view, Burton Rascoe, a Dreiser booster newly risen to critical prominence in Chicago journalism, ridiculed Sherman as a "belligerent blockhead" and called his Dreiser essay a pail of critical slops dumped over the heads of the realists, an act Rascoe saw as more damaging to the perpetrator than to his proposed victims.[19]

Dreiser himself, unhappy with John Lane's timidity regarding *The "Genius"* and because, inexplicably, they had turned down Mencken's *A Book of Prefaces* with his rousing "Bugaboo," was ready to switch publishers. When Lane's New York office closed in 1917, he was only too happy to part company and join the new house of Boni and Liveright. Horace Liveright, then at the inception of his brilliant career, promised to publish whatever Dreiser wrote and to project the long-sought uniform edition. In rapid succession he published a collection of short tales, *Free and Other Stories*; the grim drama *The Hand of the Potter*; sketches of men Dreiser had known, including the portrait of his brother Paul, *Twelve Men*; and the philosophical essays, *Hey Rub-A-Dub-Dub*.

In the Twenties Liveright issued *A Book About Myself*, followed it with a collection of sketches entitled *The Color of a Great City*, and then, to Dreiser's delight, reissued *The "Genius"* whole and entire. But the great triumph of the Twenties, of course, was *An American Tragedy*, marking Dreiser's return to the novel form. Like his trilogy, the *Tragedy* was based upon fact, was extremely long, and was written in three books. Unlike the trilogy, as if Dreiser had learned something of value from the fate of his Cowperwood story, the new novel was published complete even though two volumes were needed to accommodate its length. The resulting success relieved Dreiser's perennial money problems and lodged him as an unquestioned force in American letters; critically, even Stuart Sherman fell into line with praise. But it was to be Dreiser's last novel for twenty-one years. Other books appeared, though with less frequency than before, and his total production faltered. During the Thirties, aside from the long-withheld *Dawn*, only one full-length work appeared, *Tragic America*, in the depth of the Depression branding capitalism "a failure in America today" and excoriating the money-madness of the system with a recommendation that under the "In God We Trust" on our dollar we might well add "The Devil Take The Hindmost!" Then another decade passed before the appearance of *America is Worth Saving*, another shrill blast at American capitalistic practices and the high-level manipulation of policy by great corporations and powerful financiers. Published in 1941, it was the last of Dreiser's books to appear in his lifetime.

III

And what, in all these years, of *The Stoic*?

Dreiser's momentary pause—his "not immediately"—had dragged into a thirty-year hiatus, and still there was no sign of a conclusion for the trilogy. As a literary figure, Dreiser commanded much attention, but writers either forgot about *The Stoic* or referred to it in asides as oft-projected but never published, while now and again a lament might be raised, as when Dorothy Dudley in 1932 speculated that Dreiser perhaps had found it easier "to be a public character than to concentrate on a great project."[20]

On the contrary, Dreiser never allowed his *Stoic* project to stray entirely from his attention, but worked at it sporadically—as with *The Bulwark*—for years without completing it. That neither project ever was finally abandoned became the proof of his own deep necessity for completing them, and that urgency was more than simple German tenacity. *The Bulwark* was Dreiser's final opportunity to strike at the destructive phases of American materialism, while *The Stoic* would put his trilogy into perspective, the collapse of Cowperwood demonstrating not only life's Spencerian drift toward equilibrium but the essential fruitlessness of life itself.

A major source and inspiration for the trilogy had been Edwin Lefèvre's résumé of Yerkes' life, "What Availeth It?" to which query Lefèvre could only reply, "Nothing."[21] Originally the trilogy was planned to arrive at that same approach to nihilism, but this ending was to give Dreiser great emotional difficulty as his own life and thinking drifted toward a desperate hope that life somehow was more idealistic and spiritual than his observations seemed to prove. To strike a spiritual note in *The Bulwark*, focused on the life of a devout Quaker, was not so difficult, but to do the same for Cowperwood, the avowed materialist, would prove much more traumatic. Dreiser would waver, debate, temporize, take a position and then retreat; in the end he would reach no satisfactory resolution and would die of heart failure the day before a decision might be forced upon him.

In 1919 Dreiser, aged forty-eight and separated from his wife for a decade, met Helen Patges Richardson, a beauty of twenty-five and a cousin by marriage of his brother Edward. Her marriage also on the rocks, Helen immediately joined Dreiser in a liaison which, despite occasional rifts, became the most enduring relationship of both their lives, lasting for twenty-six years, until his death. Because Helen dreamed of a career in the movies,

within a month of their first meeting the couple left New York quietly for
the West Coast, settling in Los Angeles, where Helen played a series of
minor roles before the camera and Dreiser, supposedly working on *The
Bulwark* for Liveright, became engrossed instead in a story he referred to at
first as *Mirage* and then as *An American Tragedy*.

Late in 1922, soon after the couple returned to New York, Burton
Rascoe visited Dreiser in St. Luke's Place, where he was working a heavy
day from ten in the morning until three or four in the afternoon. Rascoe
departed under the impression that Dreiser was writing *The Stoic*, a book
whose subject he evidently had little inkling of, for he reported Dreiser also
to be writing the third volume of his Financier trilogy.[22] All Dreiser's
effort, of course, was now concentrated on the *Tragedy,* a fact he seems to
have kept from Rascoe, but he was preparing to undertake *The Stoic* soon
and with this in mind was corresponding with Benjamin Tuska, an attorney
who had represented clients in litigation with Yerkes during the 1900-1905
era. Tuska had located printed briefs prepared by his firm in the Yerkes
matters and was hoping to obtain briefs from the opposing attorneys so
that Dreiser might benefit from a full discussion of the facts. Someone in
those days, probably a member of the firm, had inquired as to Yerkes'
character, and Tuska had located a copy of the cablegram that came in
reply:

AN ADROIT UNSCRUPULOUS MERCILESS MAN PERIOD WILL HOLD TO A
WRITTEN CONTRACT.

"We have a large amount of material bearing upon the London exploits of
your subject and touching upon most of the people with whom he came in
contact," Tuska informed Dreiser in January 1923. Later that year he was
delighted to report the availability of numerous letters concerning Yerkes.
These awaited Dreiser's pleasure. Hearing nothing in reply, Tuska early in
1924 invited the author to dinner, chiding him gently in a postscript: "By
the bye, I have not heard from you about examining the two volumes of
Yerkes correspondence I wrote about."[23] Tuska could not have known
that this was a moment of all moments in Dreiser's career when it was
impossible to divert his attention from the task at hand, hard driving on
the mammoth manuscript of his *Tragedy*.

In 1926, with Dreiser somewhat rested from his labors and flushed with
unexpected financial success—a $90,000 deal with the movies had been
signed—he and Helen sailed on the S.S. *Frederick VIII* for Scandinavia, one
objective being to collect first-hand material on Yerkes' activities in London and Europe generally. But there is little evidence that he actually did
much digging, London being his last stop on a four-month, eight-country
tour, and his time there arranged by his publisher's representative, Otto

Kyllmann, of Constable and Company, who was eager to show him off to local celebrities such as George Bernard Shaw. The Scandinavian jaunt was not a total waste in terms of the trilogy, however, for Dreiser eventually used it as the basis for the vacation cruise through the Norwegian fjords taken by Cowperwood and Berenice c. 1903.

Among the Londoners Dreiser encountered was critic W. Teignmouth Shore, a devotee of the trilogy who followed Dreiser home via the mails to inquire, "When are we to have the follow-up to 'The Titan'?" and to offer his help with whatever London local color the book might require. Dreiser suggested that Shore uncover what facts he could about Yerkes, and the new volunteer went to work, elated to be a part of "Cowperwood, Act III." But within two months he was stalled by British reserve. The people who had known Yerkes were either dead or old and shy; for fear of being introduced into the novel themselves, they would reveal nothing. Some were distinguished men, wrote Shore, and such men would not allow themselves to be made use of: "London is not Chicago!!!" Sorry to be "so icebergy," he prodded Dreiser to come to London and let him squire him around. As to other sources, "Soak yourself in newspapers of that date, in the guidebooks, etc.," was his advice,[24] apparently unaware of the extent to which Dreiser already had done this, in addition to keeping abreast of press reports concerning the models for his story and the protracted legal entanglements of the Yerkes estate.

Aware from the beginning that his prolixity drew censure even from admirers, Dreiser as early as 1913 had told the Philadelphia *Record* that he hoped some day to condense his *Financier*. Nothing toward this revision having been accomplished in a decade, by 1926 it had evolved into another of his long-standing resolutions. In fact, he now intended to revise all of his novels. The compulsion both to "get it all in" and to compose rapidly had flawed the books with a manner persistently open to ridicule, and while it was one thing to dismiss criticism testily—"to talk about my splitting the infinitive and using vulgar commonplaces here and there, when the tragedy of a man's life is being displayed, is silly"[25]—but it was quite another to admit even grudgingly that the carpers perhaps had a point. This was a man who had long harbored not too secret a dream of becoming the first American recipient of the Nobel Prize for Literature and whose time, as he neared sixty, was running out. He could ill afford to let obstinacy stand in his way. If critics might be persuaded that his novels excelled in manner as well as in matter—well, he could use all the support that might be mustered, by whatever means. The bravas showered on *An American Tragedy* had sent his heart soaring and he pictured himself as within striking range of The Prize, as indeed he was.[26] Perhaps a thoroughgoing revision—was a uniform edition too much to hope for at this point?—might clinch this signal honor he coveted.

Besides composing his novels rapidly and often carelessly, Dreiser was accustomed to throwing a manuscript to his volunteer aides, even to his typists, for correction and/or editing, while his active brain impelled him into new engrossments. Now he began to rethink his oeuvre, beginning, significantly, with *The Financier*; it had always been a favorite with him, and his culpability for never having finished the trilogy weighed on him. Might not a revision both of that and of *The Titan* raise a momentum so irresistible as to carry him along immediately through *The Stoic* as well? It was an ambitious plan, overly so as it happened, for *The Financier* was the only book he managed to recast, and the job was entrusted principally to his longtime aide Louise Campbell who, whatever her abilities, was not Dreiser. When Liveright issued the new version in 1927, the book had shrunk from 780 pages to 503, yet remained much the same novel that had appeared in 1912. Emendations and deletions had been made, and with profit, yet the interminable speeches of the lawyers at Cowperwood's embezzlement trial, wisely sliced from the original version at Mencken's behest, inexplicably were reinstated. The chief effect of the new *Financier* was to underscore Dreiser's personal concern for his trilogy as a favorite among his works and to indicate his sincere, if unfulfilled, wish to see it brought to perfected conclusion.

At the invitation of the Soviets, Dreiser in 1927 undertook a prolonged tour of Russia and was elated that Gosizdat, the Russian publisher, projected publication of all his books in that country. Following his return, he wrote the critic Sergei Dinamov, with whom he had been in correspondence for some time, in hopes of drafting him as his agent. Composition of *The Stoic* was about to begin, he said, and the book surely would be ready to go within a year. So certain was Dreiser of accomplishing this that his concern centered upon presentation; the Cowperwood trilogy must be marketed as a single item, a three-volume set. His German and French connections having already agreed to this procedure, he questioned whether the State Publishing Company would be any less intelligent.[27] At the same time, he wrote to William C. Lengel, who had been his secretary while he was editor of *Butterick*, and to Dayton Stoddart, informing them of his intention to begin Volume Three in the fall of 1928.[28] But he was engaged simultaneously on the biographical sketches which *Cosmopolitan* serialized as *This Madness*, attempting to add to them and issue the whole in hard covers. And while he worked in the New York City heat of August 1929, editing proofs for the two-volume *A Gallery of Women*, *The Forum* reported him "busy putting in order the third of his novels in the Cowperwood trilogy" when in truth he had not yet taken up the project.[29] By 1930 the Wall Street crash had ushered in the great Depression, influencing Dreiser to rush into a totally new, though not unrelated, undertaking, the pessimistic elegy for capitalism he called *Tragic America*. Again, hopes for the trilogy waned.

III

Nineteen thirty-two had come before Dreiser began *The Stoic* in earnest, a time at the bottom of the economic slump when minds in the circles he habituated were focused on economics and the injustice of the social system. Intellectually, a part of Dreiser was enlisted, the national crisis looming so insuperably that late in 1930 he told Karl Sebestyén that litera- ture was the last thing he wanted to hear or know about; with the world racing toward catastrophic revolution, it was the courageous man's duty to act, not write, to charge into the arena and demand that mind replace brute force in governing world conduct. His callow admiration/envy of the great entrepreneurs had long since washed out of his system; who could possibly remain calm knowing that "plutocrats are squandering their money . . . building asinine palaces of marble and malachite" while hundreds of thousands were destitute?[30]

But creatively, carried away by the same "irresistible impulse" as other artists, he was unable to stop writing. When he began his trilogy, he had promised publicly that it would be objective, dealing equally with rich and poor, and when he was finished, its hero would stand before the world uncursed and unidealized.[31] Quite willing to write separately on the eco- nomic crisis, he was firm in his determination to preserve the trilogy from his topical anger. That Marxist critics, just then testing their power, were urging novelists to deal with the here and the now, to emphasize themes of social unbalance and to predict cataclysmic class struggle, left Dreiser well aware that his tale of Cowperwood the Superman, by now a historical topic and containing no unequivocal indictment of wealth and power, was bound to be unfashionable. To Dorothy Dudley, then concluding her extended study of his career, Dreiser admitted that most of his detractors were waiting gleefully to "pounce on [*The Stoic*] as decidedly unsocial and even ridiculous as coming from a man who wants social equity." Neverthe- less, he intended finishing his trilogy in accordance with his original plan.[32]

For help he turned to Louise Campbell, who had served him as editor/typist with *An American Tragedy* and *A Gallery of Women* and who had revised *The Financier* while he toured Scandinavia and Central Europe in 1926. Preliminary to this, he had the assistance of Kathryn Sayre in putting together coherently the masses of factual data he had saved as a basis for his story. Kathryn Sayre had written for her M.A. at Columbia in 1929 a thesis entitled "The Themes of Dreiser" and had sent the author a copy for his files. This she followed with a fourteen-page encomium called "Theodore Dreiser—Great Spirit," in which she elaborated upon his abhorrence of the hereditary advantages making it possible for one group to live richly while another must labor for every scrap of bread, a phenomenon whose blatant inequity promised to drive the United States toward Sovietization and ultimately into the embrace of Communism itself. She wrote also of his books, describing Dreiser as a punctilious historian indefatigably gathering data from court records, newspapers, and interviews about Yerkes, and spoke of his grave disappointment that *The Financier* had not been received with the cheers that met *An American Tragedy.*[33]

Miss Sayre's interest in the trilogy coincided with Dreiser's impulse to complete it, and no doubt he dropped her a note to suggest she stop by his hotel, his typical response to youthful females attracted by his writings and reputation. When they met, she fell in love, and during the 1929 summer the pair dined together at the Claremont Inn, walked the sands in the moonlight at Long Beach, parked near Canal Street overlooking the Hudson at sunset while Dreiser surveyed the conglomeration of sheds, cattle barns, railroad tracks, and commercial houses and told her that one of the best books he had ever written was *The Color of a Great City*: "It had this in it." On her part, Kay sent her idol a hand-made valentine entitled "Theodore" and cribbed from Shelley:

> Hail to thee, blithe spirit!
> Man thou never wert. . . .

When Dreiser vacationed in the southwest in the spring of 1930, secure from Helen's surveillance, Kay accompanied him, motoring through the desert. Home again, he put her to work on his files of Yerkes material, she sensing "a great power" drawing her into the creative mystery, "thrilled by Yerkes's romance and his art and homes."[34]

In 1931, Dreiser's secretary, Evelyn Light, contacted Benjamin Tuska once again in quest of the materials he had offered seven years before and inquiring whether there might possibly be other papers extant.[35] At the ornate-rustic country estate Dreiser had built at Mt. Kisco and called "Iroki" after the Indian word for "beautiful," his assistant Clara Clark worked with Kay Sayre in sifting from packed files and laying in order those notes and press clippings of potential use. Early in 1932 these had been arranged and typewritten outlines prepared from them, a new procedure for Dreiser. A ten-page synopsis of the proposed book, being a précis of the Yerkes story in its later phases and more complete than Dreiser would use, was drafted, as well as summaries of characters and actions central to the narrative. These included:[36]

Summary of Cowperwood	27 pages
Cowperwood and the London Subway System	26 pages
Summary of Aileen	8 pages
Summary of Berenice	4 pages
Summary—Settlement of Cowperwood's Property and Affairs	17 pages

Additional accounts were prepared of Yerkes' later protégées, whose stories suggested that the financier's sexual varietism continued into his ebbing years:

Summary of Gladys Unger	2 pages
Summary of Ethel Yerkes	2 pages

These "Summaries" in outline form listed all applicable references located in the files, chronologically placed, together with cross-references to specific numbers borne by manuscript notesheets on which the novelist had originally recorded his findings, in most cases decades previously. The Summaries amounted to capsule biographies of all those intimately involved in Yerkes' life; at times their actions were depicted in day-by-day sequence. When an additional effort toward typing out the original, more complete manuscript notes themselves was made, Dreiser's handwriting, although not insuperably difficult, led to confusions, an example being the typed version of his note #630:

Feb. 2, 1910—Yerkes Gallery contains 300 pictures valued at $1,500,000. Rembrandt—Picter De Hood [sic], Hobbema, Teneirs, Watteau, Ruysdael, Durer, Holbein, Frans Hals, Van Dyck, Rubens.

Misconstruing Dreiser's dash following *Rembrandt* and striving for verification of the note in order not to abrogate Dreiser's alliance with actuality, his assistants added the note: "A check of two pages of Rembrandt titles gives no picture with any name similar to Picter de Hood." By the time this note was woven into the manuscript—in the last, exhausted days of Dreiser's life—the puzzle was solved (*Stoic* 282) by deleting the name (Yerkes did possess work by painter Pieter de Hooch) and adding the names of Reynolds and Turner.

As a further aid, the girls at Iroki fused their Summary entries into a document given the theatrical title "*The Stage*: Résumé of all characters on the set at once," in whose year-by-year chronology the main actions to be developed in *The Stoic* were spelled out:[37]

1899

Berenice is installed by C. in a large Park Ave. house. She goes to Chicago to see him. Berenice has met the Washington Square society woman at Saratoga. An artist has become enamored of Berenice. When he learns through the society woman, now cold to Berenice, of her past, he tries to commit suicide. . . .

1900

. . . C. and Aileen spend the summer travelling all over Europe, but his purpose also is to get into London subways. July 26 he goes to London and looks into Charing X further. C. saw another of his glorious girls in London—Gladys Unger. . . .

1901

C. completes the sale of his Chicago holdings. Berenice and her doings with the young naval engineer. Published report of the secret elevator in her house to C.'s rendezvous on top floor. . . . C. obtains control of the Brompton and Piccadilly line subway, unbuilt, I think, and also control of one or two other subways. Mrs. C. comes to N. Y. in Oct. and he follows in Nov.

At this time no change from actuality was being made except for the substitution of fictional for real names, but of course Dreiser, who was supervising preparation of the aids, correcting and emending as they were typed, and at the same time initiating his manuscript, would manipulate the facts in the process of composing his fictional story.

Evelyn Light was instructed to answer interview requests with word that Dreiser was "devoting every minute" to completing his novel as per his publishing contract with Liveright. A research trip to England to dig out final information in London was considered, then rejected, but Dreiser contacted his acquaintance Bruce Bromley and offered to trade a dinner for advice on some of the problems he was encountering with the book.[38] In answer to inquiries as to Dreiser's progress—there were several, word having been given out that he was completing *The Stoic*—Miss Light wrote that the novel was scheduled for fall publication, and Liveright felt confident enough to prepare and issue a salesman's dummy, complete with black, white, and orange dust jacket announcing *The Stoic* with a 1932 copyright date.[39] In its business aspects, the novel was to centralize upon Cowperwood's struggle in London against the power of J. P. Morgan, for whom Dreiser had not yet indicated a pseudonym, and the few pages of text contained in the dummy began:

Despite his gloom over his great Chicago defeat, the arrival and most of all the capitulation of Berenice in this unexpected way, was sufficient to restore Cowperwood's spirits not only to their fighting norm, but far, far above it. . . .

This picked up the tale precisely where *The Titan* had laid it down, as the original version of *The Titan* had picked up the story from *The Financier* almost without dropping so much as a comma.

At sixty-one Dreiser found life's "slow sandpapering process" wearing him down as inevitably as it wore all men down,[40] and to stimulate a change he planned another trip to the Southwest, in preparation for which he wrote ahead, in February, to New Mexico, inquiring as to a small tract somewhere between Albuquerque and El Paso which he might purchase as the site for a small adobe house to work in. The building plan did not materialize, but by April he was preparing to leave. Kay Sayre would not accompany him this time, their romance having cooled; it ended with a sad letter on April 10 in which she recounted the impossible and broken dream of an everlasting love between them, heartbroken at the realization that Helen had won him back. Five days later, Dreiser sent Louise Campbell the first fifteen chapters of *The Stoic*. Except that "the changes were constant and the going hard," he would have sent these long before, and he hoped, as soon as he reached the West, for more rapid progress.[41]

In May Dreiser left on his trip, and for a while Louise Campbell, who had returned his initial chapters with her comments, received no more manuscript. The novelist stopped over in San Antonio before proceeding on toward Arizona, his success in drafting eighteen chapters in five weeks too promising a start to interrupt. He explained to Louise in June that his practice would be to mail manuscript to Evelyn Light for typing, one copy to be returned and two carbons to be retained in New York. His immediate goal was forty chapters—currently he was making headway with Chapter Thirty-Three—at which time all work to date, in corrected form and as soon as his English publishers had had a look at it, would be mailed to the Campbell home in Philadelphia for editing. Evelyn Light was to carry the major burden of preparing copy, although in later years her recollection was that the typing and research she did on what she called "the third Yerkes book" was insufficient to give her even the thread of the story.[42]

From San Antonio Dreiser wrote his friend Esther McCoy that he was seeing no one at all but working a full day every day and hoping to finish his book within a month or so.[43] This was too optimistic to be hoped for, yet manuscript accumulated rapidly enough to satisfy him. The plan for Louise Campbell to keep abreast of him in editing and revising did not leave him altogether happy, for much of her revision cut "a little too close" to suit him; he knew his typical sound and was not eager to see it altered. What Mrs. Campbell considered to be "awkward syntax" or "verbosity" had become, for better or for worse, such a hallmark of the Dreiser method that without it he could not feel himself but seemed someone new, a stranger. "I don't want my style to become too crisp or snappy," he cautioned her; "it has an involute character which to a degree should remain." Such criticism was inhibiting, and Mrs. Campbell ended her suggestions, a reaction which struck Dreiser as "ominous." He looked to her for the "severe critical sandpapering" which would shake him into "closer" writing and away from his typical prolixity, and he assured her that a number of scenes had been condensed or rearranged solely on her advice.[44]

Dreiser labored hard, and for a time this promised to be the big push that would see *The Stoic* finished. His full working day extended from nine in the morning until at least five in the evening, often until seven, and sometimes did not end until midnight. In July he returned to New York, by the end of that month reaching Chapter Fifty-Four. Miss Light managed to keep abreast of him sufficiently so that he anticipated sending Mrs. Campbell another ten chapters for editing, warning her that the manuscript—"this final draft" he called it—was going to be long; that could have been no surprise. He was full of enthusiasm, everything going so well and the book promising to contain so much of what he had hoped for it, "a lot of go & color & drama." Already he was anticipating a complete manuscript which he and Mrs. Campbell could work at condensing.[45]

Then Dreiser's problems mounted. A copy of the incomplete manuscript went to his old friend Lengel, who had risen to an editorship on *Cosmopolitan* and whose advice he respected. Although Lengel, in response, began encouragingly, pronouncing the novel "a fine book as it is," he was frank about its shortcomings. The story began too abruptly. It was, after all, nearly twenty years since the Cowperwood trilogy had been left dangling and readers would be unable to connect *The Stoic* with what had preceded it unless, as Lengel proposed, a beginning chapter of recapitulation safely bridged this void. Among the materials recommended for deletion by Louise Campbell were Aileen Cowperwood's involvement in Paris with Arabian shiek Ibrihim Abbas Bey and an extended scene of dinner with him at Orsignat's in the neighborhood of Notre Dame where the group, which included Bruce Tollifer, Cowperwood's hired gigolo, and the financier himself were entertained by a Harlequin from the Trocadero.* But Lengel was unequivocal in recommending against any cuts in this dinner scene with the "clown business." Of greater moment, Lengel found himself

*Chapter 38 of the published version.

unable to tell, even though a very substantial share of the novel was completed, whether Dreiser planned finally for Cowperwood to emerge triumphant or to be overcome by disaster. If the latter, then he thought such an ending insufficiently foreshadowed. "There is not," he wrote, "much feeling of impending battle, drama, or possible failure." If Lengel's reaction were to be taken seriously, it meant that Dreiser had mismanaged grievously and that much work must be done on sections of the book thought to be in final form.[46]

Even more alarming was the financial situation of Dreiser's publisher. He had sensed before leaving for Texas that Liveright was in trouble, for the brilliant but profligate publisher had been forced from his firm and in its reorganized state it was being managed by men Dreiser felt were no publishers. "How they can go on is beyond me," he told Louise Campbell when he returned to Mt. Kisco, apprehensive of impending insolvency.[47] His premonitions aside, he was stunned when the firm did go under, one more casualty of the Depression. Liveright had been advancing him the truly munificent sum of $1,200 a month, a sizable portion of which went into support payments for his wife, "Jug," and for aid to his brother Rome and sisters Emma, Sylvia, and Mame. The effects of his loss would be widespread.

Dreiser had never been able to get along really well with any of his publishers, mistrusting the species too much, instinctively and more often than not with good reason. But Liveright, all in all, had done better by him than anyone else, had taken him on when other houses were too timid to touch his unconventional books, and had printed whatever he submitted, even when a volume was a loss-leader with no prospect of benefiting Liveright financially however much it might enhance Dreiser's name and keep it alive in the public mind. But in 1932, in company with any number of other businesses, the Liveright firm could not survive. "Now is no time to sell books," Dreiser wrote Louise Campbell as, desolate, he faced the extinction of ninety percent of his regular income. Forced to drastic economies, he eliminated an automobile, closed up his office in the city, and sliced Evelyn Light's salary.[48]

Now more than ever he felt compelled to finish *The Stoic*, if he could manage it. The Liveright failure had eliminated its potential publisher, but the book was going so well that it should in its final form be "really dramatic," a property sufficient even in hard times to clinch a favorable deal with a new house. Because it would complete his trilogy, Dreiser hoped *The Stoic* might reawaken interest in *The Financier* and *The Titan*. He considered seriously Lengel's suggestion and proposed writing a preface which would contain synopses of the earlier volumes, and because he thought of the three books as inseparable wondered about their possible publication as a unit.[49] For a time the momentum built during the earlier months of 1932 carried Dreiser along satisfactorily. In September he was still at work on his novel, although it clearly would not be published by Liveright, nor was it in any shape for another house to bring out. On the eighth, Hutchins Hapgood was informed that Dreiser was busy on the novel and Bernard Baruch was approached to determine whether, as Dreiser had heard, his turn-of-the-century dealings with A. A. Houseman & Company had brought him into contact with Yerkes.[50] "Never answered," Dreiser later was forced to postscript this inquiry. Otto Kyllmann in London was kept supplied with manuscript as it became available, and Dreiser asked for materials on the English libel law, eager that *The Stoic*, observing actualities as faithfully as its predecessors, should not encounter problems on that score. Any materials that might help him with English social customs and titles would be appreciated, and he emphasized that his final manuscript would be different from the chapters Kyllmann had been receiving, "shorter, better dramatized (the financial part) and so on."[51]

Harper, which had let Dreiser down so traumatically with *The Titan*, showed renewed interest in being his publisher. William H. Briggs wrote that he was eagerly anticipating a look at the manuscript and felt certain it would furnish the basis for a definite Harper proposal. Dreiser must not be too particular about the condition of the manuscript; if it was "ragged" here and there, no matter. But Dreiser, perhaps recalling his earlier rebuff, seems not to have submitted the book. In October, S. A. Seligson, Director of the Group Forum, before which Dreiser had read his paper "Individualism and the Jungle," later incorporated into *Tragic America*, wished to see him, but Miss Light wrote that the novelist, occupied at Iroke, every minute devoted to concluding *A Trilogy of Desire*, could get into New York only occasionally and on these visits was most hurried. Later that month Dreiser heard from his old friend Anna Tatum, who in 1914 had delivered the bad news from Harper and with whom he no longer wished to continue an acquaintance; she wanted, she said, to express her high hopes for *The Stoic*, that book started years ago, as she recalled, and "full of the deepest richest color," potentially superior even to *An American Tragedy*.[52]

With the prospect for fall publication fully evaporated, Dreiser began slowly to drift away from his task, his attention taken elsewhere, by the new publication *The American Spectator*, for one thing, toward whose success he expended much of his effort. In addition, perenially susceptible to involvement with social problems, he had been drawn into the controversy over the imprisoned anarchist Tom Mooney and in the fall traveled to

California to join the protest urging Mooney's release from San Quentin. The year was rounded out by his return to New York, at which time he told the *World-Telegram* he was "getting along well" with *The Stoic*, fifty-five chapters written, possibly fifty more to go. When published, a prospect he declined to speculate on, he felt it would "round out a historical period such as will never come again." But it was plain to see that his interests centered on other affairs—the alarming state of the economy; the new order which seemed bound to follow the insane and demolished Twenties; the prospect of barter actually replacing money transactions (he would be glad to trade a subscription to *The American Spectator* for a nice ham and felt the exchange would have a more human quality to it); the realistic possibility that an Americanized form of communism might soon emerge, one that might provide justice, maybe not 50-50 for everybody, but at least would demolish the old ratio of 98-2—"and our American folks will like it."[53]

But despite his embrace of communism, Dreiser, always the walking contradiction, had stopped over in Hollywood long enough to manage a most capitalistic transaction, the remunerative sale of *Jennie Gerhardt* to B. P. Schulberg as a vehicle for Sylvia Sidney. The awarding of the Nobel Prize to Sinclair Lewis had weakened Dreiser's general motivation, this movie sale eased his financial straits, and altogether impetus with *The Stoic* was reduced to zero.

IV

Nineteen thirty-three began as badly as possible for *The Stoic*, with Dreiser during the first part of the year in Kentucky and Tennessee to research the 1906-7 insurrection of tobacco farmers, which he thought to make the basis for a movie script. In September he had the audacity to inform Ben Goldberg in Cleveland that he was still "at work" on his novel but admitted it was impossible to say just when or by whom it might be published. For the first time in decades he was without an operative publishing connection, a situation from which he was rescued in a year's time by Simon & Schuster. In the summer of 1934 they informed his then agent, Erich Posselt, of their wish to add him to their list as soon as the courts might determine the final nature of his settlement with the defunct Liveright firm. By September a contract had been signed.[54]

Unproductive and painful for Simon & Schuster as this new arrangement would prove to be, it began with a jubilant fanfare of publicity, the publishers advertising in the press that Dreiser's works "past, present, and future" would henceforth come from their firm, "no higher privilege" having ever been granted them. They underwrote a flashy celebration held in October on Dreiser's Iroki estate, to which two hundred columnists, actors, dancers, painters, critics, editors, writers, and publishing men plus other assorted professionals from the arts and otherwise were invited. Dreiser was given a $5,000 advance, which he needed badly, and was assured that the uniform edition he had always wanted would be produced. For his part, he promised a book of short stories and the elusive third volume of his auto-biography, neither of which materialized, then or ever. Prior to delivering these, he was to present a completed manuscript of *The Stoic* by the end of 1935, which left him at least a year in which to finish. Since his draft for the book was approximately three-quarters finished, this pledge should have spurred its completion.

But by this time a Dreiser promise to deliver signified, almost *de rigueur*, an intention to do otherwise, and within five months author and publisher were quarreling. M. Lincoln Schuster, having read Dreiser's book of poems, *Moods*, and been deeply affected by it, had arranged to reissue it as their first Dreiser offering. A suggestion that the book might be cut so enraged Dreiser that he threatened to take it out of their hands and give it to another house—not that there was any realistic possibility of his doing so, with poetry a notoriously poor seller and his own verse not the most noteworthy. In a strong letter Richard Simon reminded Dreiser that when the firm took him over "we were thinking of a five-year plan, instead of a five-month plan," and this meant exclusive rights to his books, including *Moods*, which was already in the works. "When you are ready to indicate the date you plan to finish the new novel," he added, speaking of Dreiser's major contractual obligation, "we can prepare our promotional plans in a way to lead up to its publication as a fitting climax and consolidation and as a red-letter day for American literature." Within a week Simon followed this bit of puffery with news that he intended to prepare the public methodically in advance, a letter going out to booksellers polling them as to whether *The Stoic* ought to be withheld until an effective advertising campaign had been run. From Dreiser headquarters in the Ansonia Hotel a note went to Sergei Dinamov in Russia telling him that, contrary to rumor —and to previous Dreiserian assurances—*The Stoic* was not yet issued in America, but that "Mr. Dreiser hopes to get it out by the fall."[55]

Evelyn Light must have become inured to writing such assurances, following her employer's directions whether or not she suspected—or per-haps knew as fact—that Dreiser's burning interest in *The Stoic* was nearly extinguished. His adolescent fascination with money-getters of Yerkes' stamp was almost beyond resuscitation. When he was twenty-two, hypnotized by the spectacle of great financiers lording it over the universe

—their huge factories or mills, their stone mansions, their armies of workers, their immense fortunes—he had looked down from the window of a speeding Pullman car, to him the last word in luxurious travel, and found himself capable of hoping that country workers who looked up as his train swept by might imagine him some millionaire hastening from deal to deal. But by the time of his birthday interview in 1934 he had taken his stand. That the world was divided sharply into rich and poor there was no denying, and precious little one could do to change it, but a man at least might choose where to cast his sympathy, and at sixty-three he stood foursquare with the have-nots from which he had sprung. Money was the most damnably false standard ever foisted upon an illusion-loving world. With men like Millikan, Edison, Steinmetz, or the many outstanding medical researchers enriching the world, beautifying life, what sane man could possibly be interested in the artificial precedence of wealth? "Millionaires?" he asked his interviewer; "they're petty, pathetically dumb, hams of the purest ray. They glow with futility, if you can imagine any such thing."[56]

This growing antipathy toward men of wealth made it easier for Dreiser to write books like *America is Worth Saving*, but was no help at all in completing a novel which was an implicit celebration of the cunning entrepreneur. He could do it, but only half-heartedly and only by compartmentalizing his thinking for the interim. And providing his interest survived. But even prior to signing with S & S he had strayed. Becoming intrigued with the story of Madalynne Obenchain, tried in the early 1920s for instigating a murder, he had written to his sometime-assistant Esther McCoy in Los Angeles requesting a search of newspaper files for stories on the trial and the involved personalities, asking that she "psychologize" the case to interpret the motives of those concerned and copy out for him any "good incidents" she might encounter; the notion of following *An American Tragedy* with another story based upon a killing had engaged his interest,[57] and while S & S congratulated themselves on their new prize, he concerned himself with this project, which proved abortive.

On a more speculative plane—always quicksand for him—Dreiser returned to his projected book of philosophy, toward which *Hey Rub-A-Dub-Dub* had been a first step. For stimulation in getting the book onto paper he thought of George Douglas, a newspaperman in Los Angeles, a writer of extreme proloxity who showered Dreiser with letters the length of tomes sped off his typewriter at machinegun pace, single-spaced on cheap yellow paper. In addiction to off-beat, nearly crackpot, speculative thought, Douglas was Dreiser's twin, and the novelist was convinced that flashing between the two of them was something he could only call "psychic osmosis, almost a mystical form of it," which allowed Douglas to comprehend instantly and even to predict Dreiser's meanderings. "You put in fresher and stronger phrases the very theory with which I have been fumbling for years," he wrote Douglas soon after signing with S & S, and he proposed a collaboration, Douglas coming east or Dreiser coming to Los Angeles. Either plan would suit him, the important thing being that the two work together; "I would like nothing better than to sit opposite you at a table and take up a given topic together with my theories of proofs and thrash it all out with you item by item." When Douglas responded with an invitation to stay at his home on Westmoreland Avenue, a house all windows, with a thirty-foot livingroom in which the two men might work, relaxation possible in a garden planted with figs and eucalyptus, boasting a fish pond and "a swinging summer couch for a siesta," Dreiser notified Douglas to expect him "bag in hand" at the earliest opportunity. A compelling reason for haste in reaching the Douglas Utopia was that Dreiser felt his mental state had deteriorated overnight. Weight loss and general depression, perhaps due to glandular disturbance but in any event inducing in him "the most amazing morbid fears," shook him like a "psychic earthquake." A drastic change of environment, self-prescribed, was his only hope; the therapeutic rush to Douglas' must have been equated in Dreiser's thinking with checking into a private, one-patient sanitarium.[58]

By mid-May Dreiser was on the Coast, laying out plans for a giant volume encompassing the full range of his analysis of the meaning of Life and the significance of Man. It would begin with his *Hey, Rub* essay "The Essential Tragedy of Life," then run through a maze of "Myth," "Reality," and "Reaction" essays on which a small start had been made, his "Myth of Individuality" having been placed in Mencken's *American Mercury* in 1934. The book would close with another piece from *Hey, Rub*, "The Equation Inevitable," Dreiser's version of Spencer applied to Cowperwood in the postlude to *The Titan*. "The Equation Inevitable" also formed the philosophical base for final chapters of *The Stoic*, as projected long before, Cowperwood's demise being the quintessential illustration of the principle that life drove always toward equilibrium of forces. It seems reasonable to link his contemplation of this ending, toward which he had so recently been advancing in the novel, with his reawakening interest in the theoretical volume. Once out of a dormant state, that interest flared; the mental dynamos that powered Dreiser sped close to the limits of control. Living with Douglas, talking, talking, writing, writing, through May and June until his head whirled precariously with an all but incoherent blend of science and metaphysics, Dreiser fired off esoteric queries to physicists and pathologists regarding genetics and what the "ultimate unit of protoplasm" might be. Robert A. Millikan of Cal Tech was asked whether there was "a place for the word 'chaos' in discussing the universe" and Dr. Simon Flexner, Nobel laureate of the Rockefeller Institute, was told, "I wish I could orient your personal attention to the mystery of the Autonomic System. Something creatively astounding appears to be waiting for proper biological, chemical and physical attention. Is there not someone who has written something of real importance in connection with the Autonomic System, and the true function of the Solar Plexus?"[59] He seems to have strayed precariously close to the edge.

Dreiser never was able to produce a publishable manuscript explaining his philosophical theories—the death of Douglas within the year may have contributed to this—and the major result of his spinning off on the speculative tangent was that *The Stoic*, like a scorned stepchild, was abandoned once again. If Simon and Schuster suspected, they purported not to be aware, announcing in their "Simon and Schuster News" that Dreiser's novel would be delivered sometime in 1935, and Lillian Lustig of the Production Department sent him dummies bound with sample bindings proposed for the uniform edition, including one in black and gold which she hoped Dreiser might prefer. The somewhat aberrant author was handled with kid gloves, his emotional explosion over *Moods* having demonstrated the degree to which tolerance must be exercised; at the same time, they prompted him diplomatically regarding his promises. Plans needed to be made well in advance, the publishing schedule for 1936 was waiting. Discreet inquiries flattered Dreiser with word that their prospect of bringing out *The Stoic* was the single ray of hope S & S could see in the current world of letters. From Los Angeles Dreiser replied testily that he did not wish to comment at all beyond assuring them that he was working full time, an ambiguity camouflaging the fact that his extended days involved not his novel but his struggle with *The Formula Called Man*, as he now referred to his speculations. In July Schuster himself wrote to Dreiser saying he was "literally overjoyed" to hear that notable progress had been made on "The Book," by which he meant *The Stoic*, and commenting also that he was "deeply interested in your research magnificent on your formula called MAN," which might be interpreted as, please tell us just what you are up to.[60]

Not receiving any satisfactory answer, Schuster allowed a month to pass before following up with an expression of confidence that Dreiser would not "misinterpret the spirit that prompts this inquiry," but, the publication schedule needing to be made up, he ought to report further news of the novel. Thus prodded, Dreiser dropped a bombshell; he had abandoned everything in favor of his *Formula*, for which eight or nine chapters stood ready, with some thirty topics yet to be dealt with. A lengthy, telling silence ensued, but in December Schuster found a logical pretext for further inquiry. A letter from the librarian of the Eveleth (Minnesota) Public Library asked the publication date of *The Stoic*, and this was forwarded to Dreiser as being "typical of a number of inquiries"; any information would be "doubly appreciated." But Dreiser, returned to Mt. Kisco in late October, rather than answering directly, wrote: "Don't despair. I am coming in to talk with you." Apparently he avoided making good on this promise, for the end of January 1936 brought word to Richard Simon that the novel would not be ready for spring publication. "Will it make so much difference," Dreiser asked, with thoughts only for his *Formula*, if he gave S & S "a really important book" and brought in *The Stoic* at a later date?[61]

Schuster, who may not have been apprised of the note to his partner, asked Dreiser in early February whether *The Stoic* might not be included in the Spring catalog, and Dreiser, having heard in the interim of the sudden death of George Douglas but apparently undeterred from his course, gave identical information; no, not the novel, but for the Fall list his philosophy book would be ready. He intimated that S & S might take the pressure off him by agreeing not to announce any of his work as forthcoming until the house had first had an opportunity to read it in manuscript. Schuster agreed, expressed his deep disappointment at not receiving *The Stoic*, and suggested a conference, at Dreiser's convenience, at which the S & S people might talk with him about his plans.[62]

Such a conference, with its face-to-face confrontation and its inhibitions against temporizing, apparently was the last thing Dreiser wished at this point, for mail contact dropped off precipitously. Schuster approached the author twice during April, in one note suggesting that a date be set for a conference in the city, in another offering to come out to Mt. Kisco along with Simon and Leon Shimkin of the business office for discussion of "the whole publishing program." Nearly two years had passed since signing with Dreiser and the firm had nothing at all to show for its pains—or its $5,000—except the unprofitable reprint of *Moods* and a string of broken promises. Dreiser appears to have barricaded himself behind a wall of silence, but in July Schuster broke through with a rather desperate note, in essence a capitulation, raising the possibility for making firm plans to publish *The Formula Called Man*. Another month of silence, Dreiser being in no better position to deliver his *Formula* than to bring in the novel. At the end of August came the sixty-fifth birthday interview with its hint of progress which S & S grasped as a drowning man reaches for a spar, but without any satisfactory result.[63]

Dreiser, $5,000 richer, had led S & S a merry round of delay, stalling, and duplicity. *The Stoic* was shelved, the girls at Iroki had long since been pulled off the novel entirely and set at digging into pseudo-science for the

Formula, and with that also hopelessly bogged down, prospects fell to their nadir.

In 1938 Dresier wrote to Donald McCord, brother of the Peter who had shared his walks in Philadelphia at the turn of the century when he first familiarized himself with the streets of Yerkes-Cowperwood's youth. "I know I am old," he confessed, "because I don't care a hell of a lot." He was well on the road to seventy, he had not published a novel since 1925, and was making no discernible progress with any manuscript. With his affairs taking every possible turn for the worse, so it seemed to him, one might be excused for concluding that he had come to the end of his road.[64]

V

Not until the final months of his life, when he seemed to acknowledge tacitly the imminence of death, did Dreiser work seriously on *The Stoic* again. In this time of last things long put off, Dreiser, having lived with Helen Richardson for twenty-five years, married her in 1944 and appointed her his literary executrix. Jug Dreiser, whom he had never divorced, had died two years before. Financially he was not troubled, having since 1940 sold both *Sister Carrie* and *My Gal Sal*, the story of his brother Paul, to the movies for a total of $90,000. A portion of this purchased a white stucco house on Kings Road in Los Angeles for himself and Helen, the couple moving to a new neighborhood and away from any possible embarrassment at news leaking out that they were not the married couple neighbors had taken them for. Another $8,500 was used to buy Dreiser's freedom from S & S, whom he now referred to as "those lice."[65]

Communication with S & S, having slowed to a trickle, finally died altogether. During the later Thirties various editors or the partners themselves made sporadic inquiries about *The Stoic* or, for legal protection, sent reminders of their intention to continue as his publishers. But there was nothing to publish, and they ceased pressing for the novel, asking instead, somewhat plaintively, whether he wished to let them know even his long range plans. After 1939 almost no correspondence passed, aside from essential business notes from editorial assistants. As soon as he had shed S & S, Dreiser signed with Putnam to deliver *The Bulwark* in 1942, at once began to delay and procrastinate, assuring them he was at work full time when he was far from it, and exceeded his deadline without producing anything resembling a full manuscript. Given his erratic history and the fact that he had passed seventy and was failing in health, the wonder is perhaps that Dreiser could complete any major work in the time remaining, for the vigorous figure who had begun *A Trilogy of Desire* in the 1910 era, impressing reporters as a man of gray steel, had given way to his years. W. A. Swanberg describes him as having lost thirty pounds, his hair turned altogether white and fine as down, while the famous overfull Dreiser face had sunk into withered striations that made him resemble a hound dog.

Few official honors had drifted his way, never the Pulitzer, of course, with its insistence upon wholesome views of American life, and after the pre-1930 flurry of interest he seems never again to have been a serious contender for the Nobel Prize. But in 1944 the American Academy of Arts and Letters bestowed its Award of Merit Medal, Dreiser so pleased, even if frail, that he made the transcontinental journey by railroad, alone, to receive it. He was met by Marguerite Tjader, his friend and aide since 1928; Helen, reluctant but herself unable to accompany Dreiser, and knowing no other friend both available and efficient, had asked Marguerite to serve him in an unofficial secretarial capacity during the visit. W. A. Swanberg attributes the award ceremony with stimulating Dreiser's renewed wish to complete his unfinished projects, and while it is certain that the experience was catalytic, other events played a role also. In certain favorite haunts he still was recognized despite his long absence, and some of his old acquaintances who had survived into a new era, such as Edgar Lee Masters, were there to reminisce with. His oldest friend, Mencken, in many ways Dreiser's conscience, had written to inquire whatever had become of the third volume of the *Financier-Titan* trilogy; this reminder from one who had been in on the start of that project must surely have stirred him.

Also, New York offered the opportunity for renewing acquaintance with a younger disciple, James T. Farrell. The two met in person for the first time since 1936, Farrell struck by the extent to which his idol had aged. Asked whether he would ever finish his Cowperwood story, Dreiser claimed he was already working on it, although it is certain that he was not, except perhaps by habitual intention. Marguerite Tjader, too, was eager to know his plans, whether, for instance, he was going on with *The Bulwark*, a novel whose possibilities had always intrigued her. He would bring it to an end, he answered, providing she came to California to help him. Marguerite was well aware of Helen's jealousy (usually with good reason) of any and all of Dreiser's woman friends, whoever they might be, and she acted slowly, knowing she would require Helen's permission before making any plans to travel West.[66]

The New York experience as a totality, in combination with his heightened awareness of shortened days, appears to have sparked Dreiser's final burst of creative energy. On his return to Los Angeles he at once picked up *The Bulwark*, attempted like *The Stoic* at innumerable intervals spread over thirty years. At his insistence though obviously against her own instinctual desires, Helen invited Marguerite Tjader to come and work with him, telling her that she trusted there would be no upsetting discord between them but reminding her that it takes two to prevent a quarrel.[67] Having repaid his advance from Putnam, a house he now damned in the same class with S & S, Dreiser was relieved of nagging pressures, and with Marguerite's assistance was able to finish *The Bulwark* in May 1945.

With half a year to live, he turned once more to *The Stoic*. Farrell, personally eager to see the trilogy completed as a major work in the naturalistic tradition, received word at the end of May that Dreiser was exhuming the old typescript from his "store house," expecting to have it ready by the following fall or winter. Since the book had been substantially completed in 1932, this may not have been too sanguine a prediction despite Dreiser's congenital need for hubristic optimism. Mencken, given the same word, was assured as summer yielded to September that "another week or so" would see a complete manuscript, after which a well-earned period of rest would be in order.[68]

Marguerite Tjader, to whom Dreiser was now happily referring as "my literary secretary,"[69] had returned to New York on family matters following her stint on *The Bulwark*, but prior to her departure the aging materials for *The Stoic* had been unwrapped and she examined the heaps of notes, clippings, Underground maps, synopses, and summaries on which it was based. The elaborate outlines of characters and events astounded her; the Dreiser she knew had composed in a white heat, so totally immersed in his data that he was freed from any need to lean on such mechanical props. Reading the typescript from 1932, she was distressed to find it so very unlike the old Dreiser. He had been unable to rekindle the spark; the character of Berenice, for one thing, struck her as artificial and anything but alluring, while the handling of the lives of the wealthy, always difficult for the poverty-reared Dreiser, did not ring true to her. Nevertheless, understanding the author's precarious position, knowing at once that he would never by himself be able to manipulate the complex financial matters of Cowperwood into coherent form again, she helped in outlining some fifteen additional chapters which would bring the book to the hero's death, which she understood to be Dreiser's chief objective. Dreiser seemed depressed by Marguerite's reaction to the book, and in his gloom he wondered aloud whether he should abandon it. Yet he renewed the lease on the small house Marguerite had been using so that she might have it again when she came back. He was expecting her to help him finish this last novel. She offered to cancel her trip East. All he had to do was admit he needed her and request a change of plans. But he was evasive, too conscious of the poten-

tial strife with Helen, and slid around the question by saying how marvelous it would be if she were to return soon, on her own accord, perhaps to
a position in the movies from which she could spare some time for him. So
she left.[70]

During that summer, Marguerite, always happy to oblige, made a long,
hot journey to Brooklyn's Greenwood Cemetery in order that Dreiser
might benefit from a first-hand report on the location and appearance of
the Yerkes tomb, details he felt essential to his concluding chapters. She
undoubtedly could have rendered an invaluable service, and a relatively
objective one, in finishing *The Stoic*, except that the hostility between her
and Helen, newly Mrs. Dreiser, effectively prevented it. Upon her return to
California in the fall, Marguerite found that Helen not only had stepped in
as her husband's amanuensis, but was quite definitely in charge of running
his life, something that in all their stormy twenty-six years together she
had never before been strong enough to dare. Privately she let Marguerite
know that her presence was a threat. No one else was needed or wanted at
Kings Road; Dreiser on no account was to be distracted. He seemed to fear
Helen as much as rely upon her. His independence, formerly uncurbed,
now seemed to find expression primarily in furtive trips to the neighborhood drugstore, where he might pick up a newspaper or make a private
telephone call. Outwardly Helen was cordial enough, yet during Marguerite's visits to the house she would too often discover reasons to drive
off in her car alone, on errands. She was upset, Dreiser confided, because
she thought Marguerite's return would interfere with headway on *The
Stoic*, help with which she had staked out as her own special contribution
to his writing. They could meet secretly, Dreiser suggested, but Marguerite
declined, preferring to withdraw and await proof sheets of *The Bulwark*,
leaving the field to Helen, who after a quarter-century wait was determined
to exercise her wifely prerogatives.[71]

Helen had also a personal stake in the dénouement of the Cowperwood
story, stemming from her deep fascination with mysticism and the occult,
yoga in particular. What the teachings of the *Vedanta* could possibly have
to do with the story of a street-railway monopolist might be a question to
others, but to Helen it was perfectly clear. The book would conclude on a
note of spirituality rather than on the depressing theme of fruitlessness
toward which it was headed. In her own life she had found Indian philosophy to provide answers for the puzzle of existence, and her enthusiasm was
impressed upon her husband's work. A patron of the "Vedanta Center" in
Los Angeles, she took Dreiser to speak with the Swami Prabhavananda
about her ideas for *The Stoic*, but Marguerite, checking later with the
Swami, was informed that Helen did all the talking during this interview,

while "Mr. Dreiser said nothing at all." Because they had not carried the manuscript along with them, the Swami was unable to give them an opinion as to their accuracy in portraying *Vedanta* teachings.[72]

Gradually an idea had budded that Berenice Fleming would serve as the conduit for Eastern ideas, her role in the conclusion of *The Stoic* to be expanded to that of a regenerative power, redeeming through spiritual rebirth and public beneficence both her own materialistic existence and Cowperwood's. Dreiser's basic philosophy, of course, contrasted sharply with this notion that individuals possessed any power to shape themselves or events in such a manner; as expressed in notes for his still-unfinished *Formula*, his ideas admit little interest in or influence from the East. Through Robert Elias, then interviewing Dreiser for his biography, Marguerite Tjader learned of this new development. It was disturbing news. In the preliminary work she had done, there had been no indication of such an ending for the book, and the introduction of Eastern philosophy through Berenice Fleming, of all people, "did not seem to make much sense" to her. When Marguerite attempted to discuss Dreiser's new tack with him he grew evasive, spoke in vague, uncommunicative phrases, and seemed to her either unwilling or unable to explain. His personal copy of the *Bhagavad Gita*, annotated on but a few pages, indicates that the book failed to capture his imagination. Helen, on the other hand, plunged as deeply into such teachings as she was able, and her voice was heard.[73]

Dreiser was in no condition to resist. He no longer possessed a conviction powerful enough to dominate either the domestic situation or the composition process. On the one hand, his own materialistic leanings, so invincible in younger days, had been leached from him by seventy-three years of endurance on this planet. What had fascinated him in one age now repelled. In 1914 he was still possessed by the "truly titanic mind" of Yerkes, his "rebellious Lucifer ... glorious in his sombre conception of the value of power," but the man who could be moved spontaneously to comment as he researched: "The courage of Yerkes in the future! His daring!" was no more. He came across, in his packing case of *Stoic* materials, a pronouncement made by Yerkes in 1903 and painstakingly copied out in his own hand as background for the novel. Yerkes, never shy at stating his creed, had spoken out on a man's inherent right to succeed in worldly strife, to be rewarded, and to pass on the fruits of his triumph through inheritance—and in order to facilitate this, his right to possess entire industries, whether private or "public." Reading Yerkes' words now, after the passage of forty years, Dreiser, in a shaky handwriting suggesting senility and almost indecipherable, scrawled the stern rejoinder: "Nevertheless wealth should be limited and greed regulated." It was only one indication of how far Dreiser had come from the day when the story of Yerkes and his second wife, stalking society in tandem like a pair of predatory leopards, had set him afire with the need to write it all down, to crowd it all in. The old spark, once extinguished, could never be renewed. Life had changed; he had changed. His labor became mechanical, a parody of himself in his former prime.[74]

Added to this, Dreiser had long inched—or had attempted to—in the direction of spirituality, goaded by a need to believe in some explanation of life that probed beyond empirical fact. "Well," he had declared to Marguerite Tjader on his New York visit, as soon as they were alone, "I believe in God now—a Creative Force." But it is reasonably certain that he did not, though he desired to, and his remark is likely related to his current immersion in Quaker thought preparatory to a final effort on *The Bulwark* with its hero whose "mind was on religion and the Creative Force." Forever confused and torn between belief and disbelief, his central philosophy, perennially stated, placed a question mark where others would elucidate the secret. The world creates both good and bad, he was fond of saying, and who is man to judge? His ambiguity was shown at the end, when he applied for official entry into the Communist Party and simultaneously took communion at the Congregational Church Helen dragged him to. And even this was not totally out of character, for despite raucous protestations to the contrary, religion had never quite left him, or he it. Rather, he knocked the religious coin over and honored its flip side, superstition. From his mother, who saw spirits dancing in her home, to brother Paul, for whom a hat on the bed was a sure omen of death, his family had been steeped in supernatural beliefs. Anything mystical hypnotized, as did the occult, and there must have been moments when the inexplicable conversion of Berenice seemed explicable, indeed made good sense. In any event, the principal thing now, the sole impetus, was a determination that *The Stoic*, this "definite part" of his literary program, should see the light of print, by whatever means, be it compromise, sacrifice, or surrender. In this Sargasso Sea of resignation his compositional skills lay becalmed. He had said it all many years before, calling attention to the inevitability of his title: "Everybody becomes a stoic if he lives long enough."[75]

Since Dreiser and Helen worked on the book throughout the fall of 1945 in virtual seclusion, the story of those days has had to come from her, and she tells of long discussions between them concerning the book's structure, lines of action, and specific scenes. "It was incredible the way he persisted in his job," she reports; "in fact, it was all he wanted to do." And while he rocked slowly in his chair, outside in the open if the weather permitted, she typed his words directly onto paper from dictation. In this manner work went well enough so that Dreiser felt he could tell Farrell in October that he had "just finished the long missing third volume" and would mail it to him. He was excessively optimistic. The book was not done—the conclusion was troubling Dreiser—but late in November Alvin Manuel, Dreiser's new agent, wrote to Doubleday, successor to Putnam, telling editor Donald Elder that the book would be ready to submit in two weeks. Early December had arrived before Dreiser was able to write Farrell his happy letter: "It is actually finished." A copy—the first complete typescript of *The Stoic*—was being mailed by express for Farrell's opinion and advice.[76]

VI

What sort of novel were Dreiser and Helen assembling on their California patio? Early in the composition of the trilogy, so long ago that he might be forgiven if he had forgotten it, Dreiser had described his notion of the perfect book. It would need to be daringly honest, "an absolutely accurate biography . . . a literal transcript of life as it is."[77] In transmuting Charles Yerkes into Frank Cowperwood, he had observed this dictum so scrupulously that, except for the whole being passed through the prism of his own naturalistic philosophy, the result was only a shade removed from biography and—with three volumes to move around in—a rather complete one at that. In both outline and detail, *The Financier* and *The Titan* could be considered, using the term loosely, *romans à clef*, and if anything, *The Stoic* as finally presented hews more closely to actuality—and is more drastically limited by it—than these earlier portions of the trilogy. As a basis, Dreiser returned to his earliest notes, one being the thumbnail analysis he had scribbled out to cover Yerkes' transition from Chicago to New York/London:[78]

> Problems Facing CTY at End of Chicago Career
>
> - - - - - - -
>
> His wife. On account of Emily and his immedi-
> ate future he did not want a scandel [sic] in
> connection with his wife.
>
> - - - - - - -
>
> Getting his money out of Chicago.
>
> - - - - - - -
>
> Getting a new field in which to operate—Repair
> his life.

Accordingly, *The Stoic* begins with an exposition of the "most disturbing problems confronting Frank Cowperwood at the time of his Chicago defeat" rather than with Berenice Fleming's arrival to comfort the beaten financier as the 1932 dummy had opened.

The financial sections of the novel were, fortunately, less complex than the tangled networks of business activity occupying Yerkes' Philadelphia and Chicago years, for after 1898 he was dominated by the single ambition to control the London Underground with its illimitable potential for profitable growth. In 1899 for a reputed $10,000,000 he sold control of 297 miles of his Chicago lines to the Union Traction Company (an alias for the Widener-Whitney-Elkins combine of Philadelphia), and in the following year disposed of the remaining 240 miles. Gossip put his total "take" in excess of $20,000,000. In a masterpiece of understatement, Yerkes then remarked that he would "go to London for a few weeks." It had been common knowledge that he was interested in the traction systems there, already having purchased an Underground franchise for half a million dollars and begun to burrow for a subway beneath Charing Cross, Easton, and Hampstead. But few dreamed the full extent of his ambition until 1903 brought public disclosure of his intention to spend $85,000,000—half of it from New York interests—in transforming the entire surface and underground transit system including its conversion from steam to electricity. Cognizant of the London environs being home to some 8,000,000 persons, Yerkes foresaw a financial bonanza. Some risk was unavoidable, yet he was confident. In a business one always had to take chances, but "I believe this is the best chance I ever took."[79]

For potential use in *The Stoic*, Dreiser had stockpiled as much Yerkes data as for both previous volumes combined. Cowperwood's London venture (Chapters 4 ff.) emerged from newspaper clippings containing precise details on the Charing Cross-Hampstead tube plan as well as for the total capitalization figure. As Cowperwood pursues his domination of London, Dreiser's reliance upon his notes and the summaries prepared by Kathryn Sayre in 1932 remains consistent, with each major fictional event reproducing its model faithfully. To his relief, Yerkes had found England less shaken than America by the personal scandals of his past. There was no vendetta such as that launched against him by the Chicago press; rather, the London papers, tolerant and extremely libel-conscious, praised his financial wizardry.

His purchase of the Charing Cross-Hampstead tube providing a toehold, Yerkes had applied strategy already proven successful in Chicago, moving gradually to accumulate complementary sections of London transportation. Cowperwood consolidates properties in the same sequence as Yerkes, with fidelity to the timing and even to the names of the acquired lines. He purchases first the District and Metropolitan lines, to which the Baker

Street and Waterloo subways are then added, followed by the Brompton and Piccadilly, all destined to be joined into a monopoly through the Union Traction Underground Company.[80]

Yerkes had reached this stage easily, the English willing to defer to his genius, the Americans eager to invest their dollars. But in 1902, excited by the scent of profit, a rival entered the field. J. P. Morgan, establishing his own base in the underground, applied to Parliament for a franchise which would parallel the Yerkes tube and halve the profit derivable from the area. Dreiser had taken notes on the Yerkes-Morgan confrontation, and he paraphrased them in portraying the struggle between Cowperwood and Stanford Drake, Morgan's fictional counterpart:[81]

The Notes	*The Stoic*
...Morgan has offered Yerkes 5,000,000 for the privilege of sharing that Piccadilly Circus station (Yerkes owns site—Morgan none). Also he has offered 2,500,000 if Yerkes will call off his army of lawyers who are preparing to fight Morgan's application to parliament for permission to build his proposed roads. Yerkes is considering these offers.	...Drake made Cowperwood an offer of $5,000,000 for the privilege of sharing the Piccadilly Circus Station, which belonged to Cowperwood and which would obviously be needed by Drake in his system. At the same time he also offered Cowperwood $2,500,000 if he would call off his army of lawyers who were then and there preparing to fight Drake's application to Parliament for permission to build his proposed road. Of course, the offers were refused by Cowperwood.

At this juncture, with both Yerkes and Morgan presenting franchise applications, action by the London United Company became decisive. A native firm, London United disclosed plans to connect the city with an Underground line from Hyde Park Corners, a proposal which would offer competition to both rivals and further complicate any plan for monopolizing London. This proposal and its consequences Dreiser had summarized early in his research:[82]

The London United Co. were going to build from Hyde Park Corner to Shepherds Bush. They go to Morgan and offer to unite and jointly ask for a franchise from the city to Shepherds Bush. Yerkes arrives on scene. English concern asks Morgan to operate the line as a whole when completed. Morgan refuses. Ask to be permitted to operate their section. Morgan refuses. They feel injured—sat upon. Cable Yerkes offering their section to him *although they have no franchise for it.* Yerkes cables them to see Speyer & Co. Speyer & Co., after looking into the matter, *buy.*

Their counsel then before the Parliament Tubes committee asks to withdraw their request for a franchise. As Morgan has been pleading for only *one total franchise for a year* this invalidates the whole plea. Morgan & Co. returns with a request to be allowed to obtain a franchise for their section. But their original request has called for no such thing and there is no such bill before the committee. Yerkes' counsel argues that whole matter must be thrown out.

In adapting this note for his continuation of Cowperwood's scheme, Dreiser expanded it only slightly and retained each development as given, including (except for Morgan and Yerkes) all names, even that of Speyer & Co., Yerkes' actual financial agents:[83]

At the same time there was the London United Company which was planning to build a road from Hyde Park Corner to Shepherd's Bush, the preliminary negotiations for which they had worked out. They went to Drake and offered to unite their line with his, and asked for a franchise from the city. They also asked Drake to operate the line as a whole if and when completed. Drake refused. Then they asked to be permitted to operate their section. Again Drake refused. Whereupon they offered their section to Cowperwood, although they had as yet no franchise for it. Cowperwood notified them to see Speyer & Company, a financing concern that operated not only in England and America but throughout Europe. This firm, after looking into the matter and seeing that they might, by benefiting Cowperwood, eventually benefit themselves, decided to buy all the existing rights which this particular company owned, after which they proceeded to syndicate the entire block of shares. Their counsel, then and there before the Parliament Tubes Committee on other matters, asked to withdraw their request for a franchise. As Drake had been pleading for only one total franchise for a year, this invalidated the whole plea. Drake returned with a request to be allowed a franchise for their section. But as their original request had called for no such thing, and there was no such bill before the committee, Cowperwood's counsel argued that the whole matter must be thrown out.

The House of Morgan, sensing defeat, withdrew its application from Parliament, leaving newspapers to celebrate the victor, YERKES, WHO VANQUISHED J. P. MORGAN. Having leaped a crucial hurdle, Yerkes saw his way clear to predict that his combined London Underground would be operational by January 1905. Sufficient progress was made so that when his line connecting London with Hampton Court opened in 1903, Yerkes could announce with customary pride that "in three years I hope to have a hundred miles of trainways in operation," a quotation Dreiser recorded in his notes, appending one of the ironic asides which Yerkes' career so frequently prompted: "In three years he was dead."[84]

Charles Yerkes was stricken with nephritis during the summer of 1905 and died the following December, and all events relating to his demise were transferred faithfully to *The Stoic* for the end of Cowperwood. While rumors of Yerkes' illness had swept London that summer, medical specialists were called in, and he was given a maximum of a year and a half to live. In anticipation of the inevitable, his will was drawn, but because of the effect any such alarming news might have on his half-completed traction scheme, denials of ill health were issued. In August Yerkes was sent to Paris in company of a Dr. Willard for consultation with specialists. He complained to reporters about spurious press statements which placed him at death's door, but it was apparent that his medical attendant never left his side.[85] In October, unimproved, Yerkes was back in London and making little of his illness. Met by the press, he gave an interview upon which Dreiser relied heavily in *The Stoic*. He had been working too hard, that was all; he required a good rest. A doctor did accompany him to Paris, yes, but was not needed; what better proof of good health than that his time had been spent chiefly "pottering around in an automobile"?

In arranging Cowperwood's final London interview, Dreiser paraphrased Yerkes, then went on to employ portions of his source even more directly:[86]

The Notes	*The Stoic*
He laughed merrily when the World correspondent told him of the supposed contents of the will he was supposed to have made. Whether or not he had bequeathed his priceless art treasures to the Metropolitan Museum in New York he altogether refused to say. "If people want to know what is in my will," he said, "they will have to wait until I am under the turf and I can only hope that their charity is as strong as their curiosity."	He laughed heartily when the *World* correspondent asked whether or not it was true that he had bequeathed his priceless art treasures to the Metropolitan Museum of Art. "If people want to know what is in my will," he said, "they'll have to wait until I'm under the turf, and I can only hope that their charity is as strong as their curiosity."

On November 19, establishing the pattern to which Dreiser would adhere, Yerkes arrived in New York by steamer and was whisked by ambulance to the Waldorf-Astoria, his mansion at 864 Fifth Avenue being in a state of commotion because of extensive remodeling for a new art gallery in the adjoining building he had purchased to house the overflow of his treasures. Reporters, undeceived, were aware that the revamping did not render the mansion uninhabitable for Mrs. Yerkes, that in fact she seemed to have barricaded herself within its walls as in a fortress. Using his press reports, Dreiser scarcely deviated from the actions they recorded; for instance, his introduction at this late date of Cowperwood's son and daughter from his marriage to Lillian Semple is based upon the publicized arrival from Chicago of Charles E. Yerkes and from Philadelphia of Mrs. Bella Rondinella, the Yerkes children. Also keeping vigil, but circumspectly and not cited in the press until after the death, was Emilie Grigsby, who had nursed Yerkes throughout the summer and followed him home on another steamer, as was her habit.

The death of Cowperwood, preceded by the sickbed confrontation between Aileen and Berenice Fleming, the financier's mistress, follows press accounts of Yerkes' demise. Aileen, estranged for some time and now hardened against her husband, refuses to allow his body to lie in state in the mansion, but servants in Cowperwood's employ unbolt the doors during the night so that his bronze coffin might be carried in. The subsequent melodramatic scene in which Aileen wakes in the darkness to find that the corpse has been smuggled into the reception hall has just the touch of perfect irony appropriate to a novelist's inventiveness and might be so credited were it not for Marguerite Tjader's assurance that Dreiser had been informed of this bizarre turn of events by press acquaintances who leaked the story. The funeral itself is depicted accurately: the crowds of curiosity seekers milling on Fifth Avenue, the sparse group attending private services within the home, the mourners, including Aileen, Frank A. Cowperwood, Jr., and Mrs. Anna Templeton (Dreiser adds a seat in a carriage for Berenice, an unlikely event), the interment in Greenwood Cemetery, the Greek-styled mausoleum with the Cowperwood name chiseled above its lintel, details courtesy of Marguerite Tjader.

In early 1906 the newspapers catered to wide public curiosity concerning provisions of the Yerkes will, soon probated in the courts of Cook County, Illinois (Yerkes in a sense had kept faith with the West by retaining legal residence there). Prior to public revelation, readers had been fed numerous and often conflicting rumors of bequests stipulated in the document. Read late in January, the will contained provisions which supplied Dreiser with the basic content for his fictional résumé of the Cowperwood estate:[87]

Yerkes' Will	Cowperwood's Will
Art treasures to be given to the city of New York, with a $750,000 endowment.	Art treasures to be given to the city of New York, with a $750,000 endowment.
Louis Owsley, Yerkes' personal secretary, $50,000 bequest.	Albert Jamieson, Cowperwood's personal secretary, $50,000 bequest.

Each Yerkes servant, $2,000.	Each Cowperwood servant, $2,000.
The Yerkes Observatory, $100,000.	The Cowperwood Observatory, $100,000.
The Yerkes Hospital, $800,000.	The Cowperwood Hospital, $800,000.

The dead financier safely interred, creditors closed in upon his estate. The dream of a public Yerkes Gallery and a great Yerkes charity hospital, meant to transform an outlaw's image into that of a philanthropist, soon faded. The sculptures, the paintings, and eventually even the mansion designed so that it might instantly be converted into a museum to hold them, were put on the auction block. And all of this went into *The Stoic*, sometimes in a strangely truncated form nothing at all like the familiar Dreiser manner, but nevertheless following press accounts and at times borrowing even the language of the old clippings he had saved since 1910 and earlier.

It is clear that at this stage of the composition process, with Dreiser enfeebled, his remaining life numbered in days and his spirit lifted only by the determination to complete what he had begun some forty years earlier, what he and Helen were doing was not so much writing *The Stoic* as tacking it together like a patchwork quilt. Bits and pieces from Kathryn Sayre's summaries, fashioned into sentences and placed in order, supplied a minimal pattern. Occasionally a serendipitous clipping, souvenir of an observant reporter, helped to flesh it out, but for the most part the book remained a skeletal shape on which Dreiser had lost all ability to build further.

VII

Notwithstanding his slavery to the record life had given him, Dreiser after the death of the financier made significant changes in his story, deviating from the Yerkes record in ways that both altered his plot and affected the import of the trilogy as a whole. Some of these concerned the history of Aileen Cowperwood, although for the most part Dreiser merely paraphrased his data on Mary Adelaide Yerkes, at times scarcely troubling to alter the names; thus, Mrs. Yerkes' lawyer, Clarence Knight, becomes Charles Day, and the magistrate who hears her case, Judge Cutting, becomes Judge Severing, and the name of the Yerkes financial agent, as previously noted, remains Speyer & Company.

The seventeen-page "Settlement of Cowperwood's Property and Affairs" which Kay Sayre had outlined from Dreiser's accumulated notes in 1932 was relied upon as the single source for portraying the maze of legal disputation occupying Aileen from 1906 to 1910. With numerous deletions condensing this bulky record to the space of a single brief chapter, what specifics were retained went into the novel verbatim or with slight alteration. As an example, Yerkes' secretary, Louis Owsley, had been appointed executor of the estate, but Mrs. Yerkes, who had hired Clarence Knight as attorney to represent her interests, refused to cooperate with Owsley, mistrusted him deeply as a result of his long subservience to her husband, and attempted to oust him. A number of the details of legal wrangling concern this antipathy; with Owsley appearing as the fictional Jamieson, Cowperwood's personal secretary, these are distributed throughout Chapter Seventy-Five:[88]

Settlement Summary	*The Stoic*
(Query: What did Owsley get – T.)	"What did Jamieson get out of it?" was the query.
Chas. E. Yerkes: "It is a case of a woman meddling with things she does not understand."	"It is a case of a woman meddling in things she does not understand," observed Frank A. Cowperwood, Jr.
"claim of Underground Electric for $800,000, unpaid on C's* holdings."	The London Underground company brought suit in New York . . . to collect $800,000 due them.
Owsley asked Mrs. C. to pay him 3% on her widow's award, amounting to $1,500.	Jamieson had charged Aileen $1500 collection fee when he had already been paid as executor.
Owsley asked Mrs. C. to sell house and art, giving him 6% as a fee.	"Mr. Jamieson asked me to sell my house and art collection," Aileen concluded, "and pay him 6 per cent on the transaction."
Mrs. C. has bronchitis, mild pneumonia and heart complications . . . is too ill to know about litigation or guards in the house.	William H. Cunningham as receiver . . . although Aileen was ill of pneumonia at the time, proceeded to place guards on duty at the Fifth Avenue property.
Mrs. C. filed suit in Circuit Ct. in Chicago today asking that Owsley be enjoined from exchanging	Jamieson urged the court to turn over the $4,494,000 in bonds of the Union Traction Company to

*In her Summaries, Kay Sayre continues to use the Yerkes and Cowperwood names interchangeably.

$4,494,000 of Consolidated Trac-   the reorganization committee for
tion Co. bonds for new securities   the purpose of forming a new
of Chicago Rwys. Co.   company, and Aileen's lawyers
                                         were contending the action . . .

Dreiser had the advantage of cross-reference notes which Kay Sayre had
appended to her "Settlement Summary," providing the code numbers of
the original Dreiser notes suitable for expanding her condensed notations,
as:

Dec. 4, 1919. List of moneys the particular heirs will receive. p. 627.

Elsewhere, if she questioned the accuracy or implication of the note from
which she was working, Miss Sayre might offer an interpretation for
Dreiser to consider:

Nov. 11, 1900. Signed agreement between Mrs. C. and Owsley. By it Mrs.
C. received $800,000 in lieu of dower and as a part of personal estate.
Later alleged she received $625,000 not due her. (I am sure that phrase "in
lieu of" should read "to be supplemented by" or "as part of her" Kay.)

Dreiser evidently agreeing, the rephrasing was accepted, and the printed
version of this transaction (*Stoic* 282) reads: "Aileen's lawyers, together
with Jamieson's lawyers . . . arranged a settlement whereby she would receive $800,000 in lieu of her dower rights, and as a part of her personal
estate due her."

Because acceptance of a settlement forfeited Mrs. Yerkes' right to
occupy 864 Fifth Avenue, plans had proceeded in 1910 to effect the sale
of the mansion and its contents. Except for her personal effects and certain
pictures from the collection, the auctioneer's agents admitted on March 25
tagged the hundreds of paintings, sculptures, bronzes, and rare carpets
according to their placement in the elaborate catalog being readied. Collectors, art experts, and dealers sauntered about the house, not ignoring
Mrs. Yerkes' own boudoir, openly speculating on values, eyes alert for
bargains. Wagons carted three hundred canvases to the American Galleries
on 23rd Street in a caravan rhapsodied by the press as "some rich argosy
laden with the riches of art from the East and West." Mary Adelaide
Yerkes, followed by sixty trunks and a retinue of servants, took temporary
quarters at the Plaza, then moved to the smaller home she had leased at
861 Madison Avenue. Although four stories, it measured only 32.3 by 63
feet; "And that," Dreiser had been impelled to soliloquize in his original
notes, "after her $50,000 pink marble bath!" In *The Stoic* he reduced her
accommodations a step further, installing her in an apartment rather than a
house.[89]

The auction of the Yerkes art works proved the most lucrative ever held in America. Israel's "The Frugal Meal," which Rita Sohlberg so admired when Cowperwood displayed it at his Chicago home in *The Titan*, brought only $19,500, but Turner's "Rockets and Blue Lights," heavily appreciated, went for $129,000, and the pièce de résistance, a painting Yerkes-Cowperwood had shipped home during the busiest days of his London venture, Frans Hals' "Portrait of a Woman," brought $137,000. Throughout the trilogy, Dreiser had never attempted to disguise his representation of Yerkes' purchases as Cowperwood's, and he did not now. At the mansion, attention focused (*Stoic*, Chapter 75) upon the crush of spectators pouring through the double bronze doors at last open to the wealth-adoring public. Spectators crammed the Yerkes Reception Hall, wandered up the grand central staircase, through the library, the conservatory, the Japanese room, the Italian Gardens, the Sunset Room where Adelaide-Aileen attempted suicide in *The Titan*, feasting their eyes on silk and marble, vases and Sheffield plate, torchieres and candelabra, pianos, ivories, and bronze. Whether Dreiser himself mingled with the army of sightseers is a moot question, but he was in New York, still heading the Butterick combine, he did retain a catalog of the sale, and he did clip extensively from the newspaper accounts. In *The Stoic*, as dramatic focus for the auction, he relied upon a single entry in Kay Sayre's "Aileen Summary":

Apr. 13, 1910. Auction sale in Yerkes home, prices. More elegant people there than ever came by when the Yerkes lived there. Aileen drove by and saw sale, but did not enter. p. 210.

The "p. 210" reminder was Kay's cross-reference to a press clipping in Dreiser's file, retrieved to become his chief source of elaboration for the sale. The extent to which he leaned upon the reporter's account is best understood perhaps by juxtaposing the original with the version prepared for the novel:[90]

The clipping

IN BROUGHAM, MRS. YERKES SEES CROWD THRONG HOME

———

Watches, as Carriage Slowly Passes By, Those Eager
to Offer Bids for Art Treasures Late Railway
Magnate Had Collected.

———

Motors, taxicabs and carriages hugged the curb at Fifth Avenue and Sixty-eighth street yesterday while the auction sale was going on inside the Yerkes home.

A brougham went slowly up and down two or three times. It had only one occupant, a woman, who looked at the automobiles and whose eye glided over the men and women crowding up the steps into the region of the auctioneer.

It meant much to the woman. Such a percentage of every sale. Such a final separation from her earlier ambition. Twenty years ago she was one of the most ravishingly beautiful women of this country. To a certain degree she retains something of her former spirit and bearing. She has been crushed, but not subdued. Now she is looking at the last struggle.

The woman in the carriage was Mrs. Adelaide Yerkes. She did not go in to attend the sale, yet she saw the fashionable motors at her door, motors whose owners never stopped in earlier days. Yet they were there, clamoring to get in first, women whose Summers are spent in Newport, whose town houses fill up the spaces in the social register of New York.

NOTHING STRANGE IN ATTITUDE

No wonder Mrs. Yerkes didn't want to part with her home or her treasures. The house is every bit as magnificent as represented in Park Row. . . .

From one room to another, the people with money to spend followed the voice of the auctioneer.

They saw "Cupid and Psyche," by Rodin, sold to a dealer for $51,000.

A large woman in violet, who stood near Mrs. Herman Oelrichs most of the time, always went as high as $390 on a price, never $400. . . .

When the crowd rushed into the conservatory, the auctioneer called "Don't lean against the plants."

A woman who had gone as high as $1,600 on a Bottinelli [sic] and lost it to a $1,700 voice, sighed 'neath the palms and said:

"Anyway, the air is good in here."

The Stoic

. . . And when the day of the auction finally arrived, motors, taxicabs, and carriages hugged the curb at Fifth Avenue and Sixty-eighth Street while the sale was going on. There were millionaire collectors, famous artists, and celebrated society women—whose motors had never stopped there in earlier days—all clamoring to get inside to bid on the beautiful personal belongings of Aileen and Frank Cowperwood. . . .

From one room to another they followed the booming voice of the auctioneer which reverberated through the great rooms. They saw "Cupid and Psyche" by Rodin sold to a dealer for $51,000. One Bidder, who had gone as high as $1600 on a Botticelli, lost it to a $1700 voice. A large, impressive woman in purple, who stood near the auctioneer most of the time, for some reason always bid $390 on an article, never lower, never higher. When the crowd rushed into the palm room on the heels of the auctioneer to view a Rodin statue, he called out to them "Don't lean against the palms!"

Throughout the sale, a brougham drove slowly up and down Fifth Avenue two or three times, its occupant a lone woman. She looked at the motors and carriages . . . and watched the men and women crowding up the steps into the house. It meant much to her, for she was viewing her own last struggle: a final separation from her earlier ambitions. Twenty-three years ago she was one of the most ravishingly beautiful women in America. To a certain degree she retained something of her former spirit and bearing. But Mrs. Frank Algernon Cowperwood did not go in to attend the sale. . . . Eventually she decided she could endure no more, and told the driver to take her back to her Madison Avenue apartment.

In dramatizing the period between the death of the financier (1905) and the auction (1910), Dreiser abandoned the facts he had compiled concerning Mrs. Yerkes in order to alter the life of Aileen Cowperwood. One month after Yerkes' funeral a stunning rumor hit the New York press: Mrs. Yerkes had remarried. Her bridegroom was the personable, loquacious, twenty-nine-year-old Wilson Mizner, Californian, Klondike adventurer, soon to become successful as a playwright but now a spendthrift habitué of Broadway widely regarded as a fortune-hunter, and more than twenty years his bride's junior. The news both titilated and shocked the city, furnishing the newspapers with a story whose odd combination of pathos and high comedy was irresistible. In an orgy of irreverence which would have been unimaginable during the financier's lifetime, the papers cartooned and lampooned the newlyweds as a mock Romeo and Juliet duo, abetted in their satire by every inept move the couple made.

Mrs. Yerkes-Mizner at first issued adamant denials that the ceremony had taken place, then pleaded for sympathy ("Mr. Mizner was very good to me through all my troubles. . . . I was very lonesome"), and Mizner guided reporters on a tour of the mansion, entertaining them by lounging in Yerkes' favorite armchair and drinking from his silver goblet. Pausing in the art gallery, Mizner poked fun, lecturing impromptu on the virtues of Edouard Charlemont's "The Pages" and dubbing it "Newsboys shootin' crap." The mansion was a move up, quite a change from the shanty he had occupied in the Klondike, and finally Mizner struck a pose, his hands plunged deep in his pockets: "Well, boys," he boasted, "it's all over except the cheering." But the cheers were jeers, and The New York *American*, in naïve hope or in sardonic irony, certainly with the gloomy echo of a local cliché, predicted: "The Yerkes mansion, which practically has been closed for the last eleven years, will soon be the scene of social entertainments of a character in harmony with its magnificence." So great was the notoriety that the handsome bronze fence enclosing the Yerkes property had to be boarded over to protect it against souvenir hunters crazy to obtain some little memento.[91]

At the time of the wedding, Dreiser had compiled materials adequate to rebuilding the Yerkes-Mizner marriage in the most exacting detail. Having arrived at a deep sympathy for Mrs. Yerkes, Dreiser was appalled at the journalists' mockery of her predicament. "It should be noted," he post-scripted his materials, "in speaking of Mrs. Yerkes the flippant, shameless newspaper accounts—coarse and vulgar."[92] However, he apparently intended using the event, probably for its dismal note of irony, in conclud-ing *The Stoic*. The *Synopsis* for the novel typed at Mt. Kisco in 1932 includes the marriage as an integral part of the fictional story:[93]

... Then there are his sudden return and death in New York, the attempted exclusion of his body from his own mansion, the enormous entanglement in connection with his financial affairs, the attempt of a fortune hunter to seize opportunity through a false marriage with his wife, brought about at a time when she had been made drunk, and her sub-sequent war on this ...

The marriage figures also in *The Stage* résumé which Kay Sayre prepared:[94]

1906. ... Then within a month, Aileen marries a Mr. Mizner. Extreme notoriety in keeping marriage secret.

In the summaries of Cowperwood and Aileen typed for Dreiser's con-venience, further details are supplied:[95]

Feb. 1, 1906. Aileen still denies marriage. Mizner embarrassed 165-6.

Feb. 1, 1906. All details of Aileen's denial of marriage to Mizner, as well as description and history of Mizner in interview pp. 167-172.

Feb. 2, 1906. Mrs. Yerkes-Mizner gives reasons for marriage, p. 173, 174. I think you'd be very much interested in passage I marked on interview P. 175-6, Kay. See. 177-178-179, Cartoon, 178.

Feb. 4, 1906. Mizner installed at 864 Fifth Ave, Yerkes home. He drifted into Waldorf Astoria and was immediately surrounded by friends and congratulated.

Notwithstanding his original intention, however, and the fact that from the instant of its occurrence the remarriage had prompted public reflection on the apparent fruitlessness of Yerkes' life, which was in keeping with his chosen theme, Dreiser in 1945 eliminated any reference to the event, allow-ing the dissolution of the Cowperwood estate to carry the dramatic burden in the fictional story. To keep *The Stoic* going after the death of its principal character was difficult enough, but a dead financier had no chance in competition with this lively farce. Against its melodramatic color, the portrait of Cowperwood was certain to have faded away. Whether Dreiser made the deletion purposely, on literary grounds, or whether in his final, exhausted effort he simply let it slip away as dispensable, it worked for the health of the novel.

VIII

The second of Dreiser's major changes in the record produced less happy results.

Berenice Fleming, who had entered the trilogy midway through *The Titan*, became a principal character, Cowperwood turning to her as his estrangement from Aileen hardened into a clear separation. Only the certainty of scandal with its accompanying damper upon the financier's public image kept them from divorce—that and Aileen's determination not to allow a youthful beauty to steal the husband she herself had taken from an older woman twenty years before.

As with other characters, Dreiser depended upon the Summary prepared by Sayre with its day-by-day account of Emilie Grigsby. In the main, a thin line separates Emilie from her fictional counterpart, as for instance the correspondence of Cowperwood's arrangement whereby Berenice's brother, Rolfe, becomes secretary to one of his subordinates with press reports identifying Braxton Grigsby as secretary to Yerkes himself. The Park Avenue home which Yerkes presented to Emilie in 1898 is never described in detail, probably because of the synopsis-like style in which so much of *The Stoic* is written, but Dreiser had at hand newspaper accounts sufficient to detail the mansion from cellar to attic.

By common consensus it was a palace, four stories tall, on the corner of Sixty-seventh Street, with half a block of Avenue frontage. Not more than three blocks from Yerkes' own home, it retains in fiction its actual address, 660 Park Avenue. The interior was a depository for the spillover of art trophies from foreign travels: rare porcelains, jades, Tanagra figurines, Empire furniture which Yerkes freighted from abroad. There was a vast collection of medieval ecclesiastical vestments sewn with jewels, a library of 11,000 rare volumes. The white marble of the central hall was hung with Aubusson tapestries, its staircase dominated by the Coppee portrait of Emilie "in clinging, sheer silks, with a toy dog jumping at her plump hand." Concealed within the walls, a private elevator ran Yerkes from the basement directly to the uppermost floor, where Emilie entertained him in a spacious apartment furnished "with everything that imagination could devise to make it attractive to the eye and pleasing to the senses . . . enchanting and orientally material."[96]

Yerkes set up semi-permanent bachelor quarters in the Waldorf, jokingly referred to his mansion as "Hotel Yerkes," and when he traveled, which was more and more frequently, Emilie followed within a week, on the next principal steamer. The pattern is followed in *The Stoic*, much of which takes place in London, Paris, and other centers. When the Cowperwoods, in Chapter Twenty-One, sail on the *Kaiser Wilhelm der Grosse*, Berenice follows on the *Saxonia*. In England Berenice and her mother are installed in a country house at Pryor's Cove on the Thames between Maidenhead and Marlowe, where they entertain British society and where Cowperwood may visit his "ward" whenever opportunity arises. This residence parallels the "little house at Maidenhead on the Thames [called] The Chalet" rented for Emilie Grigsby, at which "Yerkes was a frequent visitor." Here, on its broad lawns, Emilie, "clad picturesquely in flowing muslins and sometimes with a rope of lustrous pearls about her throat," danced for her guests, inspiring reciprocal invitations to nearby estates such as Taplow Court, famous home of W. H. Greenfeld.[97]

For the cruise of the Scandinavian fjords, instigated by Berenice as recreation for the financier in Chapter Fifty-Seven, Dreiser relied upon the nine-day Norwegian cruise which he and Helen had taken in 1926. Avoiding the big liners, they sailed on a small boat northward to Trondheim and into the land of the midnight sun, the same itinerary followed by Cowperwood and his mistress. Both men react to the spectacular but icy locale; Dreiser, missing "the bright colors he was accustomed to in America," was depressed, while Cowperwood is impressed by Norway's strange beauty but nevertheless thinks the fjord country "one of Nature's climatic mistakes. There's too much daylight in summer and too little in winter. Too many romantic waterways and too many sterile mountains." Moreover, the intellectual stimulation deriving from contact with the native soil of literary giants such as Hamsun and Ibsen is clearly something that Dreiser and not Yerkes-Cowperwood might be apt to experience, as admitted in Helen's *My Life with Dreiser*, where the cruise is described. Nor would Cowperwood on his return trip be likely to enjoy a stroll through Père-Lachaise in Paris, for he thrived on life, not death; in any case, although he may well have heard Sarah Bernhardt's golden voice in Chicago, it would have been impossible for him to have been stirred by the sight of her grave, for she lived until 1923, being interred just three years prior to Dreiser's own visit to the cemetery.[98]

As soon as Charles T. Yerkes was safely dead, the press glutted itself on sensational revelations concerning Emilie Grigsby; withheld for years, both facts and apocrypha poured out in a flood, providing the information on which the portrait of Berenice was founded. Included was a supposition that Emilie might actually be Yerkes' illegitimate daughter, a point upon which Dreiser causes Lord Stane to speculate in *The Stoic*. The early Berenice is faithful to all published reports of Emilie Grigsby, a girl fully as materialistic as her benefactor, who understood the use of her auburn beauty as a social lever. Throughout *The Titan* and well into *The Stoic* the girl's own personality dominates her thoughts. To a striking degree she is aware of her impact upon the world. Dreiser had called her "sybaritic," "vain," "a born actress" fond of "posing Narcissus-like before her mirror," a girl who at seventeen would write in her secret diary:[99]

'My skin is so wonderful. It tingles so with rich life. I love it and my strong muscles underneath. I love my hands and my hair and my eyes. My hands are long and thin and delicate.... My long, firm, untired limbs can dance all night. Oh, I love life! I love life!"

To undergird such remarks, Dreiser possessed notes purporting to be Emilie's description of herself at that age:[100]

"... to myself every inch of my person under my white gown and my white skin was so remarkable, so vitally individual, so full of a tingling sense of a young, pulsating life. I loved my hands because they were so fine of touch and tint, and my long, firm untired limbs, which could dance all night and hardly know it."

By way of newspaper clippings Dreiser kept track of Emilie's activities through the time he was composing *The Titan*, saving such reports as that of her 1907 lawsuit whereby she compelled the Central Trust Company to enter in her name 47,000 shares of promotion bonds of Yerkes' proposed monopoly, the London Underground Railway. In 1909 he read of a gourmet banquet at 660 Park Avenue, a bejeweled Emilie serving as hostess. Just a year after the widow Yerkes (by now divorced from Mizner) died of pneumonia, Emilie's "house of mystery," as the tabloids dubbed it, was put up for sale and its accoutrements cataloged. There was irony in Mrs. Yerkes' dying relatively impoverished, whereas the protégée had been provided for handsomely with funds untouchable by creditors.

During the reign of Edward VII, Emilie was persona grata in England, being presented formally to the King and to Queen Alexandra. But in 1911, when she sailed to attend the coronation of George V, she ran into social catastrophe, the result of publicity concerning her liaison with Yerkes. Disembarking from the *Olympic* in New York, she had considerable solace, for the headlines ran: MISS EMILIE GRIGSBY BACK WITH $800,000 IN JEWELRY. What was plainly a legacy from the streetcar king rested in a leather case borne by her maid. Custom officials took a considerable interest, the hubbub over her jewels halting work at the dock for an hour. But as her diamonds, rubies, and pearls underwent close scrutiny, Emilie remained cool, declaring for each piece that "it had been purchased in this country and that she could produce a bill for it." Satisfying the customs men with a signed affidavit certifying that her gems had not been altered while abroad, Emilie was allowed to pass.

Speculation that she had returned home to stay was absurd, said her grandfather, Hamilton Busby, who had met the *Olympic*: "She has a right to come here to attend to business matters, has she not?" Her most pressing item of business was the auction of her personal effects and the Park Avenue mansion, to which inquisitive reporters were at last admitted by the Anderson auctioneers. They produced lush paragraphs which told of "as much silver as you will find in the biggest and richest of stores on Fifth Avenue," priceless cameos and miniatures, and "all sorts of things to make a poor man feel like an anarchist."[101]

Does this sound like a girl so poor at heart that she might renounce the world to work with children in the slums? Not likely. Yet, in *The Stoic* which Farrell was given to read—and which eventually was published— Berenice travels to India, in Nagpur coming under the influence of Guru Borodandaj and through Hindu philosophy being converted to the primacy of renunciation. She returns to America to dispose of her mansion and her jewels, the proceeds being used to undertake construction of the great Cowperwood Hospital for the poor. Rejecting the material for the spiritual in this manner, she hopes to redeem herself and Cowperwood, whose life, as Berenice has been shocked to read of it in Lefèvre's "What Availeth It?" is being called a total failure.

Such a conclusion did violence to the chief strengths in the trilogy, which originally was to conclude as the dissipation of Cowperwood's worldly store achieved the "equation inevitable" prophesied in the coda to *The Titan*. Nature had created Cowperwood and caused him to produce his giant traction system to benefit the race. His purpose served, Nature, through forces of annihilation, was to spare only his material contribution. The individual was nil. Change, interplay of forces, growth, strife, equation—the evolutionary process—were all. A Cowperwood, like a Napoleon, came and went, leaving the cosmic balance undisturbed.

All this, built toward already in two volumes, was undermined and contradicted by Berenice's conversion to do-goodism, by the barest suggestion that in a universe where human endeavor by definition is vain, she might reform the world.

Yet, stranger than the fiction of Berenice's conversion was the verification for it, right there in the box of clippings Dreiser had preserved for three decades, something one would never believe without evidence. For Emilie did undertake the Indian venture ascribed to Berenice, although it occurred after the sale of her home and not prior to it. The papers for January 13, 1913, reported her departure from Paris:[102]

For several years, since the fiasco of her social aspirations in England at the time of King George's coronation, she has taken a great interest in the Yogi philosophers of Hindustan. Her trip to India will take her into the extreme interior, where ancient philosophy may bring ease to her mind and take the place of her waning beauty.

One can well imagine the spark that might ignite Helen Dreiser's imagination, running onto such a report amid the heap of data unpacked from pasteboard cartons; the needle in the haystack, found. The key to enforcing her own vision of a proper close for Dreiser's final work. And who was Dreiser, in his enfeebled condition, to argue against the fact which life placed before him, when he had always counted on life to write his plots and on the truth to buttress his inventions?

Yet Emilie of course did not bring Yerkes' dream into being. His hospital was never erected. The money for it vanished, and with it the dream. Dreiser knew this, and that is why the Summaries of 1932 contain no suggestion that the Yerkes philanthropic quest was to be realized in *The Stoic*. He knew that everything about Emilie, notwithstanding the India business—which must have seemed a jest, some reporter's practical joke on him—confirmed her unimpeachable narcissism. All other reports centered on it. "She is not given to great generosities" was the verdict of Mrs. Dunlap Hopkins, her official duenna, who must have known her better than anyone; "I never heard of her giving away anything but old clothes." And the reporters who wrote up their pre-sale tours of her home in lurid prose were convinced that Emilie's object in public disposal of the Yerkes loot was not for the millions it might bring, but which she did not need, and most certainly for no such abnegation as the finale of the novel suggests, but purely and simply "for revenge." Her Park Avenue house, they disclosed, was stuffed "from basement to roof with souvenirs and tokens from men who have sought her favors. Nearly all of these men are among the dollar princes of the world. They must bid high to gain back the gifts that they gave her."[103]

And Emilie herself had spoken out unequivocally on the subject. Personal benefaction was a joke. In 1911, leaving for permanent residence in London, where she still had great friends and where the public press was more restrained, she stripped her mansion of its most expensive furnishings and locked them away in vaults pending a further decision on whether to maintain a small New York base. Might she sell the 11,000 volume library Yerkes had given her—or perhaps donate it to the public, in her name? No. "I do not believe in the naming of libraries or institutions after private persons." For one thing, other potential donors might be put off by the very thought of perpetuating the name of someone about whom they knew nothing or "for whom, perhaps, they cared less."[104] Such a girl might auction her treasures, but she would never sacrifice everything in order to erect a Yerkes Hospital.

Unless a genuine miracle occurred. And there was no evidence that it did, as Dreiser was aware, having been diligent in saving every scrap of information he could find, including Emilie's demurrer on public benefaction. In fact, she lived out her years in England, with a house in London's Brook Street and a cottage out of Hyde Park, playing the society hostess, entertaining Lord Kitchener and other military leaders, the sculptor Rodin, whose first works in America had been brought there by Yerkes, and writers William Butler Yeats and Rupert Brook. Henry James was rumored to have fallen in love with her and immortalized her in his *Wings of the Dove*, and in the waning days of 1945, while Dreiser allowed himself to write of her conversion, she entertained in her Mayfair salon, serving her famous soup of twenty-six ingredients, thanks to Charles Yerkes an independently wealthy if much faded beauty, and she would not pass from the scene until 1964.[105]

IX

Having committed his manuscript to the mails, Dreiser was uneasy. His usual mood, completing a book and delivering it to his aides for an opinion, perhaps for some cleaning up or revision, was one of relieved finality. What was done was done, freeing him for the next pressing project. But in this instance he fretted, and shortly—as if some contingency might prevent his doing so later—he followed it with a letter to James T. Farrell asking that the book be kept until year's end and then handed directly to Donald Elder at Doubleday. That the final portions of the manuscript jarred against his original conception was obvious enough to bother him. A question nagged at his mind; he added a postscript:[106]

Would you prefer, personally, to see the chapters on Yoga come out of the book? If so, what would be your idea of a logical ending? I thought once of ending the book with Aileen's death, but later felt I had to go farther with it.

It was as though between himself and Farrell he felt spark something of that "psychic osmosis" that had brought him close to George Douglas, because Farrell on receipt of the manuscript had dropped his own work to take it up at once, eagerly, running through thirty-three chapters on the day it arrived. And as Dreiser had anticipated, he was not happy.

Dreiser having asked for a candid opinion, Farrell gave one. Dated December 19, it was massive, a letter poured out at white heat, twelve pages of single-spaced typewriting, both sides of the sheet used as if there were no time to waste reaching unnecessarily for fresh pages, an analysis of 3000 words touching upon every aspect of the novel. One imagines Farrell beating his typewriter through the night and into the dawn, rambling from point to point in an attempt to crowd his full reaction onto the pages, every so often possessed by doubts that he has adequately stressed his major thrust—or by fears that in the maze of suggestions Dreiser might find it possible to overlook or to misinterpret or to rationalize—and so spiralling always back on any pretext to his major target, the final chapters.

Farrell saw the spirit of the trilogy violated first by Cowperwood's justification of his Underground machinations as being a contribution to the betterment of life for Londoners; to Farrell this read as sentimentality, "and Cowperwood is not a sentimental man." But this flaw was minor compared to the ending, with which something, whatever it might prove to be, "must very definitely be done [and when] I speak of the ending here, I have in mind, Berenice."[107] Miss Fleming's conversion to charitable work as a means of redeeming the rapacity of Cowperwood's existence would fool no one, he warned. Readers were astute enough to see through it, to recognize that social conditions between the Cowperwood-Berenice era and the present day had not improved overnight, and on that discrepancy alone to discount the entire story. Farrell was always mindful of history, and history, he lectured his mentor frankly "does not 'cooperate' with you in giving depth" to the present attempt to close out the trilogy.

How then might the story be concluded? Farrell recounted the ways. There was Cowperwood's death and the dissolution of his treasures, all of which "casts a meaningful light on the entire trilogy." There was the demise of Aileen, where Dreiser had considered stopping, another made-to-order ending which would provide additional irony without weakening major themes. But of all possible endings, Farrell was convinced, Dreiser appeared to have selected the weakest. How was one to say it? There was no easy way, and of all times, this was not the moment for delicacy:

The ending of Berenice is not strong enough to conclude the trilogy, and not strong enough in the light of the irony of what happens to the Cowperwood fortune, and the pitifulness of the ending of Aileen.

How to close the story? In the same spirit in which you initiated it, advised Farrell.

Should Dreiser, for whatever reason, find it impossible to change the present ending, then Farrell suggested contingencies through which the story of Berenice might possibly be patched up and its potential damage mitigated. With or without her yogi philosophy, as Farrell saw it, holding the "utterly naturalistic and materialistic views" which he did, Berenice would prove to be ineffective in solving social problems through private charity. To suggest success would be a ridiculous violation of actuality. Berenice's efforts must be portrayed as pitifully inadequate set against the overwhelming misery of the race. Yes, some small measure of inner peace, the illusion of progress, might be granted her, but if the valuable Truth of Dreiser's trilogy—its irony—were to be preserved, then her efforts must lead to nothing more. Therefore, Dreiser might allow Berenice's yogaism to yield a degree of personal exculpation, if he must, but on no account must he allow it to go further; that was the only way, persisted Farrell, in which he could agree to including the yoga episodes.

To bind the entire trilogy together, the last paragraphs of *The Titan* ought to be rewritten in order that its events would conform more closely with what actually happened in the third volume and its predictions made accurate. As for the "postscript" on Good and Evil which concluded *The Stoic* in manuscript, cannibalized in desperation from an earlier Dreiser essay, that most definitely must go. In its place Dreiser should consider writing a final soliloquy "in which memories, observations AND THEIR IMPORT crowd in on Berenice." Why not something along the lines of that final paragraph of *Sister Carrie*, a book Farrell had long admired, something which might close the trilogy with a question mark, a note of ineffectuality more in keeping with the spirit in which it was undertaken and with Dreiser's lifelong convictions?

No account exists of the reception Farrell's recommendations might have received from Helen Dreiser when they arrived in the mail, but on Christmas Eve, having reflected upon his friend's candor, Dreiser himself replied in a tone of relief, even of some glee, that his own doubts had been confirmed. All that Farrell suggested was agreed to: "I also think you are dead right about the last chapter in regard to Berenice." He promised to recast this and also the next-to-last chapter. A final soliloquy might be managed, and as for the essay on Good and Evil, "that is something that can be discussed at length," Dreiser suggested, "and there is plenty of time for that."[108]

But unfortunately, there was no more time. By the time that Farrell could have received Dreiser's reply, the author was dead, suffering a severe heart attack on December 27, and dying on the 28th.

"The trouble with literary men," Dreiser once told George Jean Nathan, "is that they leave widows,"[109] an axiom never proved more accurate than in his own instance. From this juncture onward, Helen had her way. Dreiser had always recognized that the forces of life plotted stories more imaginative than any invention of the human mind, and the novelist in him would have appreciated fully this critical turning in which the influence of Farrell toward one ending was obliterated and the way laid clear for Helen's version to predominate.

She lost no time in writing to Farrell to say how happy she would be to have his thoughts if he wished to send them, adding that Dreiser had reconstructed the next-to-last chapter before his seizure. It would be no problem for her to write the last chapter herself, she thought, "but I do not want anyone to know." She regretted deeply, though, that Dreiser had not been granted time to compose a closing soliloquy "in that masterful way he had," as Farrell had suggested. To Donald Elder she wrote, not once, but twice, to say that Dreiser had revised "the last two chapters." Since Farrell still held the manuscript, with directions that it be passed to Elder, Helen requested that Elder mail her the two final chapters so that she might substitute the pair that Dreiser purportedly had revised; "he did not want the manuscript read by any other person until those changes were made."[110]

Correspondence with Elder was frequent, Helen detailing the increased responsibility Dreiser had placed upon her in recent years, the great trust he had learned to put in her judgment as it concerned his writing, with the upshot that "it is up to me to see that this last book is well edited. Exceptionally well edited." That Farrell had made some good suggestions for the manuscript and that Dreiser had approved of them was granted.[111] Simultaneously, Alvin Manuel, requesting a $5,000 advance for Mrs. Dreiser, stipulated to Doubleday that she was to have final word on the editing. Elder paused before replying. A pattern was becoming clear. When he did answer Manuel, agreeing to the advance, he also confessed his impression that Helen Dreiser seemed to propose that she would finish writing *The Stoic* by herself. This would never do. If Doubleday were to publish a Dreiser novel, then every word must be by Dreiser himself:[112]

I feel strongly that any additional material which Dreiser himself did not actually complete should be published only as an appendix, with a note designating it as uncompleted material.

Manuel relayed this condition to Helen and, the matter being put to her outright, she had no choice but to agree to the appendix route. To Elder directly she described Dreiser's last day of work, his rewriting of the next-to-last chapter, in order to establish its authenticity. As for the final section, "I know exactly what he intended to do." She conceded at the same time that probably no one but he could write it adequately, it being "one of those famous soliloquys of his." Reiterating the Farrell suggestion that Dreiser eschew generalization in order to work some actual children into the story of Berenice's slum service, waifs who would influence her to muse upon the way in which her charities amounted only to "a drop in the ocean" when the world's needs were taken into account, she was moved to lament the loss of "what Mr. Dreiser would have done with ... this soliloquy of Berenice at the last." To contemplate the irreparable loss made her ill. Nevertheless, she assured Elder, "I know just what he had in mind in connection with this story, and I am sure that my instinct will not fail me as a guide." Elder's reply was to request from her a copy of Farrell's suggestions.[113]

Louise Campbell recently had edited Dreiser's manuscript of *The Bulwark,* a job peculiarly suited to her long association with his work, and had taken pains not to transgress, by which she meant sacrificing "the famed Dreiser 'style'" for clarity's sake, appreciative that "without the awkwardness it wouldn't be Dreiser."[114] Accordingly, once firm arrangements with Doubleday were concluded, Helen mailed her *The Stoic*, minus the uncompleted appendix-chapter, and after a quick run-though Mrs. Campbell acknowledged receipt, pronouncing the book "real Dreiser." She was concerned that the chapters relating Cowperwood's financial maneuvers regarding the London Underground might prove to be overly complex. It took her three months to edit the manuscript and then, for safety's sake, the original went back to Helen in one box, the edited version and carbon in another. For most of the book Mrs. Campbell could show enthusiasm:[115]

Then when I worked over the last quarter—the part following his [Cowperwood's] serious illness, his death, his estate, and Berenice's going to India, I felt a lack. It's not as good, not as alive as most of the book.

None of this could have pleased Helen, for the adverse comments covered precisely those areas on which her influence had been most pronounced; nor could she entertain the Campbell suggestion for deleting the cruise through the Norwegian fjords, based as it was on the Dreisers' 1926 holiday; worst of all perhaps was Mrs. Campbell's straightforward comment, "I think Theodore would have improved the ending." Forwarding the manuscript to Elder, Helen pointedly included not only Dreiser's original script but "a cut version worked out by Louise Campbell," of whom she remarked in grudging tone, "Of course she does have a way of simplifying certain sentences and making the text more readable in spots." But of the basic Campbell criticism, not a word.[116]

Marguerite Tjader was cut off altogether. Having written after the author's death to re-establish relations with Helen and suggest a meeting, she was rebuffed by Helen who, for the first time in her life, could say precisely what she thought without fear of incurring Dreiser's wrath:[117]

You say in your letter that you would "love to see me." In the first place the statement is pure hypocrisy.

I do not care to see you. This, at least, is honest and direct. I, too, have a standard of life by which I try to live. It does not include service to God and Mammon.

Recounting her great contributions to "Teddie's" life, Helen spoke of occasions on which her lover was enticed from her—of one attempt by two women working in collaboration to snatch him away—and of her own pride in his invariable return to her. During the past two years, the days since their marriage, the two Dreisers had achieved an ideal union in every sense; spiritually Teddie and she spoke the same language, finely attuned to each other's faintest vibration (psychic osmosis again):

Do you think any woman could take that away from me, or spoil it with insatiable personal, or literary, or what have you, desires? No, indeed.

She wanted, at this juncture, only to be left alone.

Preparation of *The Stoic* carried over into 1947, Helen telling Mencken she expected it to be out in November. Doubleday sought protection by first sending the script to Constable & Co. in London for a verdict as to whether it might be libelous. When attorneys asked whether the book were based upon historical persons and facts, Elder forwarded the query to Helen. Somewhat taken aback, she replied that of course that was Dreiser's method, as they should well know, to gather data and facts around which his story would then be constructed. For safety's sake she cautioned that *all* names in the manuscript should be changed once again to make certain no liability existed. During the summer Mrs. Campbell's revision was selected as the script to follow, but Elder consoled Helen by pointing out that where Mrs. Campbell had taken it upon herself to assure that Berenice came out "a less romantic and idealistic person" than in the original, he had restored passages that emphasized her poetic, spiritual side and made her less of a calculating golddigger, implying he had been convinced by Helen of Dreiser's intention concerning the novel's ending. For her part, Mrs. Campbell was relieved that no one had tampered with the financial sections over which she had "sweat blood."[118]

One final dispute delayed publication. An introduction to the final chapter, submitted by Helen on September 16, inspired a telegram on the following day from Marjorie Piera, Elder's assistant. She asked approval for a revision specifying that Dreiser had projected an additional chapter, that the notes printed in its stead had been prepared not by him but by Helen, and that he had intended closing with a summary of the trilogy as a whole—a summary taking the form of a soliloquy. Helen wired back at once:[119]

I AM THE SOLE LITERARY EXECUTRIX OF THE DREISER ESTATE AND I WANT THOSE TWO FIRST PARAGRAPHS OF THE APPENDIX

TO REMAIN AS THEY ARE.... TO SAY THAT HE PROJECTED ANOTHER CHAPTER IS CONFUSING. NOT TO SAY THAT THE PRE-CEDING CHAPTER CONSISTS OF THE LAST LINES HE EVER WROTE IS DODGING THE TRUTH THAT SHOULD BE KNOWN TO THE WORLD.... DREISER MADE IT PERFECTLY CLEAR TO ME WHAT HE INTENDED TO DO AND THE WORDS STRENGTH AND WEAK-NESS GOOD AND EVIL WILL HAVE TO REMAIN IN. IF DOUBLEDAY DOES NOT WANT THIS NOTE TO COME FROM THEM THEN HAVE IT COME FROM ME BUT IT WILL HAVE TO GO IN AND THIS IS FINAL.

On September 22 Miss Piera wired a hastily prepared compromise version to Helen, who approved it via telegram on the 24th, and after a delay of thirty-three years—"not immediately," to be sure—*The Stoic* was issued by Doubleday, the company which in 1900 had done its utmost to stifle *Sister Carrie*. Dreiser's career being given to strange turnings, it seemed fitting enough that it be rounded out by this final irony.

NOTES

1 William Thackeray, *The History of Henry Esmond, Esq.* (New York: Signet, 1964), p. 66. All subsequent references to *Henry Esmond* are to this edition. Page numbers will be given in the text.

2 Henry's application of the religious idiom to Rachel is further discredited by the fact that he himself acknowledges its inapplicability, yet after that admission continues to use it. Immediately prior to his reunion with Rachel at Winchester, Esmond writes: "[Rachel] had been sister, mother, goddess to him during his youth—goddess now no more, for he knew of her weaknesses . . . but [she was] more fondly cherished as woman perhaps than ever she had been adored as divinity" (213). On the basis of this quotation, several critics have asserted that Esmond eventually outgrows his reliance on the religious idiom (see, for example, John Loofbourow, *Thackeray and the Form of Fiction* [Princeton, 1964], p. 137). The same chapter (II, 6) in which Esmond makes this assertion, however, concludes with a paragraph in which, embracing Rachel, he says, "I think the angels are not all in heaven" (218). Nor does he abandon that idiom until the memoirs themselves have ended.

3 Walter Allen, "Afterword," in *Henry Esmond*, p. 475.

4 I would like to thank Marc Wanner for locating and alerting me to this instance of contradiction as well as several others included in this essay.

5 In this instance of contradiction, as in many others, one or both terms of the contradiction are embedded in statements made by characters other than Esmond. Depending on whether we assume that Esmond is or is not quoting the character correctly, the character himself may or may not be responsible. In either case, however, Esmond himself is always responsible. That is, whenever a contradiction occurs and Esmond records it, we can assume that he is unaware of the contradiction himself, for when he records a character's statement that he knows includes an inaccuracy or contradiction, he hurriedly relays this information to the reader (32, 40, 92, 127, 214, 270, 273, 278, 284).

Two instances in which we are warned about inaccuracy are of particular interest. Esmond at one point cautions us about Holt's "trifling blunders" (270). A few pages later, Holt in turn confides to Esmond about Thomas Esmond's habit of inaccuracy (278). It remains for the reader to complete the circle: just as Henry's words about Holt are echoed in Holt's words about Thomas, so the reader should apply Holt's words about Thomas to Henry himself. Were it not that Thomas' inaccuracies are intentional and Henry's unintentional, the description of Thomas would provide an excellent description of Esmond's narrative: "His tales used to gather verisimilitude as he went on with him. He strung together fact after fact with a wonderful rapidity and coherence. It required, saving your presence, a very long habit of acquaintance with your father to know when his lordship was 1—— (telling the truth or no)" (278).

6 As the term indicates, Advent ends with the coming of Christ, December 25.

7 Most critics' readings of the novel have not taken note of these contradictions and have essentially agreed with Walter Allen's assertion that "[Esmond] is the one clear-sighted character in the novel" ("Afterword," p. 476). There are, however, at least three exceptions in the history of Thackeray scholarship. The contradictions were noted by Samuel Phillips in "Mr. Thackeray's New Novel," a review in The [London] Times, Dec. 22, 1852. Phillips, however, seeing only isolated instances of contradiction, attributed it to the author's carelessness rather than his craft: "That Steele should be described as a private in the Guards in the year 1690, when he was only 15 years old and a schoolboy at the Charter-house, is, perhaps, no great offence in a work of fiction; but a fatal smile involuntarily crosses the reader's cheek, when he learns, in an early part of the story, that a nobleman is 'made to play at ball and billiards by sharpers, who take his money;' and is informed some time afterwards that the same lord has 'gotten a new game from London, a French game, called a billiard' " (quoted in Thackeray: The Critical Heritage, ed. Geoffrey Tillotson and Donald Hawes [London, 1968], p. 156). Secondly, included in the collected letters of Thackeray is a letter from Anne Procter noting two small instances of contradiction (The Letters and Private Papers of William Makepeace Thackeray, ed. Gordon N. Ray [Cambridge, 1946], III, 128). Thackeray nowhere responds to her comments. In a footnote, the editor dismisses Anne Procter's comment, asserting that the quotations she finds contradictory are not at all incompatible.

More recently, John Sutherland has noted several instances of contradiction: for example, Webb promises Esmond his majority after Wynendale, a promotion Esmond has already received after Oudenarde. Sutherland, like Phillips, attributes such contradictions to rapid and careless composition ("The Inhibiting Secretary in Thackeray's Fiction," Modern Language Quarterly, 32 [1971], 175-188; "Henry Esmond and the Virtues of Carelessness," Modern Philology, 68, No. 4 [May, 1971], 345-354).

8 Samuel Beckett, Three Novels (New York, 1965), pp. 92, 176.

9 Samuel Beckett, *No's Knife* (London, 1967), pp. 71, 88, 79.

10 Even when the two terms of the contradiction are separated, it is often possible to locate the specific piece of subject matter Thackeray has inserted in the intervening narrative in order to obscure the contradiction. For example, the first time Harry meets Francis Esmond, Francis is rescuing Harry from the assaults of another lad who had called Harry a "bastard" (48). Later, recounting his first encounter with Francis to Dick Steele, Harry not only omits the fact that Francis was the rescuer, but asserts that it was Francis who called him a bastard (73). But between the two terms of this contradiction we have seen one of Father Holt's letters in which Holt says that Francis referred to Harry as a "bastard" (65), a piece of information that interferes with our ability to recognize the contradiction when it occurs. Again, at the beginning of the smallpox incident Esmond reports to us that Dr. Tusher brings the news that one of the maids at Three Castles has smallpox; three pages later, summarizing the incident, Henry writes, "When, then, the news was brought that the little boy at Three Castles was ill with the smallpox . . ." (86). Between the two terms of this contradiction Harry has realized that Nancy Sievewright's small brother, whom he had just seen complaining of a headache, is probably coming down with smallpox (84).

11 Included among Thackeray's working notes for *Esmond* is the following note in which he seems to be preparing for an instance of ambiguous re erence or disintegrating image: "*Exchange.*—There be many Exchanges in London, besides markets and the Royal Exchange—as that stately building called the New Exchange and Exeter Change, both in the Strand, where all attire for ladies and gentlemen is sold." (Quoted by Anne Thackeray Ritchie, "Introduction," *The Works of William Makepeace Thackeray* [New York, 1899], VII, xxix.)

12 It might be argued that the wide range of incompatible connotations surrounding single images and phrases is not the intentional result of Thackeray's craft—that, for example, the many meanings assigned to "fire" might crop up in any long novel of the period. This argument might be tenable if Thackeray nowhere showed his interest in controlling and limiting an image's connotations; but in *Vanity Fair* he had already shown both interest and considerable skill in this control and limitation. Again, the argument might be tenable if the instances of disintegrating images in *Henry Esmond* were an exception rather than the rule, but Thackeray is consistently inconsistent throughout. Most importantly, these disintegrating images occur in a novel whose theme is the invalidity of subjective truth; as will be shown, even Esmond himself calls attention to the instability of verbal communications.

13 Loofbourow, *Thackeray and the Form of Fiction*, p. 171.

14 As Alexander Welsh has shown in Part Three of *The City of Dickens* (Oxford, 1971), the equation of female figures with some form of divinity occurs throughout Victorian novels. The omnipresence of this

equation does not make its occurrence in *Esmond* any less ironic, however, since Thackeray has specifically discredited the equation within the novel.

15 There is one form of confusion in identity not included in the text of this section of the discussion because it is not immediately visible in the overt events of the plot. Thackeray continually allows Esmond to describe two different characters in the same words, or allows two different characters to utter almost identical sentences. Esmond and Steele describe young Frank Castlewood in the following way: "[Esmond] never beheld a more fascinating and *charming* gentleman [than Frank]. Castlewood had *not wit so much as enjoyment*. 'The lad looks good things,' Mr. Steele used to say; 'and his laugh *lights up* a conversation as much as ten *repartees* from Mr. *Congreve*.'" (249, 250, italics added.) A few pages later, Esmond describes Steele in these words: "There was a kindness about him and a sweet playful fancy that seemed to Esmond far more *charming* than the pointed talk of the brightest *wits*, with their elaborate *repartees* and affected severities. I think Steele *shone* rather than sparkled. Those famous *beaux esprits* of the coffee-houses (Mr. William *Congreve*, for instance, when his gout and his grandeur permitted him to come among us)..." (253). The reader interested in this form of confusion should compare Esmond's description of Lord Cutts (240) with his description of Colonel Webb (245, 281); Esmond's description of Webb's pride in his lineal descent (245) with Frank Castlewood's assertions about his lineal descent (227, 229), and again with Isabella's similar comment (55); Esmond's comment on the significance of trivialities (92) with an almost identical comment he attributes to M. Massillon (136); Esmond's descriptions of Marlborough as a god (238, 239) with Addison's (259); Rachel's complaint about the way women are treated in literature (101, 102) with Esmond's (120). One of the areas in which this phenomenon most frequently occurs is in Esmond's descriptions of Beatrix and Rachel.

1 James T. Fields, *Yesterdays with Authors* (Boston, 1899), p. 89. The letter, undated, was written sometime after the publication of *The Marble Faun*.

2 Ibid., p. 109. This statement was made to Fields in an undated letter written when Hawthorne was at work on *The Dolliver Romance*.

3 Moncure D. Conway, *Life of Nathaniel Hawthorne* (New York and London, 1890), p. 84 n.

4 Ibid., p. 98.

5 Fields, *Yesterdays with Authors*, p. 75. The letter is dated 13 April 1854.

6 Edwin P. Whipple, "Nathaniel Hawthorne," *Atlantic Monthly*, V (May 1860), 619-620; reprinted in Whipple's *Character and Characteristic Men* (Boston and New York, 1891), pp. 218-242.

7 Quoted by Austin Warren, *Nathaniel Hawthorne: Representative Selections* (New York, 1934), p. lxxxix. Clearly, I differ with Randall Stewart, who, in *Nathaniel Hawthorne: A Biography* (New Haven, Conn., 1961), attempted to picture Hawthorne as a congenial and social person.

8 *Pierre; or, The Ambiguities*, ed. Lawrance Thompson (New York, 1964), pp. 241, 90-91, 170, respectively.

9 *The English Notebooks by Nathaniel Hawthorne*, ed. Randall Stewart (New York, 1941), p. 278; *Life of Franklin Pierce* (Boston, 1852), p. 113. All subsequent references to *The English Notebooks* are to Stewart's edition.

10 R. J. Kaufman, "Tragedy and Its Validating Conditions," *Comparative Drama*, I (Spring 1967), 3-4.

11 William Braswell, "Melville as a Critic of Emerson," *American Literature*, IX (Nov. 1937), 325. As Melville failed to annotate "Self-Reliance," there is no positive evidence that he read that essay.

12 "Tale-Writing—Nathaniel Hawthorne," *Godey's Lady's Book*, XXXV (Nov. 1847), 252-256.

13 *Hawthorne* in *The Shock of Recognition: The Development of Literature in the United States Recorded by the Men Who Made It*, ed.

Edmund Wilson (New York, 1943), pp. 474, 472, 448, respectively.

14 "The Hawthorne Aspect," *The Little Review* (Aug. 1918), ibid., p. 862.

15 *The Letters of Herman Melville*, ed. Merrell R. Davis and William H. Gilman (New Haven, Conn., 1960), p. 146. The letter is dated 8 Jan. 1852. All subsequent references to Melville's letters are to this edition.

16 Foreword to *Pierre*, p. xiv.

17 *The Portable Hawthorne*, ed. Malcolm Cowley (New York, 1957), p. 609. The letter is dated 4 June 1837.

18 *The American Notebooks by Nathaniel Hawthorne*, ed. Randall Stewart (New Haven, Conn., 1932), pp. 93, 97. Except for one specified instance, all subsequent references to *The American Notebooks* are to this edition.

19 Rose Hawthorne Lathrop, *Memories of Hawthorne* (Boston, 1897), pp. 121-122. The letter is dated 28 March 1850.

20 *The Sins of the Fathers: Hawthorne's Psychological Themes* (New York, 1966), p. 260.

21 "Chiefly About War Matters," published anonymously in *Atlantic Monthly*, X (July 1862), 54.

22 Lloyd Morris, *The Rebellious Puritan: Portrait of Mr. Hawthorne* (New York, 1927), p. 272. The letter, undated, was written from London.

23 "The Old Manse" in *Mosses from an Old Manse* (1851).

24 Conway, *Hawthorne*, pp. 188-189. The letter to George S. Hillard is dated 30 Jan. 1850.

25 Ibid., p. 120. The letter to George S. Hillard is dated 9 Dec. 1853.

26 *Hawthorne* in Wilson, *Shock of Recognition*, p. 434.

27 The review, published on 25 March 1846, appears in Randall Stewart's "Hawthorne's Contributions to the *Salem Advertiser*," *American Literature*, V (Jan. 1934), 327-329.

28 *Hawthorne's English Notebooks*, pp. 432-433. The entry is dated 20 Nov. 1856.

29 *Love Letters of Nathaniel Hawthorne* (Chicago, 1907), I, 122. These statements appear in a letter to Sophia Peabody dated 1 Jan. 1840.

30 Eleanor Melville Metcalf, *Herman Melville: Cycle and Epicycle* (Cambridge, Mass., 1953), p. 90.

31 The inscription in Melville's copy of *Mosses* reads: "H. Melville, from Aunt Mary. Pittsfield. July 18, 1850" (see Merton M. Sealts, Jr., *Melville's Reading: A Check-List of Books Owned and Borrowed* [Madison, Wis., 1966], item 248). Though Melville had borrowed the original 1837 edition of *Twice-Told Tales* from Evert Duyckinck on or after July 1849, he wrote to Duyckinck on 12 Feb. 1851: ". . . I have recently read his 'Twice Told Tales' (I hadnt read but a few of them before). . . ." See Sealts, *Melville's Reading*, item 258, and *Melville's Letters*, p. 121.

32 Metcalf, *Melville*, p. 84. The letter is dated 7 Aug. 1850.

33 *Melville's Letters*, pp. 91-92. The letter is dated 6 Oct. 1849.

34 Ibid., p. 108. The letter to Richard Henry Dana, Jr., is dated 1 May 1850.
35 Ibid., p. 109. The letter to Richard Bentley, his English publisher, is dated 27 June 1850.
36 Metcalf, *Melville*, p. 84. The letter is dated 7 Aug. 1850.
37 *Melville's Letters*, p. 142. The letter is dated 17(?) Nov. 1851.
38 Leon Howard, *Herman Melville: A Biography* (Berkeley and Los Angeles, 1951), p. 175.
39 Metcalf, *Melville*, p. 90. The letter is dated 29 Aug. 1850.
40 *Melville's Letters*, p. 143. The letter is dated 17(?) Nov. 1851.
41 Jay Leyda, *The Melville Log: A Documentary Life of Herman Melville, 1819-1891* (New York, 1969), I, 438.
42 The review appeared in two installments in the *Literary World*, IX (15 Nov. 1851), 381-383, and (22 Nov. 1851), 403-404. Quotations are from the second installment.
43 I can merely suggest here that *Moby-Dick* begins where *Tamburlaine* ends. In Act V, Sc. iii, Tamburlaine announces his war against the gods in this way:

> What daring god torments my body thus,
> And seeks to conquer mighty Tamburlaine?
> . . . .
> Come, let us march against the powers of heaven,
> And set black streamers in the firmament,
> To signify the slaughter of the gods.
> . . . .
> Why, shall I sit and languish in this pain?
> No, strike the drums, and, in revenge of this,
> Come, let us charge our spears, and pierce his breast
> Whose shoulders bear the axis of the world,
> That, if I perish, heaven and earth may fade.

In "The Quarter-Deck" chapter, Ahab announces his war against God in these terms: "He tasks me; he heaps me; I see in him outrageous strength, with an inscrutable malice sinewing it. That inscrutable thing is chiefly what I hate; and be the white whale agent, or be the white whale principal, I will wreak that hate upon him. Talk not to me of blasphemy, man; I'd strike the sun if it insulted me."
44 As H. Bruce Franklin said in *The Wake of the Gods: Melville's Mythology* (Stanford, Calif., 1963), p. 61: "Despite all the heterodoxy of opinion on *Moby-Dick*, few critics doubt that Moby Dick is a god." That being the case, scholars have turned their attention to an investigation of possible influences—philosophical, religious, mythological, and literary—that led to Melville's quarrel with God. But a crucial question that still goes begging is why Melville began his most sustained quarrel with God at this point in his psychological career.
45 See, for instance, Hugh W. Hetherington, *Melville's Reviewers, British*

and American, 1846-1891 (Chapel Hill, N.C., 1961) and *The Recognition of Herman Melville: Selected Criticism Since 1846*, ed. Hershel Parker (Ann Arbor, Mich., 1967).

46 *Pierce*, p. 117.

47 As the crucial date of the composition of this essay is surmised, not known, scholarly opinion, when recorded at all, is divided as to whether the essay was written just before or just after Melville met Hawthorne. Leyda, *Melville Log*, I, 387, noted: "August 11. . . . *M begins a critical essay, 'Hawthorne & His Mosses'*. . . ." Metcalf, *Melville*, p. 87, wrote: "*Evert Duyckinck departed August 12 with the manuscript of Melville's essay, 'Hawthorne and His Mosses'*. . . ." Howard, *Melville*, pp. 156-159, reviewed the available evidence to show that Melville wrote the essay after he met Hawthorne. On the other hand, Stewart, *Hawthorne*, p. 108, observed in passing that the essay was written shortly before Melville met Hawthorne, but he seems to have based his conjecture on the date "July 18, 1850" that appears on the flyleaf of Melville's copy of the *Mosses* volume (see note 31 above). Hennig Cohen in the three versions of his edition of *Selected Poems of Herman Melville* likewise wrote that Melville reviewed *Mosses* shortly before meeting Hawthorne, as if it were established fact. The dilemma is made most evident by Newton Arvin's *Herman Melville* (New York, 1961), p. 136: "Probably just before the Stockbridge party [at which Melville and Hawthorne first met], though possibly just after it," Melville wrote the essay. My reasons for saying that the essay "in all likelihood was written on August 11" are evident in my discussion.

48 *Melville's Letters*, p. 113. This letter to Evert Duyckinck is dated 16 Aug. 1850.

49 Julian Hawthorne, *Nathaniel Hawthorne and His Wife* (Boston and New York, 1884), I, 384-385.

50 Metcalf, *Melville*, p. 90.

51 *Melville's Letters*, p. 121. The letter is dated 12 Feb. 1851.

52 Sealts, *Melville's Reading*, item 253. I am not suggesting that Melville first read *The Scarlet Letter* in 1870; I am suggesting that he did not read that novel before he wrote the *Mosses* review. In discussing *The Scarlet Letter* in that essay, Melville adopted the same strategy of generalization he adopted in speaking of *Twice-Told Tales*, whose stories, he later confessed, he "hadnt read but a few . . . before." In treating of Hawthorne's works in the *Mosses* review, he said: "I have thus far omitted all mention of his *Twice-Told Tales* and *Scarlet Letter*. Both are excellent, but full of such manifold, strange, and diffusive beauties, that time would all but fail me to point the half of them out." That is why Melville was also able to declare with such aplomb in the *Mosses* review that "whatever Nathaniel Hawthorne may hereafter write, *Mosses from an Old Manse* will be ultimately accounted his masterpiece." When, in fact, he finally read *Twice-Told Tales in toto*, he

wrote to Duyckinck: "... I think they far exceed the 'Mosses'" (*Melville's Letters*, p. 121). What would he have said had he read *The Scarlet Letter* at that time?

53 *Melville's Letters*, pp. 124-125. I am not the first to notice self-projection in the *Mosses* essay. Willard Thorp, *Herman Melville: Representative Selections* (New York, 1938), pp. xxxv-xxxvi, long ago observed that the "picture that he draws of Hawthorne in 'Hawthorne and His Mosses' is projected from his own mind." Likewise, Edmund Wilson in *Shock of Recognition*, p. 185, said that the *Mosses* essay "must have been inspired by his sense of his own genius rather than by any clear perception of the quality of Hawthorne's."

54 Metcalf, *Melville*, p. 92. The pioneer study of the Melville-Hawthorne relationship was done by Harrison M. Hayford, "Melville and Hawthorne: A Biographical and Critical Study," unpublished Ph.D. dissertation (Yale, 1945).

55 *Hawthorne's American Notebooks*, p. 232.

56 Lathrop, *Memories of Hawthorne*, p. 200. This letter, undated, was sent by Sophia to her mother from Liverpool.

57 *Melville's Letters*, pp. 142-143. This letter is dated 17(?) Nov. 1851.

58 *Hawthorne*, p. xix.

59 Lathrop, *Memories of Hawthorne*, pp. 136-137. This undated poem, according to the author, was found among "my mother's early letters to my father...."

60 *Love Letters of Nathaniel Hawthorne*, II, 36. This letter is dated 3 Sept. 1841.

61 Lathrop, *Memories of Hawthorne*, p. 214.

62 Ibid., p. 150.

63 Leyda, *Melville Log*, I, 389, 391, 408, 410.

64 Ibid., I and II, *passim*.

65 *Melville's Letters*, p. 129.

66 Metcalf, *Melville*, p. 93.

67 *Hawthorne and His Circle* (New York and London, 1903), p. 33.

68 *Melville's Letters*, p. 126. This letter is dated 1(?) June 1851.

69 That Melville had to urge Hawthorne to "show all our faults and weaknesses" may seem odd indeed, for Hawthorne himself had written in the conclusion of *The Scarlet Letter*: "Among many morals which press upon us from the poor minister's miserable experience, we put only this into a sentence: 'Be true! Be true! Be true! Show freely to the world, if not your worst, yet some trait whereby the worst may be inferred!'" Clearly, it is easy enough to recognize a significant principle, quite difficult sometimes to practice it—another instance of the head-heart dichotomy that marks not only Hawthorne's fiction but Hawthorne himself.

70 These quotations are drawn from *Melville's Letters*, pp. 119, 126, 128, 132, 135.

71 Ibid., p. 127. This letter is dated 1(?) June 1851.
72 Ibid., p. 152. This letter is dated 17 July 1852.
73 *The Complete Writings of Nathaniel Hawthorne*, Old Manse Ed. (Boston, 1900), XVIII, 252. This passage is derived from Mrs. Hawthorne's 1868 edition of the *American Notebooks* rather than from Randall Stewart's because the original notebooks from 25 Sept. 1838 to, coincidentally, 25 Sept. 1841 have been lost.
74 Conway, *Hawthorne*, p. 57.
75 *Our Old Home: A Series of English Sketches, Centenary Edition of the Works of Nathaniel Hawthorne* (Columbus, Ohio, 1970), V, 300-301. All subsequent references to *Our Old Home* are to this edition.
76 *Hawthorne's English Notebooks*, pp. 275-276.
77 Ibid., p. 277.
78 *Our Old Home*, pp. 304-305.
79 *Melville's Letters*, p. 142. This letter to Hawthorne is dated 17(?) Nov. 1851.
80 *Love Letters of Nathaniel Hawthorne*, I, 223-226. This letter is dated 4 Oct. 1840.
81 Julian Hawthorne, *Hawthorne and His Circle*, p. 6.
82 *Melville's Letters*, p. 144. This letter is dated 17(?) Nov. 1851.
83 *American Notebooks*, p. 220. The entry is dated 1 Aug. 1851.
84 *English Notebooks*, p. 432. This entry is dated 20 Nov. 1856.
85 A legend in the scholarship is that Melville wrote the two stanzas of "Monody" on the title page of *Our Old Home*, though he recorded only Hawthorne's death date there. William H. Shurr in *Mystery of Iniquity: Melville as a Poet, 1857-1891* (Lexington, Ky., 1972), p. 166, agrees with my speculation that the first stanza was written earlier than the second, and he worked with the manuscripts and consulted with Robert Ryan, editor of the forthcoming definitive text of the poems. "The first stanza of the poem," Shurr writes, "appears to have been written shortly after his [Hawthorne's] death. . . . The second stanza, with its reference to the word 'vine' may have been written while he was developing his Hawthornesque character of Vine for *Clarel*." Be that as it may, many commentators have demonstrated similarities between the subject of "Monody" and the character of Vine in *Clarel*. Bezanson points out, among other things, that Vine's "motives are at times ruthlessly linked with passive ennui, overt anti-intellectualism, pride, and some ambiguous hidden fear . . ." (p. xcix). Robert Penn Warren in *Selected Poems of Herman Melville: A Reader's Edition* (New York, 1970), pp. 392-396, 438-439, also comments on the Vine-Hawthorne parallel and concludes: "In the light of the record, there seems little doubt that Vine is a projection of Hawthorne."
86 *Hawthorne and His Circle*, p. 33. See also "Hawthorne at Lenox," *Booklovers Weekly*, No. 10 (30 Dec. 1901), pp. 229-230. Julian

Hawthorne, to be sure, is not always reliable, but in these interviews he seems to be so, for his statements are corroborated by the known facts and by Melville's own, though more complex, view of Hawthorne in the character Vine (see note 85 above).

87 *Melville's Letters*, p. 92. The letter, dated 6 Oct. 1849, was written to Lemuel Shaw.

88 The "Agatha story" involved Agatha Hatch, who had been deserted by her sailor husband. Melville was concerned with the "great patience, & endurance, & resignation" represented by Agatha, a theme that became central to such tales and sketches as "The Encantadas," "Bartleby," and "Cock-a-Doodle-Doo!" See *Melville's Letters*, esp. pp. 153-161, and Patricia Lacy, "The Agatha Theme in Melville's Stories," *University of Texas Studies in English*, XXXV (1956), 96-105.

89 *Melville's Letters*, p. 121. This letter, dated 12 Feb. 1851, was written to Evert Duyckinck, their mutual friend.

90 *English Notebooks*, pp. 271-272. The entry is dated 16 Jan. 1856.

91 Samuel G. Goodrich, *Recollections of a Lifetime* (New York, 1856), II, 270.

92 Fields, *Yesterdays with Authors*, p. 62.

93 Metcalf, *Melville*, p. 106. The letter is dated 2 Oct. 1851.

94 *English Notebooks*, pp. 271-272. The entry is dated 20 Nov. 1856.

95 Ibid., p. 98. The entry is dated 28 Dec. 1854.

96 Ibid., p. 225.

97 *American Notebooks*, pp. 209-210.

98 *English Notebooks*, p. 225.

99 Warren, *Hawthorne*, p. xvi. In "A Reading of 'Rappaccini's Daughter,'" *Studies in Short Fiction*, II (Winter 1965), 154-156, I speculated that, as Giovanni has unresolved feelings about Beatrice, so Hawthorne had unresolved feelings about Sophia during his courtship of her, an irresolution that, to his credit, he managed to overcome.

100 W. H. Auden, Introduction to the Modern Library edition of *The Tales of Grimm and Andersen* (New York, 1952), p. xx.

101 Robert Penn Warren, recognizing that art "is often confessional and penitential," observed that "the sense of guilt may sometimes lead to the yearning projection of the self-that-might-have-been, the idealized self acting out a redemptive drama. That is, art can be . . . readily summoned to repair the defects of our moral nature . . ." (*Selected Poems of Melville*, p. 81). While Hawthorne often used his fiction to repair his moral nature, he is more confessional than penitential in *The Marble Faun* (Ch. XXXI), if we take Kenyon's view toward Donatello to have any connection with Hawthorne's view toward Melville. "I do not pretend to be the guide and counsellor whom Donatello needs," Kenyon says to Miriam, though he recognizes Donatello's "bitter agony"; "for, *to mention no other obstacle* [italics added], I am a man, and between

man and man there is always an insuperable gulf. They can never quite grasp each other's hands; and therefore man never derives any intimate help, any heart sustenance, from his brother man, but from woman,—his mother, his sister, or his wife. Be Donatello's friend at need, therefore, and most gladly will I resign him!"

Much of the information derives from Dreiser's manuscript notes, a sequence of several hundred sheets arranged chronologically and containing data from newspapers, etc., relevant to the Yerkes story from 1898 onward. Most sheets are numbered consecutively, but in some instances, such as full-page press clippings, dates are substituted, such dates always concerning the historical occurrence of events and not Dreiser's transcription of the materials. Dreiser's manuscript notes exist at Charles Patterson Van Pelt Library, University of Pennsylvania, and references here to the sequence are labeled *DMN* followed by the number and/or date of the notesheet. In other instances where materials from the library's Dreiser Collection are used, as in the correspondence, the label *UP* identifies the University of Pennsylvania.

1 "Dreiser, at 65, May Quit Reds For Roosevelt," *New York Times*, 22 Aug. 1936.
2 Schuster to Dreiser, 26 Aug. 1936; Simon to Dreiser, 22 Sept. 1936. UP.
3 "Theodore Dreiser On The Novel," *New York Evening Sun*, 28 Sept. 1912, p. 7.
4 Theodore Dreiser, "My Uncompleted Trilogy," *New York Evening Sun*, 30 May 1914, p. 7.
5 Montrose J. Moses, "Theodore Dreiser," *New York Times*, 23 June 1912, p. 378.
6 "Theodore Dreiser On The Novel."
7 Guy J. Forgue, ed., *Letters of H. L. Mencken* (New York: Alfred A. Knopf, 1961), p. 36.
8 *Chicago Journal*, 18 Mar. 1914, clipping pasted in Dreiser Scrapbook. UP. The Chicago papers appear to have had continued difficulty with describing Dreiser's novels, Lucian Cary (*Chicago Evening Post*, 22 Nov. 1912) having accurately pointed out the parallels between Cowperwood and Yerkes but mistakenly identified Emilie Grigsby as the second Mrs. Yerkes.
9 Robert H. Elias, ed., *Letters of Theodore Dreiser* (Philadelphia: University of Pennsylvania Press, 1959), I, 162; also, Tatum to Dreiser, 18 Mar. 1914. UP.
10 For a more complete history of Emilie Grigsby, including the use of her

life in *The Titan*, see Philip L. Gerber, "The Alabaster Protégé," *AL*, 43 (May 1971), 217-230.

11 Dorothy Dudley, *Forgotten Frontiers: Dreiser and the Land of the Free* (New York: Harrison Smith and Robert Haas, 1932), p. 302.

12 Forgue, *Letters*, p. 55.

13 "Theodore Dreiser On The Novel."

14 Elias, *Letters*, I, 164-165.

15 George Jean Nathan, "Three Friends: Lewis, O'Neill, Dreiser," *The Borzoi Reader*, ed. Carl Van Doren (New York: Alfred A. Knopf, 1936), p. 611.

16 Stuart P. Sherman, "The Naturalism of Mr. Dreiser," *Nation*, 2 Dec. 1915, pp. 648-650.

17 H. L. Mencken, "The Dreiser Bugaboo," *Seven Arts*, 2 (Aug. 1917), 507-517.

18 Helen Thomas Follett and Wilson Follett, *Some Modern Novelists* (New York: Henry Holt & Co., 1918), pp. 350-352.

19 Burton Rascoe, *Before I Forget* (New York: The Literary Guild, 1937), p. 408.

20 Dudley, *Forgotten Frontiers*, p. 472.

21 Edwin Lefèvre, "What Availeth It?" *Everybody's*, 24 (June 1911), 836-848.

22 Burton Rascoe, *We Were Interrupted* (Garden City: Doubleday & Company, Inc., 1947), p. 297.

23 Tuska to Dreiser, 4 Jan. 1923; 10 Feb. 1923; 17 Nov. 1923; 21 Jan. 1924. UP.

24 Shore to Dreiser, 16 Nov. 1926; 9 Dec. 1926; 19 Feb. 1927. UP.

25 Alfred Kazin and Charles Shapiro, eds., *The Stature of Theodore Dreiser* (Bloomington: Indiana University Press, 1955), p. 60.

26 Dreiser had the possibility of a Nobel Prize in mind from at least 1911 when Grant Richards, helping him with Yerkes research, encouraged him to believe he might win it. Dreiser proposed that Mencken nominate him, the two of them to share the award if their campaign proved successful. In 1927 he asked Louise Campbell to approach either F. P. Adams or Heywood Broun and promote a nomination for him. In 1930, when the Swedish Academy decided to give the Nobel Prize for literature to an American, the contest was between Dreiser and Sinclair Lewis, with Lewis winning.

27 Dreiser to Dinamov, 14 Oct. 1928. UP. Also, Elias, *Letters*, II, 476-478.

28 Dreiser to Stoddart, 10 Oct. 1928. UP. Also, Elias, *Letters*, II 479-480.

29 "Toasts," *Forum*, Nov. 1929, p. lxvii.

30 Karl Sebestyén, "Theodore Dreiser at Home," *Living Age*, 30 Dec. 1930, pp. 375-378.

31 Moses, "Theodore Dreiser," pp. 377-378; also *Chicago Evening Post*, 24 Nov. 1911, cited in Robert H. Elias, *Theodore Dreiser: Apostle of Nature* (New York: Alfred A. Knopf, 1949), p. 160.

32 Elias, *Letters*, II, 583.
33 Kathryn D. Sayre, typescript of "Theodore Dreiser—Great Spirit," pp. 3, 11-12. UP.
34 Kathryn Sayre recorded her meetings with Dreiser on separate sheets which amount to an informal diary; present citations are to entries for 11, 13, and 21 July 1929; 18, 20, and 24 Apr. 1930. The valentine is undated. Also, Sayre to Dreiser, 5 Feb. 1932. UP.
35 Light to Tuska, 9, 29 May 1931. Light to Dreiser, 30 May, 10 Aug. 1931. UP.
36 The Sayre Summaries exist in typescript at UP.
37 *"The Stage"* exists in typescript at UP.
38 Dreiser to Bromley, 22 Apr. 1932. UP.
39 Light to Klima, 19 Mar. 1932; to Smith, 2 Apr. 1932; to Sakoski, 16 May 1932; to Mackey, 7 June 1932. UP. A copy of the 1932 dummy of *The Stoic* prepared by Liveright is in the library of Cornell University, the gift of Robert H. Elias.
40 Dreiser to Campbell, 15 Apr. 1932. UP.
41 Ibid. Also, Sayre to Dreiser, 10 Apr. 1932. UP.
42 Elias, *Letters*, II, 589-590. Also, Light to Helen Dreiser, 4 May 1946. UP.
43 Dreiser to McCoy, 9 June 1932. UP.
44 Louise Campbell, *Letters to Louise* (Philadelphia: University of Pennsylvania Press, 1959), pp. 77, 80. Also, Dreiser to Campbell, 23 July, 8 Aug. 1932. UP.
45 Elias, *Letters*, II, 593.
46 Lengel to Dreiser, 12 Aug. 1932. UP.
47 Dreiser to Campbell, 23 July 1932. UP.
48 Elias, *Letters*, II, 591.
49 *A Trilogy of Desire* was eventually issued as a single volume (New York: World Publishing Co., 1972) with a descriptive introduction by Philip L. Gerber.
50 Light to Hapgood, 8 Sept. 1932; Dreiser to Baruch, 8 Sept. 1932. UP.
51 Dreiser to Kyllmann, 12 Sept. 1932.
52 Briggs to Dreiser, 22 Sept. 1932; Light to Seligson, 10 Oct. 1932; Tatum to Dreiser, 23 Oct. 1932. UP.
53 "Dreiser Overlooks His Former Experience with Hollywood, for Things Will Be Different in the Filming of 'Jennie Gerhardt,' " *New York World-Telegram*, 15 Dec. 1932.
54 Dreiser to Goldberg, 11 Sept. 1933; Shimkin to Posselt, 29 Aug. 1934. UP.
55 Schuster to Dreiser, 9, 15 Feb. 1935; Light to Dinamov, 20 Feb. 1935. UP.
56 Theodore Dreiser, *A Book About Myself* (New York: Boni and Liveright, 1922), p. 362; also "No 'Sitting In Shade' for Dreiser, At 63," *New York Times*, 28 Aug. 1934, p. L 19.
57 Elias, *Letters* II, 684, 687.

58 Ibid., pp. 720, 727. Also Douglas to Dreiser, (n.d.) 1935; Dreiser to Douglas, 16 Mar. 1935. UP.
59 Dreiser to Millikan, 16 Mar. 1935. UP. Also, Elias, *Letters*, II, 745.
60 "Simon and Schuster News," 5 Oct. 1935; Lustig to Dreiser, 25 Oct. 1935; Schuster to Dreiser, 29 July 1935. UP.
61 Schuster to Dreiser, 20 Aug. 1935; Dreiser to Schuster, 27 Aug. 1935; Schuster to Dreiser, 21 Dec. 1935; Dreiser to Schuster, 27 Dec. 1935; Dreiser to Simon, 21 Jan. 1936. UP.
62 Schuster to Dreiser, 3 Feb. 1936; Dreiser to Schuster, 12 Feb. 1936; Schuster to Dreiser, 14 Feb. 1936. UP.
63 Schuster to Dreiser, 13, 22 Apr., 6 July 1936. UP.
64 Dreiser to Donald McCord, 5 Jan. 1938. UP.
65 W. A. Swanberg, *Dreiser* (New York: Charles Scribner's Sons, 1965), p. 484.
66 Marguerite Tjader, *Theodore Dreiser: A New Dimension* (Norwalk, Connecticut: Silvermine Publishers Inc., 1965), pp. 143-144.
67 Helen Dreiser to Tjader (Harris), 27 June 1944, quoted in W. A. Swanberg, *Dreiser*, pp. 505-506.
68 Dreiser to Farrell, 26 May 1945; to Mencken 5 July 1945. UP.
69 Dreiser to Elder, 21 June 1945. UP.
70 Tjader, *Dreiser*, pp. 200-202, 207.
71 Ibid., pp. 227-228.
72 Ibid., pp. 230-231. Also, R. N. Mookerjee in "Dreiser's Use of Hindu Thought in The Stoic," *AL*, 43 (May 1971), pp. 273-278, explains in considerable detail the superficiality of Dreiser's knowledge of Eastern philosophy and reaches the conclusion that Berenice Fleming's ludicrous interpretations of *Bhagavad Gita* excerpts are actually those of Helen Dreiser.
73 Tjader, *Dreiser*, p. 230. Also, Mookerjee, "Dreiser's Use," p. 273.
74 Dreiser, "My Uncompleted Trilogy," p. 7. Also, DMN, notes numbered 758 and 719.
75 Tjader, *Dreiser*, p. 127. Also, "Dreiser Overlooks His Former Experience."
76 Dreiser to Farrell, 24 Oct. 1945; Manuel to Elder, 26 Nov. 1945; Dreiser to Farrell, 5 Dec. 1945. UP.
77 "Theodore Dreiser On The Novel." For further information on Dreiser's adherence to the biographies of Yerkes and other financiers as the scientific basis for his realism, see: Philip D. Gerber, "Dreiser's Debt to *Jay Cooke*," *Library Chronicle*, 38 (Winter 1972), pp. 67-77; also Dreiser's Financier: A Genesis," *JML*, 1 (March 1971), pp. 354-374; and "The Financier Himself: Dreiser and C. T. Yerkes," *PMLA*, 88 (January 1973), pp. 112-121.
78 DMN, note numbered 40-10, in Dreiser's hand. UP.
79 DMN, note numbered 452, consisting of a newspaper clipping, mounted

and inserted in sequence, carrying in Dreiser's hand the date 28 Nov. 1903. UP. Also, *Chicago Tribune*, 28 Feb. 1901, p. 1.

80 Chapters 32 and 50 of *The Stoic* are compared with pp. 5-9, 13-15 of the typescript "Summary of Cowperwood" at UP.

81 DMN, note numbered 408, dated in Dreiser's hand 14 Oct. 1902 (UP) is compared with p. 205 *The Stoic*.

82 DMN, note numbered 409, dated in Dreiser's hand 22 Oct. 1902 (UP) is compared with pp. 205-206 *The Stoic*.

83 See note 82, above.

84 DMN, notes numbered 413, 436. UP.

85 DMN, note numbered 489. UP.

86 DMN, note numbered 491, dated in Dreiser's hand 28 Oct. 1905 (UP) is compared with p. 242 *The Stoic*.

87 The report in *New York Times*, 3 Jan. 1906, p. 1, is compared with pp. 277-278 *The Stoic*.

88 Pp. 3-5, 8, 16 of the typescript "Settlement of Cowperwood's Property and Affairs" (UP) are compared with pp. 279, 280, 282 *The Stoic*.

89 DMN, notes numbered 212, 584, 596, 628, 629, 635, 740; also, typescript "Summary of Aileen." UP.

90 DMN, note numbered 210, being a clipping, mounted and dated 13 Apr. 1910 (UP), is compared with pp. 284-285 *The Stoic*.

91 DMN, notes numbered 175, 176, 179, 521.

92 DMN, note numbered 30.

93 Typescript of "The Stoic—Synopsis" dated 6 June 1932, p. 3. UP.

94 Typescript of "*The Stage*," p. 4. UP.

95 "Summary of Aileen," p. 5. UP.

96 DMN, notes numbered 15-16, 73. Both are newspaper clippings. Note 15-16 consists of two pages and carries in Dreiser's hand the heading "History of Emilie Grigsby"; note 73 has the headline: "Emilie Grigsby's 'Revenge' Sale in House of Mystery: Public Gets Its First Peep into the Home of Yerkes's beautiful Protegee." UP.

97 DMN, notes numbered 62 and 15-16. UP.

98 Helen Dreiser, *My Life with Dreiser* (Cleveland: World Publishing Company, 1951), pp. 130-131.

99 Theodore Dreiser, *The Titan* (New York: John Lane Company, 1914), p. 352.

100 DMN, note numbered 666. UP.

101 DMN, note dated 5 Sept. 1911. UP.

102 DMN, note numbered 729. UP. The note consists of a clipping with the headline: "Emilie Grigsby Goes to India for Health," dated 13 Jan. 1913.

103 *Chicago Daily Tribune*, 3 Jan. 1906, p. 2. Also, DMN, note numbered 73. UP.

104 DMN, note numbered 67 and dated in Dreiser's hand 11 May 1911. UP.

105 Leon Edel, *Henry James: The Master* (Philadelphia: J. B. Lippincott Company, 1972), pp. 174-180; also, "Miss Emilie Grigsby," *Times* (London), 12 Feb. 1964, p. 15a; also, "Emilie Busbey Grigsby Dead; American Hostess in England," *New York Times*, 14 Feb. 1964, p. 29. The New York reference treats Emilie's association with Yerkes, the London reference does not.

106 Dreiser to Farrell, 14 Dec. 1945. UP.

107 Farrell to Dreiser, 19 Dec. 1945. UP.

108 Dreiser to Farrell, 24 Dec. 1945. UP.

109 Nathan, "Three Friends," p. 614.

110 Helen Dreiser to Farrell, 8 Jan. 1946; to Elder, 14, 25 Jan. 1946. UP.

111 Helen Dreiser to Elder, 26 Feb. 1946. UP.

112 Elder to Manuel, 6 Mar. 1946. UP.

113 Helen Dreiser to Elder, 13 Mar. 1946; Elder to Helen Dreiser, 3 Apr. 1946. UP.

114 Campbell to Elder, 22 Sept. 1946. UP.

115 Campbell to Helen Dreiser, 4 July 1946. UP.

116 Helen Dreiser to Elder, 10 July 1946. UP.

117 Helen Dreiser to Tjader (Harris), 17 June 1946. UP.

118 Helen Dreiser to Elder, (n.d.) Feb. 1947; Elder to Helen Dreiser, 5 Aug. 1947; Campbell to Elder, 26 Aug. 1947. UP.

119 Helen Dreiser to Piera, 20 Sept. 1947. UP.